CLEAN START

THE GUILFORD SUBSTANCE ABUSE SERIES

Editors

HOWARD T. BLANE, Ph.D.
Research Institute on Alcoholism, Buffalo

THOMAS R. KOSTEN, M.D.
Yale University School of Medicine, New Haven

CLEAN START
An Outpatient Program for Initiating Cocaine Recovery

WILLIAM E. McAULIFFE, Ph.D.
JEFFREY ALBERT, M.S.W.
Harvard Medical School
at The Cambridge Hospital

Foreword by Barry S. Brown, Ph.D.

THE GUILFORD PRESS
New York London

Library of Congress Cataloging-in-Publication Data
McAuliffe, William E.
    Clean start: an outpatient program for initiating cocaine
recovery / by William E. McAuliffe, Jeffrey Albert.
        p.   cm. – (The Guilford substance abuse series)
    "The Cessation and Early Recovery Program of the Harvard Cocaine
Recovery Project."
    Includes bibliographical references and index.
    ISBN 0-89862-190-9 – ISBN 0-89862-194-1 (pbk.)
    1. Cocaine habit–Treatment. 2. Group psychotherapy. I. Albert,
Jeffrey. II. Harvard Cocaine Recovery Project. Cessation and Early
Recovery Program. III. Title. IV. Series.
    [DNLM: 1. Cocaine. 2. Substance Dependence–therapy. WM 280
M478c]
    RC568.C6M33 1992
    616.864706–dc20
    DNLM/DLC
    for Library of Congress   92-1528
                                                                   CIP

To Donna and Kaitlyn McAuliffe

To my children,
Jordan, Jessie, and Ben Albert

About the Authors

William E. McAuliffe, Ph.D., is Associate Professor in the Department of Psychiatry, Harvard Medical School at The Cambridge Hospital, and in the Department of Health and Social Behavior, Harvard School of Public Health. He is Director of Substance Abuse Research at The Cambridge Hospital. A clinical sociologist who received his doctorate in sociology from The Johns Hopkins University, he is Principal Investigator of both the Harvard Cocaine Recovery Project and Project Outreach. He is coauthor of several relapse prevention manuals for drug addicts, including *Addict Aftercare: Recovery Training and Self-Help, Addiction and the Vulnerable Self,* and *Recovery Training and Self-Help: Relapse Prevention and Aftercare for Drug Addicts.* He has published numerous articles on problems of drug abuse.

Jeffrey Albert, M.S.W., has worked extensively as a counselor of addicts who are in the initial stages of recovery. Mr. Albert was an original leader of the Clean Start group and, with Dr. McAuliffe, designed its curriculum. He has written a manual for individuals who wish to detoxify from methadone maintenance, as well as numerous articles about addiction treatment. Mr. Albert currently leads groups of incarcerated addicts, and he has designed a model program with a video component for addicted prisoners and their counselors. He is also completing a series of essays on the role of self-help groups in recovery.

Kathleen Ackerman, B.A., is a coauthor of the second chapter in this book. She has worked with Dr. McAuliffe on the manual *Recovery Training and Self-Help: Relapse Prevention and Aftercare for Drug Addicts,* and is a coauthor of a paper written with Dr. McAuliffe on health care and public policy issues concerning drug abuse. She is a student at New York University Law School.

Contents

Foreword

In 1972, President Richard M. Nixon declared a war on drugs and, in conjunction with a unanimous Congress, provided funds to initiate a nationwide program of community-based drug treatment. In the intervening years, succeeding presidents have joined that war albeit with varying degrees of enthusiasm and vigor. Still, it is useful to take note of the initial thrust of that war, even as it was to develop with bipartisan frustration into continuing stalemate. An early objective was not only to expand the availability of treatment, but to move treatment from the two large institutional settings (Lexington and Fort Worth), to which drug abuse clients were expected to move, to facilities in their own communities. Through the use of community-based facilities, drug abuse clients could have available to them the supports of family and community, they could resolve problems in living specific to the environments in which they were located, and new support systems could be developed to assist clients' efforts at drug-free living. While this use of local resources was a significant factor in the planning for community-based treatment, all too often the community receded from view and the clinic or residential setting became the only environment of interest. In large measure, rehabilitation took place in counselors' offices or the conditioned passages of the therapeutic community, and while few argued with the role of external community—of family, friends, work setting, school, church, support systems—few made efforts to incorporate that community into the work of treatment. Treatment programs achieved a great success in reducing, and eliminating, drug use for individuals in treatment, then experienced frustrating rates of relapse as the client left the program, and the supports and structure of treatment were thereby removed. In the face of treatment's incomplete success, two somewhat competing explanations were constructed. On the one hand, in the absence of either virus or bacterium, policy-makers came to characterize drug abuse as a chronic, relapsing disease. On the other, the drug abuser who did not respond to treatment was seen as not yet ready for treatment. Treatment failure was the consequence of disease or of limited motivation on the client's part. Treatment itself was largely absolved.

In fact, we have not lacked for evidence of the importance of community in client rehabilitation. Numerous studies have built on Wikler's 1965 findings of the importance of conditioning in triggering relapse, and those studies have themselves been buttressed by clinical accounts of craving and relapse brought on by visits to old neighborhoods after years of incarceration, or reports of craving and relapse brought on by internal cues of depression or anxiety. It is these cues to relapse—external and internal—with which the client must cope effectively if he or she is to become and remain drug free, and it is the effort to build a program that prepares clients to be aware of those cues—to avoid them where feasible, to recognize and respond to them effectively where avoidance is not feasible—that has distinguished some few new initiatives in drug abuse treatment over the past decade. It is these initiatives, taking the task of rehabilitation beyond institutional walls, that give promise of breaking the cycle of treatment abstinence and community relapse.

The effort to take greater account of the capacity of community either to frustrate or to support recovery has come variously to be called relapse prevention, aftercare, and continuing care. The different terms used are not without some significance. Whereas relapse prevention is most largely a client-centered, behavior skills training program preparing the individual to recognize and cope with the inevitable cues and situations inviting relapse, aftercare is often a more largely community-centered program of building family, peer, and organizational supports to the maintenance of a drug-free life. Obviously, there is room and logic to the combining of both approaches to defend against relapse. Just as the individual needs to develop the skills—and a confidence in the skills—to avoid relapse, there will likely be a need to reshape the client's community to modify the family's role expectations for the recovering client, to locate or develop social networks that will act as alternatives to drug-using networks, and to develop work and leisure activities that fill the recovering client's time until the client learns to structure time for himself or herself.

This combining of skills training with the development of community support systems into a comprehensive program of recovery is the singular contribution of Clean Start and of its authors, William E. McAuliffe and Jeffrey Albert. They describe a coordinated initiative involving an assessment of the triggers (i.e., cues) to relapse, and the building of walls (i.e., defenses) against relapse. Those walls are constructed in part through the development of coping skills to deal with triggers, and in part through the development of a body of social supports designed to remove potential triggers. Throughout, the effort to maintain abstinence is a joint undertaking of client and staff, with the client taking increasing responsibility for his or her recovery in conjunction with the client's increasing confidence in his or her own abilities. Through a series of commitment steps that are, in fact, strides away from drug use, the client builds that confidence and, with it, a life in which drugs no longer have any place.

Clean Start builds on the highly successful Recovery Training and Self-Help model developed by McAuliffe in conjunction with Fred Zackon and James Ch'ien. That model targeted the special needs and concerns of heroin users whereas Clean Start is directed to cocaine users.

In this regard it meets a particular void in our treatment resources. Cocaine use continues to challenge traditional forms of drug abuse treatment. Treatment of opiate use is hampered by clients' continuing (or newly initiated) involvement with cocaine while the nonopiate cocaine client appears particularly vulnerable to relapse. Indeed, so powerful is the attraction of cocaine, and so extraordinary the threat of relapse, that cocaine use has resulted in a redefinition of the term addiction. No longer is addiction to be conditioned on a drug's capacity to produce physiological withdrawal; instead, the extraordinary reinforcing quality of cocaine has come to define that drug as addicting. Little wonder that massive energies and dollars are expended in a quest for that medication that can neutralize the effects of cocaine and for those psychosocial interventions that can counteract its attraction. Clean Start, with its combination of skills training and the creation of community supports, offers an important and hopeful new addition to our programming for cocaine users.

A particular feature of this volume is the authors' ability to combine theory and study with a step-by-step manual designed to guarantee that the results of a research program obtain clinical expression. Sadly, that effort to make the products of research accessible to the service community remains an isolated occurrence. The authors are to be congratulated for stripping their work of research jargon and for making use of a language and format that allows their program to be implemented by the service delivery community. In the continuing effort to develop

effective strategies for coping with drug dependence, this volume
should provide not only a model for working with cocaine abuse, but a
model for the integration of efforts between the research and service
delivery communities.

BARRY S. BROWN, Ph.D.
Chief, Community Research Branch
Division of Applied Research
National Institute on Drug Abuse

Preface

A "clean start," as we use the term in this manual, is more than a beginning. It is a new departure that requires a fundamental change of outlook, style, and direction. This manual is a guide to helping chemically dependent outpatient clients take the critical first steps of such a departure. It describes the initial month-long cessation and early recovery group (the "Clean Start" group) of the Harvard Cocaine Recovery Project (HCRP), a randomized clinical trial of group treatments for cocaine addiction funded by the National Institute on Drug Abuse (NIDA). The main purposes of the Clean Start group were to help clients achieve stable abstinence and to prepare them for long-term treatment. The first half of this manual examines the rationale for these goals and our overall approach to achieving them. It discusses the needs of newly recovering clients in terms of a social conditioning model of addiction, and it describes a coherent step-by-step program to meet those needs. The program is intended to be both theoretically sound and practical. It builds upon 20 years of advances in research and clinical applications, and includes a sequence of carefully developed, well-tested "scripts" for leading structured drug-free group sessions. The scripts were tested and refined during 4 years of repetitions (1987–1990) in the HCRP and Project Outreach, an AIDS prevention study also funded by NIDA. The second half of the manual contains the actual scripts for the sessions.

The manual is intended primarily as an easy-to-follow practical guide for group leaders, but is adaptable to the uses of individual counselors and other clinicians as well. Its applications of theory to practical, tested strategies should make it relevant to anyone interested in chemical dependency and its treatment. Our program also may be of interest to those who are concerned with drug treatment policy. The

ongoing cocaine epidemic has strained society's drug treatment resources beyond their capacities. The Clean Start program builds on
recent findings (Amini et al., 1989; Hayashida et al., 1989; Miller &
Hester, 1986) that outpatient treatment, at approximately one-tenth of
the cost of inpatient treatment, is just as effective in the long run and
much more attractive and feasible for many members of the new
generation of addicts. Unfortunately, until now there has been no fully
articulated model of outpatient, drug-free cessation from drugs such as
cocaine or heroin that is the functional equivalent of the residential
treatment model.

Although the Clean Start program was designed for the specific
needs of cocaine addicts, its principles and strategies are adaptable to
the treatment of most chemical dependencies. Achieving stable abstinence is a necessary first step in the treatment of any addiction. Other
key elements of recovery such as achieving biological and psychological
stability and repairing and extending supportive social connections both
consolidate and build upon this step. Individuals who have been
severely addicted to substances that cause life-threatening withdrawal
symptoms may require a short period of hospitalization before entering
a program like Clean Start. However, our experience in Project Outreach, where most of the clients were heroin addicts, has shown that a
sufficiently intensive outpatient cessation and early recovery modality
can help a broad spectrum of addicts.

Working at the very gates of recovery can be a daunting responsibility. Clients come in fear and confusion, asking us to save their lives.
They say, in essence, "My way has failed repeatedly, I am losing
everything that matters: show me a way that works." No individual
clinician or researcher can presume to have The Way. We must resort to
our best collective experience and thinking to offer one way. For the staff
as for the clients of the HCRP, participating in many clean starts
required us to learn together from several false starts. Like the clients,
each staff member of the HCRP learned to trust and consult others. Like
the clients, we were able to take calculated risks together that we could
not have accomplished alone. A growing sense of confidence not in our
individual opinions but in the collective judgment of a committed staff
was one of the most gratifying aspects of working in the HCRP. It
allowed us to give back to the clients some of the energy that their new
departures into recovery gave to us.

WILLIAM E. MCAULIFFE
JEFFREY ALBERT

Acknowledgments

We are grateful to the clinical, research, and administrative staffs of the Harvard Cocaine Recovery Project. They include Geoffrey Carpenter, Tim Flynn, Lauren Goldsmith, Edward J. Khantzian, Richard LaBrie, Eliot Levine, Elizabeth Stone Maland, Kum Kum Malik, Norah Mulvaney, Stephanie Pearlman, Guillermo Rivera-Pagan, Susan Robel, Beth Rosner, JoAnn Scherer, Dori Singer, Patricia Song, Mary Ann Touchette, Linda Watson, Cynthia Webnar, Laura Wetterau, and Larissa Wilberschied. Special thanks to Georgia Cordill-London, Sam Erban, Amy Ferber, Thomas McGarraghy, Elizabeth McMahon-Cicerano, Michael Pelham, and Hope Podell, who were leaders of Clean Start groups. Their experiences and ideas contributed significantly to the development of the model.

Barry Brown, Edward Khantzian, Kurt Halliday, Hil Ohrstrom, and Dwayne Simpson read earlier versions of the book and made helpful suggestions for improvement.

Readers of the *Recovery Training and Self-Help* manual (Zackon et al., 1985) will recognize the great contribution of RTSH to the Clean Start model. The sessions "A Road Map to Recovery," "Coping with Dangerous Situations," and "Family and Partners in Early Recovery," in particular, are adaptations of sessions in the RTSH manual. We are indebted to James Ch'ien and Bob Benfari for many of the ideas regarding interventions, program structure, and the understanding of self-help, and especially to Fred Zackon for the group techniques, a developmental approach to recovery, and the format of the sessions.

The Department of Psychiatry of The Cambridge Hospital and the North Charles Foundation provided support for the study. Myron Belfer, Glover Taylor, Peter Kastner, and Helen Modica were particularly important in this regard. And the many treatment agencies, individual clinicians, and Employee Assistance Programs (EAPs) that referred their clients to us contributed in an important way to the success of the project.

This work was supported by grants from the National Institute on Drug Abuse (5 R01 DAO4418; 5 R18 DAO5271; 5 R01 DAO7063) and from the Office of Substance Abuse, State of Rhode Island. Barry Brown and Rebecca Ashery have been continuing sources of moral support for this research.

Jeffrey Albert is grateful to the following people who have helped him immeasurably: Fred Zackon, Marty Seligman, Georgia Cordill-London, Hil Ohrstrom, Stephanie Pearlman, Tim Flynn, Kurt Halliday, Rob Schneider, Thomas McGarraghy, and Sam Erban. He also wishes to thank Beatrice Albert for her love and faith; his late father, Sidney Albert, for encouraging him by precept and example to try to help others; Jordan Albert, Jessie Albert, Ben Albert, Nora Albert, and Barbara Albert; Gail Weiss, whose skills and support went far beyond those of child care; and Diane Juster for her exceptional critical judgment and her warm support.

William McAuliffe wishes to acknowledge his intellectual debt to Robert A. Gordon, Robert L. Hamblin, and George C. Homans. He owes more than he can say to his aunt and uncle, Belle and Irv Rubinstein, and to his daughter and wife, Kaitlyn and Donna McAuliffe. He also wishes to remember Harold Goldsmith and Charles Alpert.

Finally, the development of this treatment modality was made possible only because there were recovering people who took a chance by participating in the program. Without their efforts to achieve recovery, nothing that we did could have made a difference.

Handouts

The reader is encouraged to reproduce and modify these handouts to make them better suited to specific needs. We recommend enlarging each handout prior to giving it to clients.

All are architects of fate,
Working in these walls of time,
*   Some with massive deeds and great,*
*   Some with ornaments of rhyme.*
                    —H. W. LONGFELLOW

PART I

PROGRAM THEORY AND DESIGN

CHAPTER ONE

Introduction

This manual for group leaders is a product of the Harvard Cocaine Recovery Project (HCRP), which was a randomized clinical trial of group treatments for cocaine addiction. The study was funded by a grant from the National Institute on Drug Abuse (NIDA). During the course of the project, Recovery Training and Self-Help (RTSH) (McAuliffe & Ch'ien 1986; Zackon et al., 1985), one of the methods of group treatment and relapse prevention being studied, was expanded into a more comprehensive system of recovery based on principles of social learning and behavioral conditioning (Bandura & Walters, 1963; Skinner, 1953). The new system was designed as an outpatient drug-free alternative to existing drug treatment modalities. It includes a month-long group cessation program, individual counseling, a 6-month recovery group, and participation in Cocaine Anonymous (CA) or other self-help fellowships.

The manual describes the month-long cessation and early recovery phase of the system. It presents a sociobehavioral system for helping groups of addicts to separate themselves from drug use and lay the foundation for further recovery. This component of the system is designed as an alternative or supplement to the residential chemical dependency and hospital detoxification modalities that have become popular in the past decade. Although aimed at a broad range of drug treatment providers, the manual is especially designed for group leaders who would prefer a detailed "cookbook" for conducting successful outpatient cessation groups. However, we feel that the coherent view of addiction and recovery that unifies the manual makes it relevant to students or to anyone interested in the problems of helping people change addictive behaviors. The topic-centered sessions, which constitute the second half of the manual, can easily be adapted to the uses of individual counselors or to inpatient programs.

What Is the Need for an Outpatient Cocaine Cessation Program?

The need we found for inexpensive "ground-level" treatment services is as widespread as the cocaine epidemic. Cocaine is as addictive as heroin (Hasin et al., 1988), and ten times as many people nationwide have used cocaine as have used heroin (National Institute on Drug Abuse, 1990). In many states cocaine addicts outnumber those in treatment for any other addiction (McAuliffe et al., 1988). Cocaine accounts for more emergency room visits than heroin or any other controlled substance (Drug Abuse Warning Network, 1989), and the number of babies born addicted to cocaine has increased dramatically. Cocaine-related murders have become standard fare in the daily news, and the human and financial costs of cocaine addiction are immeasurable.

The suddenness and scope of the cocaine problem caught the treatment community without an adequate response to the number of people seeking help. Cocaine addiction was rare from the 1950s to the early 1970s, when the major modalities of drug abuse treatment were being developed, and so these modalities were designed primarily to treat the abuse of depressants such as alcohol, heroin, or barbiturates. In the absence of specific treatments for cocaine addiction, existing outpatient and residential drug-free modalities were adapted to cocaine treatment during the 1980s. However, the adaptations were not based on the evidence of clinical research trials. There is reason to believe that the cocaine problem requires treatments suited to the specific effects of the drug and to the particular characteristics of the affected population. In many cases of addiction to depressants, close medical supervision may be necessary during detoxification because of the physiological withdrawal symptoms that those drugs can produce. However, despite the great addictiveness of cocaine, its withdrawal causes comparatively few physical symptoms (see Gawin, 1991, for a dissenting view). In this respect, cocaine is comparable to nicotine or marijuana, drugs for which outpatient cessation is a logical first option.

In contrast to heroin addicts, for whom many of the current drug treatment resources have been designed, many of today's cocaine addicts have relatively short histories of severe addiction and reasonably intact work and family support systems. They are reluctant to disrupt their lives and responsibilities more than may be necessary. A growing number of these addicts recognize the need for a period of intensive, structured treatment, but they are unwilling or unable to spend weeks in residential care. The same supportive life circumstances that could contribute to their success as outpatients discourage these addicts from seeking inpatient treatment. No modality of treatment is useful if it is not used.

Most of the current outpatient alternatives for such clients are also inadequate: Instead of providing an unnecessarily high level of external support, they do not offer enough. The once- or twice-a-week counseling sessions provided by the average existing outpatient program are not sufficient to counteract the effects of a drug as powerfully addictive as cocaine (Kang et al., 1991). Nor is the content of most existing outpatient counseling programs well designed to deal with the specific problems of abrupt cessation from such a highly addictive drug. Cocaine cravings can be much more intense and pervasive than cravings for alcohol or even heroin. They must be countered by an intensive learning process, one that helps clients to monitor relevant aspects of their daily lives and that facilitates their achieving a new social identity. These goals usually cannot be accomplished in a single weekly counseling session.

Recent research has shown that outpatient professional treatment for substance abuse is as effective as inpatient treatment in many cases (Amini et al., 1989; Miller & Hester, 1986). Yet, ironically, many patients who enter residential treatment relapse upon discharge precisely because of the perceived discontinuity between residential "treatment" and outpatient "aftercare." Addicts and their families too often think of inpatient treatment as "The Cure." In fact, the hardest work of recovery begins on the outside. After discharge from residential treatment, one is confronted with temptation, increased stress, and substantially reduced supports. Having achieved abstinence and feeling relieved of the pressures that motivated cessation, many newly discharged inpatients are unwilling to undertake the critical lifestyle changes required to sustain long-term recovery. In contrast, outpatient cessation requires one to make many of those lifestyle changes while still desperate to become drug-free. Thus, although outpatient cessation is more difficult than inpatient cessation, the probability of remaining abstinent after outpatient cessation is greater. For many cocaine addicts who are not physically dependent on other drugs, it is feasible to begin this work "in the field." The intimacy and efficiency of a unified, structured program are also attractive to clients who are put off by the seeming looseness or spiritual emphasis of 12-step fellowships such as CA. Many clients can use the support of intensive outpatient treatment to ease their entry into the recovering community, and many can use it to complement their participation in fellowships.

The argument for making outpatient cessation a first option for many cocaine addicts becomes more compelling in light of the high cost of residential treatment. Residential treatment costs about $10,000 a month, more than 10 times as much as our outpatient cessation treatment. Residential treatment is simply too expensive for the many cocaine addicts without Medicaid or private insurance. Indeed, many addicts with private insurance often rapidly exhaust their benefits; insurance companies are increasingly reluctant to pay for extended residential treatment, with early discharges increasing the demands on outpatient support systems.

In addition to being feasible and cost-effective, an outpatient cessation group also offers specific programmatic advantages. Rather than disrupting a longer-term recovery group or endangering it with insufficiently committed or nonabstinent clients, a short-term cessation program gives staff members the chance to assess clients' readiness for outpatient treatment, and at the same time gives clients who are not ready a chance to select themselves out. A comprehensive two-stage program also helps to retain those clients who are ready for longer-term treatment. Recovering addicts who form their first critical connections to counselors and other members at one site are most comfortable entering extended treatment at the same site.

In summary, our experience strongly suggests that, for a sufficient number of addicts who are not physically dependent on other drugs, the time is ripe and the price is right for intensive outpatient cessation and early recovery programming.

How Did the Harvard Cocaine Cessation and Early Recovery Program Evolve?

The HCRP was undertaken to develop and test new outpatient group treatments specifically for cocaine addiction. One of these treatments was an adaptation of RTSH (McAuliffe et al., 1990–1991; McAuliffe & Ch'ien, 1986; Zackon et al., 1985, 1992), and another was Modified Dynamic Group Therapy (MDGT) (Khantzian et al., 1990). Clients were randomly assigned to RTSH, MDGT, or a "no group" condition. Clients in all three conditions received weekly individual counseling and were encouraged to attend 12-step fellowship meetings.

Many addicts seeking treatment from the HCRP needed a more intensive period of support than the long-term RTSH or MDGT programs provided. Some study applicants had not yet achieved stable abstinence. We initially referred these clients to inpatient facilities, but few of those we referred returned to our program. Many applicants who were referred to us directly from inpatient detoxification and residential rehabilitation programs were not yet sufficiently stable as outpatients to be members of the long-term RTSH or MDGT groups. Others, who had achieved abstinence on their own or with the help of 12-step fellowships but who had never been in treatment, needed more basic orientation than the RTSH or MDGT groups provide. Some prospective clients who had established brief periods of abstinence on their own needed intensive help to consolidate their gains and move forward. Others who had relapsed briefly after a period of sustained abstinence required highly structured support, but not inpatient treatment.

These newly or unstably abstinent clients needed immediate exposure to specific sorts of information and support. Their needs included orientation; stabilization; assessment; highly focused direction; information about the elements of addiction, cessation, and recovery; help in identifying and overcoming the initial internal and external obstacles to recovery; a motivating group culture; guidance in attaining maximum family support; and strategies for avoiding and surviving crises while building secure foundations for further recovery. Some of these elements are available in the long-term RTSH regimen. However, because RTSH groups are open to new members at any time, and because the topics of the Recovery Training sessions are on a 26-week rotation, the entering client might have to wait weeks or months for the more "basic" sessions. Moreover, the RTSH program assumes that drug use has ceased, and therefore does not address cessation explicitly. An unstructured group, such as MDGT, runs the risk of being preoccupied with the frequent crises of newly abstaining clients, and thereby inadequately addressing the issues of slightly more advanced recovery. We found that a short cessation program could meet these clients' immediate needs and thus complement the long-term program.

Like the topics of RTSH, the topics of the cessation program were initially based on theoretical analysis, but then evolved and were refined through much trial and error. Each session was repeated many times over the course of 2 years. The Cessation and Early Recovery Program of the HCRP was subsequently adapted for a similar program in Project Outreach, an NIDA-funded clinical trial of interventions for drug users at risk for AIDS. Gradually, as a clearer idea emerged of the specific techniques that would meet the needs of our clients, some topics were dropped while others were expanded or added. The most important modification in the program was its expansion from a 2-week cycle of 6 sessions to a 4-week cycle of 12 sessions. The expansion allowed us to address additional topics important to early recovery and to adjust to the actual rate at which clients were able to progress. In practice, clients who were using cocaine up to the point of admission, or who had had no previous treatment, usually required a month or more to make the initial changes necessary to function well in long-term outpatient treatment. A minimum of 4 weeks of regular, drug-free attendance at the cessation sessions usually indicated sufficient stability and commitment to succeed at longer-term outpatient treatment. In addition, if a client was willing to take actions to reduce immediate dangers to recovery, he or she was deemed eligible to advance to RTSH or other relapse prevention programs such as MDGT. Although designed according to the RTSH model, the Cessation and Early Recovery Program was meant to serve the needs of clients entering all three of HCRP's treatment conditions. Clean Start's success as a stepping stone to several modalities of longer-term treatment has proven its wide applicability.

Whom Did the Cessation Program Serve?

The cocaine addicts for whom this program was developed were recruited principally by referrals from other treatment programs or agencies, public service announcements on radio and television, public transit advertisements, drug hotlines, employee assistance programs (EAPs), public interest newspaper stories, and word of mouth (see Ashery & McAuliffe, 1992). Word of mouth was the single most productive source of clients. Prospective clients completed a brief telephone questionnaire to determine their eligibility for the program. HCRP was designed only for people interested in long-term recovery. Both research and clinical considerations dictated the study's eligibility criteria. All subjects had to:

- have had a primary cocaine addiction during the past year
- meet DSM-III criteria for cocaine abuse
- be 18 years or older
- be willing to commit to abstinence from all controlled substances and alcohol for the entire period of treatment
- have no pending legal cases that could result in imprisonment (which would interrupt the treatment course, disrupt the group, and might cause the client to be lost to research either during the treatment phase or during the follow-up)
- have no physical or psychiatric condition serious enough to interfere with drug abuse treatment
- have no plans to move out of the Boston area for a year
- be willing to postpone any vacations until the completion of treatment

In our view, it makes clinical sense to select clients carefully for outpatient cessation treatment because this modality is not appropriate for all cocaine addicts who seek help. With fewer external supports than are available for inpatients, outpatients must bring more to treatment initially. For example, severely addicted individuals without a strong incentive to change or who cannot establish a reasonably safe living or working environment may need a period of residential, halfway house, or day treatment. Addicts with concurrent medical or psychiatric problems that warrant close medical monitoring should start recovery in a hospital. In addition, many clients are not ready to make the changes that successful treatment requires, and many simply do not want to recover. An appropriate process of selection will include clients who are in the best position to make use of the treatment, and will exclude those with a low probability of success who would endanger the recoveries of those better suited for outpatient treatment.

Were the people who entered our program representative of the larger population of cocaine addicts? Yes and no. Our clients were heterogeneous, including a wide spectrum of personal, psychological, socioeconomic, and racial characteristics. Nonetheless, a comparison of clients who attended at least one cessation group in our program with those who entered outpatient programs funded by the Massachusetts Department of Public Health (DPH) during the same time period in the greater Boston metropolitan area shows that our population was somewhat better educated, older, and more predominantly male (Halliday, 1992). One reason for the difference was that many of the people in the DPH sample were not part of our target population. A large portion of the addicts treated in the DPH sample did not seek treatment voluntarily: They were referred to outpatient counseling by the courts as a condition of probation or parole, and some were required to enter treatment by the Department of Social Services in order to keep or regain custody of children. Nor did the DPH sample exclude people under 18 years of age or with severe medical or psychiatric disorders. Finally, the DPH sample was usually not required to commit to long-term abstinence or to make as great a commitment of time to treatment (one or two weekly counseling sessions was typical for the DPH sample vs. the three or four required contacts per week in our program).

The subjects who completed the cessation program were also more select than those who applied. Of the 755 clients who came to the initial orientation session, 40% completed the program. The majority of the noncompleters dropped out before the fourth session. Those who completed the program tended to be slightly older and better educated. The completers were more likely than the noncompleters to have had job-related motivations.

It is not surprising that clients who enter and complete a program with stringent eligibility and program requirements have characteristics repeatedly shown by research to predict good treatment outcomes (McLellan, 1983; Ogborn, 1978). Older, better-educated clients who are not legally constrained to enter treatment are more likely to have stable marriages, jobs, and friendships. Clients with jobs or good job prospects are more likely than others to be socially stable and more likely to have the motivation and support needed for recovery. Higher educational level correlates positively with higher socioeconomic status and social stability, and it correlates negatively with having an antisocial lifestyle. It is therefore likely that relatively more clients with these characteristics would voluntarily enter and complete a program with stringent requirements. In summary, the combined eligibility and program requirements of Clean Start, especially the exclusion of legally coerced clients, probably selected a sample with relatively high motivation, stability, and support.

This is not to say that younger, poorer, more severely addicted "street" addicts cannot succeed in an intensive outpatient program like ours. Many of them did. However, it seems that in order for outpatient treatment to succeed, an addict must have *some* strong source of motivation and support. For example, one inner-city client who successfully completed both the cessation and RTSH groups had a good job and a supportive union steward who was a member of Alcoholics Anonymous (AA). These circumstances probably helped to offset the effects of his drug-ridden family and neighborhood. Others from pervasively addicted backgrounds and environments succeeded with the help of unusually strong social skills, close relationships with supportive family members, or strong preexisting personal or family connections with 12-step fellowships. One of the jobs of cessation treatment is to ensure that clients identify and make maximum use of such assets.

How Should This Manual Be Used?

Ideally, this manual should be read through from beginning to end. Readers can gain a clear picture of the approach more quickly by reading Chapters Five (Program Design), Six (Sessions Format), and Eight (Sample Session). For those already familiar with *Recovery Training and Self-Help*, reading Chapter Five would suffice. Group leaders who decide to adopt the approach will need to read most intensively the second part of the manual, which contains the actual "recipes" for the sessions. However, one cannot do total justice to recipes without understanding the principles of good cooking and nutrition. One should understand the reasons for our selection and arrangement of specific topics and exercises in order to be able to convey their spirit to clients. At the same time, a familiarity with the groundwork of the whole program will help one respond creatively to the many situations that the best plans cannot anticipate.

The treatment program described in this manual is based on a specific theory of addiction and recovery. This theory and some of its implications for early treatment are the subjects of Chapter Two. Chapter Three applies the theory to our observations of clients' needs during the cessation phase of treatment. Chapter Four discusses the program goals suggested by client needs; Chapter Five gives an overview of the program we designed to meet those needs. Chapter Six presents the thinking behind our choices of topics for the sessions, describing the rationales and goals that underlie the topics and their order. Chapter Seven explains the "master" format of all of the sessions, their underlying unity of structure and its rationale. Chapter Eight illustrates how a Clean Start session works by providing a sample session. Chapter Nine concludes the first part of this book with a discussion of relapses and some of the other major problems that confront group leaders.

The second part of this manual contains the formats of the actual sessions, the directions for leading them, and the handouts for group members.

Theoretical Foundation

At the start of our work on this treatment modality, we asked ourselves whether *outpatient* cessation and initial recovery were possible for persons addicted to a drug as powerful as cocaine. Although cessation from cigarettes is routinely accomplished on an outpatient basis, and although cocaine does not involve severe physiological withdrawal, the conventional wisdom in the drug treatment field has been that adequate drug-free treatment of major addictions requires an initial inpatient or residential stay. In 1985, when we planned our experimental study of relapse prevention for cocaine addiction, we assumed that we would recruit all of our clients from residential chemical dependency programs. However, once the study was under way, persons who had stopped using cocaine without professional help began applying for relapse prevention treatment. They had either stayed locked in their rooms "kicking the habit cold turkey" (as it had been called in an earlier era with regard to heroin addiction), or they had achieved abstinence by attending 12-step fellowship meetings. We also discovered a new study describing "spontaneous recovery" from heroin addiction (Biernacki, 1986), and learned that several of our new colleagues at Cambridge Hospital were interviewing cocaine addicts in Cambridge who had stopped using on their own (Shaffer & Jones, 1989). If some addicts could stop heroin or cocaine use on their own as outpatients, it seemed reasonable that others who had failed on their own might succeed as

This chapter closely follows McAuliffe et al. (1990–1991). Kathleen Ackerman is a coauthor.

outpatients with the help of a group, professional counselors, and a carefully designed program. The challenge we then faced was having to design the modality ourselves because we knew of no existing model.

Although most of the major modalities of drug treatment have been developed with little attention to theoretical concerns, we began this effort with the assumption that, to develop a new form of treatment, one should theoretically analyze the condition being treated, examine the specific problems involved in its treatment, and derive principles by which the condition could be changed. This chapter describes the psychosocial theory that resulted from that analysis.

We begin this chapter by briefly reviewing the basics of our conditioning theory of addiction and discussing its implications for the goals of drug-abuse treatment. We describe clinical applications of the conditioning model to relapse prevention. However, conditioning analysis is not confined to relapse prevention, and in the second part of the chapter we show how it can be fruitfully applied to cessation of drug use, on both an inpatient and an outpatient basis. We also analyze in detail the period of early recovery, which we define as the first month following cessation of cocaine use. For example, we describe how responses to relapse triggers should vary, depending upon the stage of recovery and on the nature of the trigger. We describe a new concept that derives from the social conditioning model of recovery—the "commitment step"—which we believe is an especially effective tool to help persons in early recovery overcome their ambivalence about making difficult changes. In the final portion of the chapter, we expand the conditioning theory analysis to include sociological variables that we believe are essential for treating addiction to illicit substances. Of special importance is the role of the recovering addict community in resocializing the newly abstinent addict.

Conditioning Theory of Addiction

The approach described in this manual is based on a theory of addiction (McAuliffe, 1989; McAuliffe & Gordon, 1974, 1980) that uses a combination of the principles of operant conditioning (Deese & Hulse, 1967; Skinner, 1953) and those of social learning theory (Bandura & Walters, 1963). In our view, application of conditioning principles to drug abuse has revolutionized the field's understanding and treatment of addiction. The theory provides a unified and powerful explanation of what were once the most mysterious and intractable aspects of addiction and relapse. How can a person be "taken over" by drugs to the exclusion of everything else? Why does this happen even with a drug such as cocaine, which causes no gross physiological withdrawal symptoms (Gawin, 1991)? Why are long-abstinent institutionalized addicts still vulnerable to relapse upon discharge? Why does a person become strongly readdicted more rapidly than he or she originally became addicted?

The roots of answers to these questions can be traced to the late 1950s, when John R. Nichols and his coworkers demonstrated experimentally that rats would "relapse" to ingesting opiates as a result of conditioning following repeated drug reinforcement (Nichols, 1965; Nichols & Davis, 1959; Nichols et al., 1956). The animals that were previously trained to ingest opiates to relieve withdrawal distress *but that were no longer experiencing withdrawal symptoms* returned to drug-seeking behavior when exposed to environmental cues associated with their previous drug ingestion. These experiments stimulated a large body of research with animals (Grabowski & O'Brien, 1981) and humans (Meyer & Mirin, 1978). Studies found that animals would self-administer all substances that humans abused (Bigelow et al., 1984), that withdrawal distress was not a necessary condition for sustained self-administration, and that the reinforcing effects of drugs of abuse conformed to all the major principles of *operant conditioning*. Operant conditioning, briefly, refers to the strengthening of responses that operate on the environment to produce rewarding effects. Thus, drug addiction is the great strengthening of the drug taking response; it results from the cumulative effects of taking drugs to produce their reinforcing effects.

The drug self-administration studies and the epidemic of cocaine addiction (a drug that produces all the behavioral manifestations of addiction but does not produce a physiological withdrawal syndrome of the sort associated with opiates, alcohol, or sedatives) caused theorists to change their understanding of the nature of addiction (Akers et al., 1968; Edwards et al., 1982; Lindesmith, 1968; Vaillant, 1969; Wikler et al., 1965). Scientists and the public alike once believed that physiological dependence, like that produced by opiates and alcohol, was the sine qua non of addiction (Lindesmith, 1947), and that the essence of treatment was detoxification. Scientists now accept that cocaine can be as addicting as any other drug of abuse (Gawin, 1991). They recognize that drug reinforcement is the essential causal factor in addiction (Edwards et al., 1982; Lindesmith, 1968; Vaillant, 1988). Both the World Health Organization (Edwards et al., 1982) and the American Psychiatric Association (1987) have accordingly revised their definitions and diagnostic criteria for addiction in line with this new theory.

The forms of drug reinforcement may vary from the relief of unpleasant states (e.g., withdrawal symptoms, emotional distress, boredom, and physical pain) to the production of euphoria (e.g., rush). However, the basic process of conditioning is the same. With repeated use, the individual becomes increasingly attached to the reinforcing stimulus and is more likely to emit the behavior that produced it. Craving is a subjective experience of this addiction, and may be an indicator of its severity. Other indicators may be behavioral, including the criteria typically used to diagnose addiction (e.g., spending large amounts of money and effort to obtain and use drugs, being unable to stop using despite important negative consequences, using drugs in inappropriate circumstances, being preoccupied with use to the exclusion of other aspects of life, and tending to relapse). Because this attachment increases (and decreases) incrementally, we recognize that addiction is a continuous rather than discrete state. How addicted the individual is at a given time is thus a matter of degree. Because individuals with preexisting emotional problems may use drugs to relieve negative states as well as to produce euphoria, they have more sources of reinforcement and have a built-in stimulus for relapse during periods of abstinence.

Extinction or Deactivation of Addiction

It follows from this conditioning analysis that the essential therapeutic event in successful drug treatment is extinction. Consequently, the goal of addiction treatment should be the systematic extinction or "deactivation" of the drug conditioning by (1) the cessation of drug use and (2) the strengthening of alternative responses to stimuli that evoked drug-use responses in the past. Extinction of conditioning occurs when one responds repeatedly to the drug-use stimuli without using drugs and being reinforced by the effects. The drug-craving response is extinguished with sustained nonuse over the relevant range of conditioned situations. This range is usually very broad because most addicts get high in many habitual times, places, moods, and social settings. The degree of addiction is reduced only by a small fraction during a month of inpatient treatment, because extinction at that time occurs over a relatively narrow range of situations and during a time span that allows for a small number of extinction experiences. Even after months of drug-free residential care and an apparent end to drug cravings, addicts often resume drug use immediately upon discharge when exposed to unextinguished triggers. Thus, reduction of a high degree of addiction to the very low levels that make relapse unlikely usually requires a substantial amount of time, typically several years.

We refer to extinction as "deactivation of craving" in our clinical work because most clients are not familiar with the Skinnerian concept, and we want to emphasize to them that the potential for rapidly reactivating addiction by drug use is never lost.

The initial cessation of drug use is only an essential first step in the long-term process of reducing the strength of the drug-use response. In this model, detoxification per se (medical treatment of physiological symptoms to provide relief) is no longer considered *the* central objective of drug treatment, even when the drug in question is one that produces classic withdrawal symptoms. Surely, relieving withdrawal distress is important because it is humane and eliminates a major stimulus of relapse during early recovery. So-called protracted withdrawal distress (low-grade physiological abnormalities that persist for months after drug use ceases) also contributes to explaining relapse. But most scientists do not hold that physiological dependence constitutes a drive state that is essential to explain why addicts react in special ways to drugs. Experts know that, although detoxification is usually quickly and easily accomplished, the problem of addiction persists well after physiological dependence has been resolved. Relapse often occurs long after detoxification because drug use is reinforced by much more than relief of withdrawal.

Clinical Application: Relapse Prevention

Relapse prevention, one of the components of RTSH (McAuliffe & Ch'ien, 1986), was one of the first clinical applications of conditioning theory to achieve wide acceptance in the substance-abuse field (e.g., Marlatt & Gordon, 1985). Relapse was a natural target for early behavioral addiction theorists (McAuliffe & Gordon, 1974, 1980; Vaillant, 1969; Wikler, 1965) because relapse after a long period of abstinence could not be explained easily by a theory that depended on withdrawal sickness as the essential cause of compulsive drug use. Many conditioning principles are useful for understanding relapse-related aspects of addiction. For example, a fundamental law of conditioning theory is that relearning occurs much more quickly than original learning. That principle explains why abstaining addicts find that resuming drug use causes readdiction much more rapidly than initial drug use caused addiction. Another conditioning principle predicts that intermittent reinforcement (such as "slips") produces "resistance to extinction," which helps explain why craving for drug use can persist for a long time when clients use on occasion during recovery. Conditioning studies predict that an addict will occasionally experience a "return of responding" even after a long period of continuous extinction (Deese & Hulse,

1967). This phenomenon is quite common among recovering addicts who have remained abstinent for years.

One method of relapse prevention explained by conditioning theory is administration of naltrexone. Naltrexone is a medicine used to block the reinforcing effects of opiates and thereby prevent relapse. The treatment approach is highly effective if the naltrexone is taken consistently. After one or two tries, most addicts do not use opiates again while on naltrexone. Unfortunately, only highly motivated addicts are willing to take naltrexone over a long period of time.

Other examples of conditioning factors in relapse prevention are the threat of incarcerating a probationer if he or she has a positive urine test (i.e., of punishing the drug-taking response) or the reminder by an employee assistance program (EAP) counselor that the addict will lose his or her job as the result of relapse. Impaired professional committees perform the same monitoring function for addicted doctors and nurses. A formal application of this form of conditioning theory to relapse is known as "contingency contracting" (Anker & Crowley, 1982). Relapse is prevented by making a severe punishment contingent upon relapse. For example, a patient and therapist agree that if the client returns to drug use the therapist will send a letter to his or her spouse, boss, professional licensing board, or someone else in a position to bring about sanctions. Previously prepared by the client, the letter confesses that the client is actively using again. Although not widely used in its pure form, this approach highlights the concept of contingencies in conditioning theory, an idea that our program employs with regard to natural reinforcers (see the discussion of commitment steps below).

Perhaps most important for applications of conditioning theory to relapse prevention strategies were experimental studies that have shown that relapse can be induced by exposure to conditioned "discriminative stimuli" (Grabowski & O'Brien, 1981). Many formal relapse prevention programs now counsel clients to identify and avoid these "craving triggers," "high-risk situations," or "dangerous situations" (Annis, 1986; Daley, 1987; Marlatt & Gordon, 1980; McAuliffe & Ch'ien, 1986). In addition to the personal triggers that each client must identify, there are some situations that are dangerous for most clients. It is not surprising, for example, that having cash in hand is dangerous for most newly recovering addicts, for cash was consistently associated with their drug use. The existence of a large number of common relapse triggers is one reason that group approaches to relapse prevention are efficient.

Conditioning Analysis of Halting Active Drug Use

The usefulness of conditioning theory is not, however, limited to relapse prevention. Conditioning theory may also be used to analyze cessation from illicit drug use. Methadone maintenance eliminates illicit drug use by preventing withdrawal distress and by satiating the craving for opiates so that environmental triggers are rendered ineffective. Incarceration can end drug use simply by making access too difficult; craving in response to internal cues declines with recognition of the unavailability of drugs and with frustrated attempts to obtain them.

Residential treatment achieves abstinence by a combination of strategies. It removes the client from any easy opportunity to obtain drugs (suddenly and substantially increasing the effort required to use) and from the external stimuli (including paraphernalia, other users, and dealers) that trigger craving and use (Malow, 1989). Residential clients experience a total break with their previous daily routines and lifestyles. They are kept busy in therapy and self-help sessions and other recovery-supportive activities, and they are thereby prevented from dwelling on internal stimuli that produce craving. If there is discomfort due to physiological withdrawal, medical staff may ease it with a short course of medication. The staff monitors the client's progress and intervenes when there is trouble. The clinicians also establish norms and values that are inconsistent with the drug culture and replace it with the culture of recovery. The presence of other residents going through the same process also helps to provide support and social reinforcement for stopping drug use. This combination of elements in residential programs is apparently highly effective in helping addicts stop drug use while in the institution (Edgehill Newport, no date; Miller et al., 1990). What happens to them when these supports are suddenly removed through discharge is another issue—the one at which the early recovery component of our program is directed.

Outpatient Cessation

The outpatient cessation component of our program uses strategies that are similar to the conditioning ideas inherent in residential cessation programs. The person must first be separated from drugs. Although the physical restraints of residential treatment are absent in outpatient treatment, outpatients can make using drugs much more difficult by restricting the clients' access to intoxicants. Clients can get rid of any drugs in their living spaces (including home, job, and recreation), destroy paraphernalia, and arrange for others to keep intoxicants out of the house during this especially vulnerable period. They can then take effective steps to limit their exposure to drug-related external stimuli outside the home (e.g., avoiding old friends or places where people use drugs). A person in cessation treatment can get others (e.g., a spouse) to help with activities (e.g., food shopping) that might expose the recovering person to places where drugs are sold. Newly recovering persons can have someone else hold their cash, and they can destroy dealers' telephone numbers. Of course, group and individual counseling can be delivered as well in an outpatient setting as in a residential facility. Clients can build further support for recovery by going to self-help meetings and by surrounding themselves with supportive people who express values and norms of the recovering community. These activities also keep the newly recovering person busy. The client can inform family members, his or her boss, and important others that he or she is in recovery; they will then be able to help monitor the recovering person's progress and help avoid major stresses. Thus, a conditioning analysis allows a newly recovering addict to construct outpatient mechanisms that are functionally equivalent to the effective elements of residential cessation treatment.

Early Recovery

Recovery includes more than the processes of cessation and extinction. The harm done by years of the disease process must be repaired. That includes physical disease, cognitive and psychological pathology, and relations with family, friends, employees, credit agencies, and society at large. The factors that led to addiction initially (psychological problems, deviant associates, etc.) must be eliminated or dealt with in new ways. The mechanisms (social skills, attitudes, and values) needed to achieve a healthful, nonaddict life need to be strengthened, learned, or re-learned.

We define *early recovery* as the first month following stopping of drug use. When we began developing this treatment modality, we thought that persons who stopped use as outpatients would need approximately 2 weeks to stabilize and learn the basics of recovery before moving on to long-term outpatient treatment (a recovery group and individual counseling in our case). We also assumed that 2 weeks of orientation and of making basic adjustments to outpatient drug-free living would be sufficient for the many clients who had achieved abstinence in residential programs but were not ready to enter a long-term recovery group. Our subsequent experience indicated that 4 weeks was more nearly correct for both types of clients.

As we proceeded with the outpatient cessation design, we analyzed the behavioral elements of early recovery in order to structure a program that met the specific needs of early recovery. Most of the elements essential for outpatient cessation continue to be needed in early recovery, but in addition the process of repair must begin. Because responses to most external discriminative stimuli, or triggers, are still unextinguished when a newly recovering addict is discharged from inpatient detoxification or completes outpatient cessation treatment, most triggers must be avoided, at least temporarily. Newly recovering clients must be willing and able to avoid drug use and users, throw away any remaining drug-associated possessions, avoid unnecessary cash, postpone or be accompanied in stressful situations, and keep busy at work or in recovery meetings from morning until night. They also must continue to surround themselves with supportive people, which maximizes incentives not to relapse. Damaged relationships with family and friends must be rekindled. During their first weeks as outpatients, clients need intensive training and support for these strategies. They need to know what to avoid and how and why to avoid it. They also need to make drug use as difficult as possible by limiting access and encouraging others to monitor "slippery" behavior. The newly recovering person must also initiate planning for long-term recovery and take the first irrevocable steps in the process of rehabilitation.

The "Walls"

In effect, both cessation and early recovery require constructing outpatient psychosocial "walls" that approximate the effective physical restrictions of inpatient treatment. The highly restricted daily routine for a newly abstaining addict may start with a period of planning for the day, followed by going to work in the morning, a Narcotics Anonymous (NA) or CA meeting at noon, a quick dinner at home or with a temporary sponsor or recovering friend, a cessation-group meeting, and then another NA meeting before bedtime. On weekends, a person might attend as many as three NA meetings daily and have a bite to eat with group members after the last meeting. Whenever he or she begins to feel shaky, he or she must immediately go home or seek support at an NA meeting or from a recovery counselor.

Many clients who reluctantly accept these restrictions at first eventually come to view them as necessary first steps in recovery. The abstaining addict must surrender the notion that recovery can be achieved by merely stopping cocaine use; for, as later sections show, cocaine use does not take place in a vacuum but is part of an integrated lifestyle, a "fabric" in which each thread is intertwined with all the rest. Whether addicts recover in treatment or on their own (Biernacki, 1986; Shaffer & Jones, 1989), experience indicates that major restructuring is required. A new lifestyle fabric must be woven. Helping clients to accept that the beginning of this process requires restrictions and demonstrating how to make necessary changes are thus central tasks of outpatient cessation programming.

The need for restrictions can be explained to clients by drawing a parallel with the restrictions placed on a person who is recovering from a broken leg. In the hospital, the patient with a broken leg must stay in bed most of the time. When discharged, a period of bed rest is common. A cast and crutches provide support but impose restrictions. Once the cast is removed, the patient must still undergo rehabilitation before returning to normal activities, and an even longer period is needed before demanding activities such as sports are possible. When compared to recovery from a broken leg, the restrictions imposed by recovery from cocaine addiction do not seem to be quite so onerous or exceptional.

With sufficient time for extinction and new learning at every step, the client can lower the restrictive "walls" gradually. Although with each lowering of the "walls" the recovering person should expect to experience new challenges and some resulting craving (thoughts of drugs, wishes to return to the former lifestyle, or desires to use), the objective is to make the process so gradual that the craving is manageable. If craving becomes too threatening, the client must back up and proceed more slowly. A "relapse," even a very brief one, is usually a clear signal that the client has not begun with high enough walls, or has lowered them too quickly. In many cases, a relapse in early recovery may mean that a more intense level of support (such as a halfway house) is necessary.

Coping with Craving

However solid the "walls," the newly recovering person will undergo a substantial amount of drug craving and should develop strategies for coping with it from the outset. Despite comprehensive efforts to avoid external triggers, some are unavoidable (see below), as are internal triggers (emotions, time of day, and so on). A variety of methods are available for reducing the intensity of craving: meditation, distraction, cognitive "debating," social support, and so on. These techniques require learning and practice if they are to be effective, and should be part of any early recovery program.

Differentiating Relapse Triggers

As a result of focusing upon one stage of recovery, we realized the importance of differentiating among triggers and that the ideal response to them varied as the client progressed through the stages of recovery. Triggers or dangerous situations may be divided into three types:

1. *Triggers that should be avoided permanently from the beginning of recovery.* These include active users, drug dealers, bars, and shooting galleries. If these cannot be avoided on every occasion, the client must learn to leave the scene as quickly as possible. Whereas some behavioral programs have recommended "desensitization" exercises (such as injecting with water) to extinguish these triggers, we believe that because such triggers are at the core of the addict lifestyle, they should be permanently left behind.

2. *Triggers that cannot be avoided.* These cues include internal stimuli such as stress, depression or anger, and excitement. They may arise from experiences common to early recovery (dealing with creditors, going to court, job stress, and unexpected family crises). Less common, but especially threatening, events include the death of loved ones or being treated with pain medication by a physician. They may also include long-standing emotional or interpersonal problems that predated and often contributed to the development of addiction. Cessation counseling must help clients handle these triggers by teaching specific coping mechanisms (see below) and by addressing the source of the undesirable stimulation where possible—for example, resolving tensions between the newly recovering person and drug-using family members.

3. *Triggers that should be avoided in earlier stages of recovery when possible, but that must be dealt with eventually to achieve a full recovery.* These triggers are essential aspects of conventional life that have become associated with drug use during active addiction, and need to be transformed back into neutral stimuli. They include sex and intimate relationships, handling money, and major life decisions such as having a child or changing careers. They may also include long-standing interpersonal issues (e.g., marital problems). These stimuli should be avoided initially because of their strong associations with drug use and because they can distract the addict from the work of early recovery. However, resolving chronic problems and converting triggers such as sex or cash into positive forces or coping with them effectively must eventually become central parts of the recovery process (Annis & Davis, 1988). A primary task of cessation therapy is to help new clients understand and accept their temporary limitations.

Because clients' needs vary during the course of recovery, the same topics (e.g., the family in recovery) may be handled somewhat differently in the present program and in long-term treatment, such as our RTSH groups, or in an advanced recovery program.

Commitment Steps

Most clients in early treatment are still ambivalently attached to the old reinforcers and naturally resistant to making difficult and frightening changes. Because a client's willingness to make commitments to change is a critical variable in early recovery, clinicians need effective social and behavioral techniques to assess and increase this willingness. A special alternative response that facilitates willing commitments to a new lifestyle at the cessation phase is what we call a *commitment step*. Commitment steps are concrete actions that bind one more tightly than before to a new course of action. The ideal commitment step is one that positively rewards the recovering person in a drug-free manner *and* makes drug use more difficult or more costly. Each such step makes further steps more likely by increasing new social rewards, making backsliding more difficult, and giving one more to lose from failure.

For example, a client might disclose to the group that he or she has been thinking about getting high on Saturday night. This might result in a public commitment to attend, instead, a Saturday night NA meeting with the group. Thus, the addict has in a single stroke invoked a group sanction against getting high on Saturday night and created a situation in which he or she is likely to be rewarded for abstinence by group acceptance and drug-free fun. Because we recommend that learning new behaviors occur in a series of discrete actions (successive approximations of the new behavior) that are likely to succeed, we refer to these actions as steps in an ongoing process. (There is no connection with the 12 steps of NA.)

Disclosing one's recovery to loved ones, co-workers, or employers is another such step. Many cocaine addicts have concealed their use from the potentially supportive nonusers in their lives. These people usually know that something is wrong, but they do not always know what. Being open about recovery rebuilds bridges to significant others. It also protects newly recovering people from casual offers of drugs or alcohol, allows others to understand demands on the clients' time for meetings and therapy, and invites friendly overtures and support from other recovering people. Being open (with discretion, of course) also makes returning to drug use more difficult, because persons who know about the recovering person's past will be more alert to the possibilities for backsliding. Such steps can begin to move a client "off the fence" about recovery.

Becoming friendly with long-term recovering people is another important commitment step that can simultaneously satisfy the need for company and guidance and make returning to drugs and drug-using friends more difficult. The closer the client becomes to long-term recovering friends, the further he or she is removed from the places and occasions of drug use, and the more invested the client is in these new friends, the more he or she stands to lose by associating with old drug-using friends.

The superiority of commitment steps to other avoidance responses can be illustrated by the difference between the recovering addict's putting his or her free-base pipe away in a cabinet and destroying it. The latter course makes returning to drug use a little more difficult, and it invites praise from one's cessation group. Dealers can be avoided by simply not calling them; destroying one's telephone number book, changing one's own number, and exchanging the new number with people who are solidly in recovery are commitment steps. The commitment step helps to close doors on the addict lifestyle as it opens doors to the recovering lifestyle.

Giving up ready access to cash in early recovery may be accomplished by a variety of commitment steps such as tearing up cash cards, arranging for paychecks to go directly toward paying bills, and having a spouse or other trusted person hold one's cash. Such steps not only avoid a major trigger (cash in hand) and make it a little more difficult to obtain money for drugs in a weak moment; they also help to reestablish credit and reassure family members about the willingness to become responsible.

In advanced recovery, becoming involved in a healthy and honest intimate relationship with a nonuser or a person who is also in advanced recovery is an important commitment step. It not only helps to prevent relapse via casual sex, but it also leads to further investments in a conventional lifestyle (a house, children, and so forth) that make drug use increasingly alien. Spending free time with people who do not use substances and who know about the client's history of drug abuse helps to protect the client against exposure to temptation and sets up powerful contingencies against relapse.

As these examples illustrate, there are gradations of commitment steps. Not surprisingly, counselors and group leaders often have difficulty convincing clients to carry out major steps. We find that one effective behavioral strategy is to encourage a series of small, manageable steps. Attending a single NA meeting, for example, is a small commitment step because it identifies a person as being in recovery and provides support for that identification. A limited commitment option, with no stated obligation to return for another meeting, is particularly important for the client who still may be ambivalent about long-term abstinence. For clients who resist taking even this limited step, an even smaller step, such as meeting just once in private with a counselor or senior recovering person, may be a reasonable start.

It is unwise to encourage clients to undertake commitment steps that are beyond their current ability. Failure in early recovery can be demoralizing. However, when someone has failed to sustain abstinence or make progress because of insufficient commitment, clinicians must help him or her to determine the largest realistic step of which he or she is capable. Many prospective group members in our program are recovering people who have attended 12-step fellowship meetings regularly, have experienced some success, and are ready to invest and risk much more. Joining a recovery group that meets three times a week for 6 months is a substantial commitment; if the client then stops attending the group, he or she might feel guilty, alarm a spouse or employer, receive a call from the leader and other group members, and so on. Recognizing that prospective members may hesitate to make such a commitment, we have always allowed prospective RTSH members the smaller initial commitment step of visiting the Recovery Training sessions up to four times to decide whether they want to enter the program (Zackon et al., 1985). This process may result in the new client's making friends with members, finding the group helpful, and recognizing the value of making a larger commitment. Because the Clean Start program lasts only 4 weeks, it too is a less demanding commitment than entering long-term treatment, and thereby serves as a bridge from addiction to recovery.

The Social Dimension of Recovery and the Recovering Addict Lifestyle

"High-risk" situations are only part of a broad range of stimuli that have been conditioned in varying degrees by an addict's drug use. Triggers of cocaine craving do not exist in isolation. They are part of an organized pattern of behaviors, attitudes, and symbols that we call the addict lifestyle. Relapse prevention models to date have paid relatively little attention to social context or the dramatic lifestyle changes needed for recovery from cocaine or heroin addiction. This neglect is probably due to the models' origins in psychological research on alcoholism, eating disorders, and tobacco smoking, where clients are less likely than illicit drug addicts to be members of deviant subcultures. When lifestyle has been addressed, it has often been from a middle-class orientation. For example, Marlatt (1979) prescribes a "balanced lifestyle" including jogging, working fewer hours, and meditating. Although this regimen might be sufficient for recovering cigarette smokers, cocaine and heroin addicts require a much more radical and comprehensive restructuring.

In contrast to tobacco and alcohol addictions, cocaine addiction is a disorder of subculture: Many cocaine addicts are former heroin addicts who are deeply enmeshed in a subculture of illicit drug use, unemployment, crime, violence, and disease. The addict subculture sustains itself with a complex system of institutions, values, norms, beliefs, and rituals. More than just creating discrete high-risk situations, drug addiction systematically corrupts virtually every aspect of life. Retaining this subcultural lifestyle, even in part, is antithetical to recovery. Yet many cocaine and heroin addicts have never functioned in conventional society and have nothing to return to when they renounce the addict subculture (Biernacki, 1986). We believe that the success of therapeutic communities, self-help groups such as NA, and religious conversions in promoting recovery (Biernacki, 1986) is partly a result of the replacement of the addict's subculture with social support and a system of prosocial institutions, values, and beliefs.

Even middle- and working-class cocaine addicts who have retained some investment in conventional society tend to see conventional lifestyles as boring or "square." For these addicts, giving up cocaine means giving up the glitter of nightclubs, drug-oriented music, unconventional sex, alcohol and marijuana, cash cards, drug dealing, and drug-using associates. It can feel like giving up excitement itself.

Indeed, these subcultural elements are usually inherently positively reinforcing or through association with drug use have become valued by the addict (Corcoran & Carney, 1988). In many instances, cocaine addicts are strongly addicted to the triggers themselves. Sex and alcohol are two examples. Clients are naturally ambivalent about giving up triggers that are intensely rewarding on their own. Newly recovering persons may deny the need to do so ("Why can't I hang around with my old friends if they promise not to use around me?"; "Cocaine, not alcohol, was my problem. Why shouldn't I have a beer at the ballpark?"). In the same way that a recovering person relapses to cocaine use, he or she may relapse to the behaviors associated with cocaine. In short, avoidance of triggers per se is not a self-sustaining strategy, because the avoided stimuli are not naturally repelling.

One approach to this problem is to teach alternative responses that have inherently rewarding consequences. If it is not wise to go to a bar during leisure hours, then the recovering person must have an alternative place to go. Many clients have never attended a social function without being intoxicated, and they experience great anxiety in drug-free interactions. When they stop using, many recovering people are at a loss as to what to do and with whom to do it. The alternatives to learning new social and recreational skills are returning to past associates and pleasures or living without people and without enjoyment. Both options lead to relapse.

If we ask clients to forsake an entire social and recreational lifestyle, then what do we offer as a replacement? Clinicians usually view such issues as important topics for therapeutic discussion but believe that directly providing solutions is beyond the scope of professional involvement. By contrast, we believe that program-sponsored solutions to such issues in early recovery should be part of drug treatment. We encourage group members to socialize with one another, and often with the group leaders, after weeknight group meetings. We strongly recommend that members participate in NA and CA; we encourage them to make friends with other recovering people they meet there and elsewhere. We also advocate participation in NA service and recreational activities. In accordance with this treatment philosophy, RTSH groups plan social–recreational activities for all weekends and holidays, when drinking heavily is a societal norm and drugging heavily is an addict norm. Clean Start introduces persons newly in recovery to this idea of group-sponsored recreational and social activities. However, because Clean Start clients are often too vulnerable and preoccupied to participate in demanding social situations, the activities are less ambitious (e.g., going to a restaurant for coffee after a group meeting rather than planning to meet for dinner).

In short, we urge our clients to adopt in place of the addict lifestyle a "recovering addict lifestyle" with new self-sustaining satisfactions. What is unique about recovery from drug addiction, as opposed to smoking cessation, for example, is the availability of a ready-made pattern of alternative responses. Just as the triggers which a recovering cocaine addict must avoid tend to be part of an organized pattern of behaviors, attitudes, and symbols, so are many of the most available alternative responses. A community that models norms of safe and satisfying recovering behavior already exists. One function of the cessation group is to prepare members for that community and to facilitate their gaining membership in it.

Social Learning in the Recovery Group

A recovery group must support each member's efforts to replace chemical rewards with social ones. Like the long-term RTSH group on which it is based, the cessation group uses many small-group processes and social learning techniques such as modeling, social facilitation, and group rewards and sanctions to help individuals overcome resistance to change. Seeing others make changes gives clients a clear picture of how change is accomplished, and provides motivation to try a little harder. The group can provide social backing to a member who needs to confront a family member or boss. It can examine a problem, identify options, and apply its collective experience to solutions. The group can praise honest effort and signs of progress as well as identify backsliding or stagnation. Each success that is reported to and applauded by the group fosters a groupwide sense of accomplishment.

Abstinence is not the only healthy norm of recovery learned socially in the group. Members also learn together and from one another the values of responsibility, promptness, planning, foresight, patience, tolerance, honesty, frugality, humor, and respect. One of the great pleasures of leading a cessation group lies in witnessing the energy that is released as members begin to help and trust one another and experience nonexploitative friendships. Those more experienced in recovery reach out to those less experienced, and in areas where everyone is relatively inexperienced, a spirit of commonality and cohesiveness develops.

The prosocial abstinent culture in the cessation group prepares clients for membership in long-term groups and in the recovering community, just as the latter prepares them for fuller participation in larger society. Indeed, smaller recovery groups can function in the recovering community as the family of origin functions in conventional society. The newly recovering person can feel secure sustaining recovery in a group where he or she is already accepted and knows everyone. At first, the cessation group itself may be the center of the client's new social life. Initial entry into the broader recovering community is a difficult step for many clients. They may yearn to meet more recovering people, but feel uncomfortable speaking in large NA meetings. Many clients express reservations about the spiritual orientation of 12-step fellowships. These reservations are often overcome when other group members explain the 12-step traditions and norms, testify to the value of fellowship participation, and accompany new members to meetings and activities.

With each step into recovery, clients internalize more of the new values and norms of their groups and community. Acting like a recovering person results in being treated like a recovering person and vice versa. Thus, recovery gains momentum. Although the initial steps toward social values at the cessation stage can be among the most halting, they are also among the most crucial. The social limbo of the newly abstinent client becomes an opportunity for him or her to make critical new connections.

The Recovering Community

The recovering community is an important addition to our model of the sociology of the recovery process. When we began our research on recovery groups in 1979, there was no organized recovering drug addict community in Boston. By "recovering community" we mean individuals in drug treatment, members of recovery groups, people who participate in 12-step fellowships, recovering people who work in treatment, and people who let others know that they are recovering and who interact with other recovering people.

Our recent work has convinced us that without an organized recovering community, the newly recovering person's task is more difficult. For many recovering cocaine and heroin addicts, immediate integration into conventional society is mined with dangers, stresses, and frustrations. Addicts have often destroyed their relationships with nonaddicts who may be unwilling at first to forgive and forget. Many nonaddicts do not understand the process of recovery. They may deny that long-term treatment is necessary or, conversely, that recovery is possible. Society is permeated with drinkers and drug users who pose an obvious danger to newly recovering people and who often reinforce denial about the addict's inability to drink or smoke marijuana in safety. Consequently, we counsel most newly abstinent addicts to spend a transitional period in the recovering community. Within this protective community, a newly recovering person can develop coping and inter-personal skills while deactivating addiction and gradually lowering the walls to fuller social participation.

The recovering community thus provides a safe haven during the fragile period of early recovery and is an essential bridge between addict and conventional lifestyles. Like immigrant communities in broader society, the recovering community consists of members with similar backgrounds who can empathize with one another. In this community, a drug-addict past is a ticket to acceptance rather than a stigma. For people who have often felt like outsiders, this acceptance is critical. Also, as in immigrant communities, members of the recovering commu-nity perform formal and informal sponsorship roles for new members.

The recovering community can provide a broader base of abstinent social support than can a small cessation or recovery group. Like a smaller group, it offers a supportive value system, norms, rituals, and a theory of addiction and recovery; in the recovering community, this culture is not limited in time and extent as it must be in a smaller group. Furthermore, the powerful social cohesion in this community can often help one to achieve abstinence and adherence to other norms of recovery more effectively than can professional therapy alone. The many senior role models and peers in the recovering community are sensitive to backsliding, dishonesty, and lingering attachment to addict subcultural values. Deviations from community norms are quickly confronted. Moreover, a steady stream of new members in the community reminds the client vividly of the ravages and foibles of addiction. Finally, the community is a source of free and available treatment for addicts and their families, and of practical support, such as safe housing, when one needs it most.

In time, as craving diminishes and the client fine-tunes new coping skills, he or she begins to look beyond the solid base of support in the recovering community to career advancement and broader social involvement. Some people who have become drug counselors may begin to pursue careers other than drug counseling. Friendship networks expand to include nonrecovering people who may have similar career, family, or recreational interests. Integration into conventional society occurs gradually with the increase of the recovering person's commitments, coping skills, and enjoyment of conventional rewards.

Thus, we have described a three-stage model of lifestyle change during cocaine recovery: (1) a brief period of stringent restrictions (the "walls") gradually grows into (2) a recovering lifestyle and involvement in the recovering community, which in turn slowly expands to (3) a drug-free conventional lifestyle. The speed and completeness of this transformation depend upon how severe addiction was at the start, whether there is substance abuse during recovery, how deeply entrenched the user was in the addict lifestyle, and how fully the recovering person is willing and able to make commitments to a new lifestyle.

The Causal Context of Recovery

The process of addiction occurs within a causal context; long-term recovery requires changes in the context or at least in the way one responds to it. Persons who become addicted to cocaine tend to be socially or economically impoverished, thrill-seeking, psychologically unstable, or otherwise maladjusted. Addiction and its termination tend to exacerbate all of these deficits. Although the beginning of recovery may be the time to learn to cope with, rather than resolve, many problems, sooner or later they must be addressed. Frequently, membership in cohesive groups that help clients separate from cocaine also helps them take the initial steps to address these preexisting deficits (Khantzian et al., 1990).

Client Needs during Cessation and Early Recovery

"Someone I knew pulled up to the bus stop where I was waiting and said, 'I've got it.' My heart started racing and I felt like puking, but I did what I'd planned to do in [the group]. I took off in the other direction. The only thing that saved me was knowing that I was coming here tonight."

This journal entry comes from a cessation-group member. All literate clients were required to make short daily journal entries. Because the journals often speak eloquently of the needs of clients in a cessation program, additional examples follow:

"I'm starting to feel some hope. Before I didn't know there *was* recovery and I wouldn't have believed you if you told me. But here it's spelled out, and I can *see* it. There are rules in this game."

"I need to keep my mind on recovery rather than getting high. I can see it working for others. But every little thing sets me off . . . someone saying 'product,' the sight of baking soda . . . but if I were more busy it would help. Tell me what to do."

"I know I can't drink when I think about it logically . . . but there's this other voice that says I can."

Effective treatment must clearly address the needs of its intended patients. We designed our program for the addict seeking treatment in the earliest stages of recovery. For reasons explained in the previous chapter, such addicts enter treatment in personal and social disarray. Addiction has become inviable, but it has not yet been "extinguished" and replaced with alternative responses. Consequently, the client in early recovery has many needs. This chapter sets forth the most salient of these needs so that the reader will better understand the purpose of the overall treatment model and of the individual sessions.

Safety, Reassurance, and Hope

Addicts come to an outpatient cessation program for a great variety of reasons. Many are under pressure from employers, loved ones, courts, or child welfare agencies. Many are trying to avoid the more drastic step of inpatient treatment. Some have already tried inpatient treatment and feel the need for intensive transitional support or further intervention in the face of relapse or feared relapse. Some have been severely shaken up by financial losses or health problems. Others have had relatively few adverse consequences, but are dismayed by their repeated failures to control their use on their own and the prospect of serious problems if their use continues. Some come hoping to learn how to succeed at becoming controlled users. Others are tentatively trying out the idea that they are addicted and need treatment.

Even though some have been traumatized or pressured more than others, most of the clients who show up for the first time at a cessation group have the dazed look of earthquake survivors. They seem bewildered by the extent of their loss of control. "The world I thought I was on top of turned upside down on me," as one young man put it. Cocaine works its devastation rapidly, and the first needs of its survivors are for safety, stability, and reassurance. They need to know that they are in a sympathetic, understanding, and drug-free setting, that they are in competent hands, and that there is reason for hope. Like anyone entering treatment for a suddenly devastating and life-threatening illness, they need to feel that they are in the right place.

The message of the early cessation sessions must therefore inspire confidence, and so must the messengers. The leaders must be well prepared, calm, and orderly. Because many clients are completely unfamiliar with the nature or requirements of treatment, and because their attention and comprehension may be impaired in the wake of their drug use, the program and its administrative details must be explained slowly and carefully, as must the principles underlying the treatment model. A clear diagnosis of addiction can be calming and reassuring. In addition to sympathizing with the clients' distress, leaders must offer an explanation and description of the causes and symptoms of addiction that rings true to the clients' experience. Even for clients in denial (see below), the diagnosis of addiction usually makes sense at some level and offers great relief.

One message repeated in various ways in the early sessions is that addiction is a deceptive and devastating condition, but a treatable one. The diagnosis of addiction is made more acceptable to the degree that it is paired with realistic and hopeful information about treatment and recovery. The negative cultural connotations of "addict" need to be counterbalanced by the positive identity of "recovering addict." It is reassuring to know that craving and confusion are normal consequences of addiction, if the recovering addict also knows that they can be gradually reduced in recovery.

In sum, the cessation group is, for an addict, a welcoming port in a storm. It is a safe and caring drug-free center of early recovery. Once safe within it, clients can begin to learn about their disease and help one another make the prescribed changes. From it, they can slowly venture out to practice drug-free living and to expand their systems of support.

Instruction, the Foundation, and the Walls

The first priority of recovery is to stay substance free on a daily basis. (The theoretical basis of this assertion was given in Chapter Two.) To this end, clients need easy-to-remember instructions to stop drug use, to avoid common dangers, and to deal with unavoidable crises. The new client must understand the concept of the "foundation" and the "walls" of recovery. The walls and the foundation are our terms for the system of steps that creates a life space that is free of drugs and that ensures support for recovery. Clients are not likely to recover if they are routinely exposed to powerful but avoidable craving triggers. Four conditions can be thought of as the cornerstones of the foundation for recovery: (1) a drug-free residence; (2) a reasonably drug-free workplace or source of financial support; (3) drug-free places to spend leisure time; and (4) drug-free social support (including treatment, the family, the self-help community, and other sources of help and guidance). If the cornerstones are not in place, the outpatient's first task during the cessation phase is to begin to put them into place. A client's willingness to take foundation-building steps is one of the best indicators of his or her readiness to take on the responsibilities of outpatient treatment.

The walls of early recovery can be thought of as the extension of the principles elaborated in Chapter Two to all daily activities. In the cessation phase, the *minimal* walls can be conveniently summarized as the three "A's"—Abstinence, Attendance, and Avoidance (of avoidable threats to recovery). The client who is not seriously open to the idea of abstinence from all mood-altering substances is unlikely to benefit from outpatient treatment. The same is true for the client who is not willing to avoid users and opportunities to get high or who cannot show up regularly for treatment. Avoiding unnecessary exposure to craving triggers includes ending relationships with drug-using friends and dealers. A continuing theme of this manual is that no task is more central to clients' early recovery than their changing of friends and associates. In addition, they must stay out of bars, rock concerts, and other places associated with drug and alcohol use; and they must get rid of posters, records, magazines and other artifacts of the drug-using lifestyle. As one client expressed it, "You need to do a whole personal and social 'makeover.' "

As we suggested in Chapter Two, "commitment steps" can make drug use more difficult for the new client while providing positive incentives to recover. Telling as many people as possible about being in recovery is a strong deterrent from drug use. Inconvenience, embarrassment, and the prospect of social losses are all formidable obstacles to backsliding. At the same time, clean people can also be models of recovery who provide encouragement and information. Family members, fellow clients, therapists, and friends can help monitor and reinforce the newly recovering person's behavior.

Another key wall is *scheduling*, that is, filling the days with planned activities. Addiction loves a vacuum. Time which is fully planned and occupied is protection against the common dangers of boredom and loneliness. Many successful clients arrange to work overtime during the initial months of recovery, and many schedule the end of the workday to coincide with the starting time of a recovery meeting. Obtaining guidance and support from professional treatment and self-help recovery meetings is a cornerstone of the foundation, and *frequent* attendance is among the most important walls. The very knowledge that there is "an appointment with recovery" in the evening adds direction to the day. The cessation program, therefore, maximizes treatment contacts. It insists on a "commitment policy" of 100% attendance (see Chapter Five) and on supplementing the cessation group meetings with required NA and CA meetings, especially on weekends.

"Portability" and Dealing with Unavoidable Crises

Not even faithful attendance and careful self-restrictions can protect a recovering addict from all temptations and stressful situations. Drugs and alcohol are pandemic in society. A special advantage of outpatient cessation treatment is that it helps clients to learn early to cope with or escape unavoidable dangers. They learn how to set priorities, think cravings through, ask for appropriate help, and occupy and distract themselves.

Clients can rehearse these coping strategies in the cessation group, but it is also essential to create as much continuity as possible between treatment sessions and home, work, and recreational settings. We therefore give clients as many portable "wall bricks" as possible, including handouts with tips for dealing with crises, a chart for monitoring and evaluating one's planning and daily activities, and fellowship meeting lists.

Overcoming Denial

Tools are useless if the client is not disposed to use them. Building a foundation and walls is a demanding job requiring the sacrifice of powerful reinforcers. It is not surprising that some of the biggest obstacles to recovery are internal. Clients new to treatment are in an awkward position. They must accept that what had appeared to be their salvation has become, or soon will become, their downfall. They have lost "everything," and they have nothing yet with which to replace it. The prospect of developing alternative answers may seem unattractive or impossible. Too often, the new client tries to obviate the need for painful solutions by denying the severity of the problem or the need to make major changes.

Many early-stage cocaine addicts, who do not fit the stigmatizing heroin-based stereotype of the hopeless street addict, say, "This can't be addiction. I have a good job, a good family, and some successful friends who tell me I'm not an addict. Furthermore, I have stopped using for weeks at a time." Fortunately, such objections are usually weak and doubt ridden. By the time an addict is trying out the notion that he or she needs help, denial is usually significantly eroded. The person may protest, "Not me," but does so with diminished conviction. Nevertheless, given the volatility of early recovery, denial tends to flare up inopportunely. One antidote to it is clear, consistent information. Our program helps each client to view his or her situation in light of standard diagnostic criteria. These criteria are derived from the conditioning theory described in Chapter Two. We present facts about the problem, coupled with hopeful information about the solution. Addiction is an insidious and devastating condition; the client's recognizing it as such makes it more treatable.

Just as important, clients need the examples and shared experience of other group members. Theories of progressive addiction become undeniably real when the client can recognize the progression of his or her disease in the other group members. Frequently, a client who still hopes to be able to control cocaine use learns from the examples of those whose similar hopes have been dashed. He or she may also learn from the experience of those who have tried to use alcohol safely.

Support for Change

Most new clients know at some level that change is necessary. However, accepting the idea that change is necessary does not in itself ensure change. Attachments to the life of addiction are deep and extensive, as is the fear of doing things differently. Even small steps into recovery are likely to be difficult. Clients come to treatment because they have been unable to take these steps without help. The cessation program helps by identifying problems, instructing clients in specific strategies, breaking actions down into manageable steps, and monitoring client progress. The group process confronts resistance, models progress, encourages concrete action, and rewards success.

A first objective is to demonstrate that change is a function of action. Once clients achieve a degree of abstinence, they too often substitute the wish for recovery and the words of recovery for its substance. Inertia is understandable but dangerous, especially at the cessation phase of recovery. Early recovery has been described as a slope that is steepest at the beginning. In the first months, the client requires some momentum and some steady forward motion in order to avoid sliding backward.

The program counters the tendency to slip backward and the failure to move forward by promoting commitment steps. Commitment steps are actions that lead to a recovering lifestyle while making returning to the addict lifestyle more difficult and less desirable. For example, by disclosing his or her recovery to a family member, the client is likely to receive approval and acceptance contingent on continuing to recover. The knowledge that a loved one who has been educated about the threats to recovery is watching acts as an additional protective barrier against these threats. Because commitment steps are socially rewarded within and outside of the group, they make further commitment steps more likely. Commitment gathers momentum with each rewarded effort.

Ambivalent clients continue to hang on to some dangerous piece of the old life. Consider the case of "Paul," who admitted in the cessation group that he was continuing to visit a nightclub on Saturday nights with a drug-using friend (but was "not using"). After determining that part of the problem was Paul's lack of clean friends, the group recommended that Paul regularly attend a Saturday night NA meeting frequented by several of the group members. In addition, he committed himself to accompanying the other members for coffee after the meeting. This step was effective because it discouraged dangerous behavior while providing a positive alternative.

"Judith" was 20 minutes late to two cessation sessions because of "work obligations." The leader asked whether her supervisor knew of her recovery. Disclosure, she objected, "could cost me my job." A closer examination revealed that disclosure, on the contrary, probably would have gained Judith support for recovery. What *might* have caused her to lose her job would have been a subsequent relapse. It was the leeway to relapse that she had been protecting. Rather than disclosing her recovery to employers, Judith dropped out of the cessation program and relapsed. Ultimately, she took the appropriate commitment step and was readmitted to the program.

Not all of the small, productive steps supported by the cessation group are commitment steps. Sometimes, for example, clients might be encouraged to speak more often in group meetings or to attend the group's delicatessen outing for 15 minutes instead of 5 minutes. When clients are not making at least minimal progress (e.g., if they are avoiding drug use by isolating themselves at home after work or after treatment), they tend to tire of recovery. Unable to move forward into new satisfactions, they slide backward into the accustomed ones. Conversely, obtaining new social and recreational rewards, however small initially, can make abstinence self-sustaining.

Another case is that of "Jack," who was too anxious to tolerate drug-free social situations. He found himself unable to accompany the group to the delicatessen. He could not remember ever having been drug free in adult society, and had no idea what to say. The leader made two suggestions. The first was for Jack to ask openly at the next group session whether other members had experienced similar fears and, if so, how they had dealt with them. The second suggestion was to accompany the others for coffee for only 10 minutes. Jack followed both suggestions. He discovered in the next session that intense social anxiety is normal in early recovery and that it was acceptable to the group. Indeed, one member expressed appreciation to Jack for having voiced *her* fears. Another member reinforced the leader's suggestion that the feared behavior be broken down into manageable steps: "Sometimes when you're afraid of a new thing it feels like you've got to do it all at once. You don't." Someone else offered to demonstrate progressive relaxation techniques. Another member remarked that Jack didn't have to say anything at all: "Being there and listening can be enough." This combination of behavioral coaching, peer acceptance, encouragement, and role models was enough to help Jack begin to move forward.

Self-Assessment and Information about Treatment and Recovery

Jack was ready for outpatient treatment. Once shown where to dig the foundation, he needed only some ongoing encouragement and the tools for digging. Others are less prepared for the size of the job. They may have no idea of what is involved, what help is available, or how to obtain or utilize that help. They may expect drug-abuse treatment to be like an antibiotic that will somehow "cure" them without their taking active responsibility for getting better. Some are simply not ready for recovery. Others may require a period of residential treatment. Nevertheless, almost all will benefit from assessing their situations in light of the usual needs and course of recovery.

A realistically optimistic picture of treatment and recovery can help the client to accept the addict diagnosis. It makes possible the *"recovering addict"* identity. It can also temper unrealistic expectations, and, as in Jack's case, can help the client to define what is normal and appropriate to an early stage of recovery. "The big picture" of recovery can clarify the client's immediate task.

An effective overview of treatment and recovery needs both breadth and depth. It must clarify a wide range of resources and shine a headlight on the road ahead. Clients need to understand their roles in relation to groups, self-help fellowships, and individual counselors. They should become acquainted with the effective elements of treatment, and they should learn what it means to say that treatment works. They need to know what the cessation group offers that is different from what NA offers. Some clients have had no experience in groups and need basic practice in how to listen and participate. Others need an introduction to more sophisticated group-membership skills such as how to respond helpfully. Most new clients must consider carefully how much treatment is enough, in terms of both intensity and duration. Finally, they need a sense of destination. This can be provided in part by examining the relationship between the cessation group and long-term treatment, and why it is desirable to graduate from one phase to the next. An advantage of group treatment is that the clients with more skills and relevant experience in these areas become resources and models for clients with less.

A Group Culture

Clients "come in from the cold" of addiction with all of their affiliations and values devastated. For many, the cessation group offers a reintroduction to humanity. Usually, the gratification of finally belonging somewhere and of sharing values and goals bursts forth like a pent-up natural force. The leaders must nurture this spirit, because it is powerfully motivating, but at the same time must temper and channel it practically lest everyone get carried away with pseudofellowship. Leaders must not allow the new culture of abstinence to become so militant that members feel inhibited from revealing cravings or relapses.

Liberal cheering and applause are very useful, but are no substitute for thoughtful group problem-solving, a behavior that the leader must model. Good-natured laughter is one of the best corrections for those who get carried away. It also helps break the ice and to foster group cohesiveness. The group's sense of its culture can be nurtured by stories about specific crises overcome and about the origins of group sayings and principles. Graduates of the group invited back to tell about their recovery experiences contribute powerfully to the group's identity and offer a useful introduction to long-term treatment.

Bringing the Family into Recovery

As indicated, the client's "walls" must extend beyond the formal treatment sessions. No source of support is more potent than loved ones. Many clients are motivated to seek treatment by the loss or threatened loss of support from someone close to them. By the same token, many clients protect their "relapse room" by leading double lives, not disclosing or incompletely disclosing their recoveries to family members. Such disclosure is a key commitment step during the cessation phase.

In order to bring loved ones into the client's recovery efficiently, family members must be invited to treatment. There they can be educated about what clients need—for example, why intensive, long-term treatment is necessary and why stopping drug use is only the beginning of recovery. They can also learn about the difference between supporting recovery and "enabling" addiction, and why loved ones themselves may need support separate from that of clients. At the same time, clients must learn to take responsibility for putting recovery first in dealing with family members.

Clients also need to understand clearly the dangers of associating with family members who use drugs or otherwise threaten recovery.

Many clients continue to deny their vulnerability to loved ones who are users. The group must be sensitive to the pain of having to separate from loved ones, and to some degree, the group itself can fill the void caused by such separations. These issues, like the others identified in this chapter, must be addressed systematically by the structure of the program and by the content of the clinical sessions.

Program Goals

The goals of the Clean Start program are implied by the needs of the clients at the cessation phase. Like those needs, the goals are interrelated. Briefly, the goals are to:

- help clients to achieve and sustain abstinence from all mood-altering drugs;
- help to relieve the pain of this process;
- educate clients about the disease of addiction and its treatment;
- prepare clients for long-term treatment;
- assess with them their appropriateness for outpatient treatment and any referral needs for additional outpatient services;
- resolve attitudes, such as ambivalence about recovery, denial, and resistance to change that could interfere with long-term treatment;
- resolve external obstacles to treatment (e.g., work and child-care schedules);
- resolve immediate dangers to recovery (e.g., habitual attendance at a nightclub);
- begin to build a foundation for long-term recovery (including appropriate social supports);
- create an experience of positive membership in a recovery group; and
- support advancement from the Clean Start group to the long-term treatment as a significant achievement.

These objectives overlap. The achievement of stable abstinence, the primary goal of the cessation regimen, is a necessary preparation for long-term treatment. It is essential to the client's foundation for recovery, and it protects the integrity of advanced groups. Many of the measures that build a foundation for long-term recovery also help the client to stay abstinent on a daily basis. The ability to resolve situations such as the use of psychotropic prescription medications or scheduling conflicts that could interfere with long-term treatment also help clinicians and clients to assess clients' readiness for outpatient treatment—as does the ability to initiate foundation-building steps. Finally, achieving a sense of membership in a mutually supportive group is preparation for other group memberships. Although the goals of the program are separated for purposes of coherent discussion below, the reader should keep in mind that, in practice, achieving any one of these goals is likely to entail progress toward the others.

Cessation

The primary goal of cessation treatment is to help clients achieve and sustain abstinence for the first month of recovery, for without abstinence nothing else is possible. As we made clear in Chapters Two and Three, the techniques and strategies for achieving stable abstinence include, but are not limited to, the traditional strategies of relapse prevention. Craving triggers are embedded in integrated styles of social behavior. Changing these styles amounts to changing one's core of motivations. That is why the goals of stable cessation and those of stable early recovery are consistent. Techniques such as commitment steps help newly recovering addicts to separate from drugs more securely by fostering changes in their social affiliations. The best barriers to relapse are also incentives to growth.

Clients who have not yet established a period of abstinence on their own, including those who use only on weekends, need to stop using immediately in order to attend the sessions. This requires an intensive, multifaceted program of education, self-restrictions, incentives, and supports for not using. The client must learn what triggers to avoid and how to avoid them; how to cope with withdrawal and craving; how to use natural barriers (time, distance, inconvenience) against relapse; how to use financial and social barriers (restricted access to cash and the valued opinion of others); and how to fill daily schedules with activities that support and reward recovery. (Also see the section on the "walls" in Chapter Two.) Because the goal is abrupt cessation, these measures must be undertaken simultaneously in a group milieu that supports radical changes of behavior and attitudes.

Clients who come directly from an inpatient setting and have not been abstinent as outpatients and those who have achieved some outpatient abstinence but are having trouble sustaining it may require less basic education about addiction than the others. But all clients need support for eliminating weak spots in the walls and executing commitment steps. Discharge from inpatient treatment is almost always a time of shaky abstinence. (The reasons for this, including unsupported exposure to stress and unextinguished craving triggers, are discussed in Chapter Two.) In addition, some clients leave a residential setting feeling "cured." They may have quickly grasped the principles of cessation at a cognitive level, but they are unprepared to make the sweeping behavioral changes that those principles imply. Such clients often reveal signs of overconfidence and secret reservations about full compliance with the program.

The reasons to achieve stable abstinence are repeated in some form in every session, and they are set forth most extensively in the session titled Erecting the Walls. They are, in short, that the use of any intoxicant reactivates addiction or may result in a substitute addiction; that any drug use makes drug-free learning unlikely; and that any drug or alcohol use by group members threatens the entire cessation group and is a barrier to membership in the recovering community. The "whys and hows" of abstinence are explained repeatedly, and clients are commended for "being here and being clean" as critical first steps, whatever else they have or have not accomplished.

However, to say that achieving stable abstinence is a necessary goal of the cessation program is not to say that it is an ultimate goal of recovery. We emphasize that recovery is never just about *not* doing something; it is about doing something different and better. Thus even for the earliest craving crises, we counsel clients to practice healthy alternative responses such as socializing, eating, exercising, and meditating. When a client is applauded for a day, a week, or a month of abstinence, the leader habitually should ask, "What are you doing instead of drugs?" The ultimate goal of recovery, if it is to be successful, is a drug-free life that is more satisfying than one dependent on drug use.

Comfort and Encouragement

The goal of cessation is more feasible if a program can allay the pain of cessation. A withdrawal syndrome, for example, can become more manageable through education and support. It is soothing to know that restlessness and depression are shared, stage-normal conditions, and that they pass. Explanations of withdrawal and techniques for coping with it recur throughout the program, but they are most extensively addressed in the Erecting the Walls and Problems and Progress sessions in this manual.

Withdrawal is not the only source of pain associated with cessation and initial recovery. All members share the dilemma of having to give up a way of life with no assurance that it can be replaced. Although they are ashamed of the consequences of their addictions, they are frightened of living drugfree. Once again, it helps them to know that they are not alone. Grief, shame, and fear are universal and natural feelings that can be overcome by adhering faithfully to a proven regimen of behavioral change. Helpful peers and rational, sympathetic leaders can help each member endure these feelings while identifying their causes and taking the initial steps to reduce them. The goal of comfort and encouragement overlaps extensively with the goal of achieving positive membership in a recovery group. Both goals are pursued most explicitly in the Problems and Progress sessions.

Preparation for Long-Term Treatment

The cessation program seeks to lay the necessary groundwork for participation in long-term treatment. This groundwork includes but is not limited to the achievement of stable abstinence and education about addiction and treatment. A new member who is not securely abstinent poses an obvious threat to members with more advanced recovery. One may seek alliances with other vulnerable members and become a kind of "Typhoid Mary" of drug use. An early introduction to the behavioral theory of addiction and craving reduction supports the goal of stable abstinence. It is especially important to offer this underpinning before one enters the RTSH group where, in the 26-week rotation of topics, Deactivation of Craving is not likely to be scheduled in the first month.

Even new members who are not actively using but who remain uninitiated in the norms of the recovery group present the group with a special set of difficulties. Members of long-term groups develop a language and a culture of recovery. The group culture depends not only on shared goals and experiences but on a level of shared background knowledge about addiction, treatment, family issues, the recovering community, and appropriate group participation. It can be time consuming and distracting for the leaders and the other members to have to translate concepts such as "commitment to recovery." Moreover, other group members may react hostilely to members who appear not to share their new norms. One function of the Clean Start program is to socialize members into the group culture. This is accomplished not only by explicit education but by exposure to a structured therapeutic regimen and by group processes such as role-modeling and "partner communications." The graduate of Clean Start is prepared in this way to take an active part in further treatment.

Clients who are new to treatment often have little sense of the purpose of therapy groups or of how to behave in them. Some initially try to use the cessation group as a platform to air resentments at family members, spouses, or employers. Others sit passively waiting to be "fixed" by the leaders. Those who have never been in treatment need to understand such elements of appropriate group participation as regular and punctual attendance. Yet many newly abstinent people have not attended *anything* regularly and punctually for years. Others who are willing to make an extraordinary effort for a short period do not understand why a longer-term commitment is necessary. Thus, an important part of preparing clients for long-term treatment is persuading them of this necessity. Even clients who are familiar with treatment and recovery need to learn about the rationale for our particular approach and how we view the immediate and longer-term tasks of recovery.

People who have always functioned reasonably well in groups may take for granted the many requisite skills and attitudes. Becoming "group-worthy" entails their learning to listen well, to be honest and open, to seek and accept help, to come to the point when they speak, to cooperate, to reach out to other members, to give and receive constructive criticism, to take responsibility for doing their part in accomplishing the group's goals, to respect the recoveries of other members, and to persevere throughout the ups and downs and fits and starts of a recovery group. Because many addicts have had little experience of membership in conventional groups and organizations, these skills and attitudes must be modeled and explained in the Clean Start group. Although it is not a realistic objective to create socially competent members in a month's time, most clients can make a beginning. Disruptive clients, for example, can become aware of their impact on others.

Initial Foundation-Building

The discussions of supporting change and commitment steps in previous chapters are comprehensive enough to obviate an extended discussion here. We wish only to reemphasize that at the cessation stage the *initial* steps toward building a foundation for long-term recovery may be small. Clients can demonstrate their willingness to make larger social changes by attending their first NA or CA meeting with other members of the cessation group. If they are not ready to disclose their recovery to their employers or supervisors, they might try disclosing it to a co-worker as an interim measure. Such a step might make obtaining or using drugs just a little more inconvenient, risky, or embarrassing than it would be otherwise.

In cases of immediate and obvious danger, certain minimal changes may be needed. For example, if the newly recovering addict cannot immediately separate from a spouse who is using drugs, he or she can set other explicit limits on the circumstances of the drug use, such as refusing to allow drugs or paraphernalia in the apartment and trying to arrange an intervention with an individual or couples counselor. Most clients in the Clean Start program can at least begin to minimize danger and maximize support from family members, intimates, and other recovering people. If they cannot move or change jobs immediately, smaller intermediate steps are possible. For example, they might seek support from nonusers at work, leave work temporarily or when in danger, ask for a transfer, seek explicit help from their employers, get information about other jobs, or announce at an NA meeting that they are seeking a safe job (or roommate). Any of these steps might indicate a level of commitment sufficient to build on.

Although group leaders should not pressure clients to commit to changes that they are not ready to make, in order to graduate to long-term treatment, clients must take *some* actual steps to eliminate immediate dangers. If such steps cannot be taken while they are in crisis and have the group's support, they are not likely to be taken until there is a relapse. The Clean Start group presents the optimal conditions for action, if action is at all possible.

Positive Membership

The cessation program seeks to take advantage of the unique powers of group membership. As indicated in Chapters Two and Three, most new clients are as hungry for a sense of healthy belonging as they are unused to it. For many, the cessation group represents reentry, if not first entry, into society itself. Leaders should warmly welcome new members and respectfully acknowledge the difficulty and the importance of their asking for help. The discovery that they are accepted precisely for facing the source of their shame provides motivation when it is needed most. Moreover, the fact that they have a *shared* condition implies that members have a special understanding of one another and can help one another to get better.

Although the ingredients of mutual help are spelled out in the content of the sessions (especially in the sessions Making the Most of Treatment and Problems and Progress), precepts are of limited usefulness without concrete examples. The leaders must consistently model the attitudes and techniques of respectful listening, of cooperative decision-making, of reaching out and risking rejection, and of bringing the group's collective wisdom to bear on individual problems. They also must continually commend and encourage clients who exemplify these behaviors, and they must review the connection between desirable group behaviors and the larger goals of the group. Clear reminders of the group's shared mission are themselves powerful catalysts to group cohesiveness.

The creation of a group identity and conscience is aided by ceremonies and rituals. A written group philosophy from which members read aloud at the close of each session can be helpful. Posting group slogans such as "Being Here, Being Clean," "Learning Together," and "Freedom through Actions" reinforces the group's self-awareness. The leaders can also collect and repeat at relevant moments the stories, sayings, and jokes of successive "generations" of group members. Such verbal culture helps to bear the group's tradition, and it may be powerfully supplemented by the live recovery stories of visiting members who have moved on to long-term treatment.

Resolving Time Conflicts and Obstacles to Treatment

Many clients enter the cessation program despite obvious obstacles to full participation. If a work schedule conflicts with treatment times, the usual course is to make explicit work-schedule alterations with the employer. We have found most employers to be accommodating. Some employers or EAPs may wish to contact program staff. Consent to release information forms should be made available to clients for this purpose. Unwillingness to disclose their recovery to the appropriate employers or supervisors in order to make the necessary arrangements may indicate a lack of sufficient commitment to recovery. We have found that clients who can arrange to attend all of the cessation sessions on time can also make arrangements for a more extended commitment. The cessation sessions must demonstrate the primary importance of treatment to clients and the consequent need for arranging their schedule around it.

Because many clients omit mentioning possible sources of conflicts, the leaders must be alert to any lapses in attendance or punctuality. During orientation, and again before clients advance to long-term treatment, each client should be questioned about any prior commitments. Clients should also be questioned about transportation arrangements, vacation plans (the program prohibits vacations; see Chapter Five), and legal or medical issues that could affect attendance. Clients with prescriptions for psychoactive medications must sign release forms so that the leader or individual counselor can speak to the physician. Normally, admission to a drug-free, long-term group would require that such medications be discontinued.

Some clients with physical or psychiatric disorders will have to undertake or complete concurrent treatment for those conditions before graduating. Such conditions might range from a toothache to suicidal depression.

Completing the Program

Fulfilling the requirements for moving ahead to long-term treatment represents the achievement of a significant commitment step. Completion requires, briefly, "Being here and being clean" for 12 consecutive sessions, actively participating, and completing one's Ownwork (see Chapter Five). For many, this will be the first completed commitment in years, and it merits public recognition as such. In the graduation ceremony, clients briefly recount their progress in the Clean Start group and indicate their most important next steps in recovery. They are awarded certificates of completion signed by the leaders.

Program Design

Clean Start is an outpatient drug-free early recovery program for cocaine addicts. It is a group program that lasts at least 1 month and is co-led by a professional and a recovering group leader who follow a structured format consisting of 12 sessions. Upon completion of the program, graduates are ready to advance to longer-term recovery treatment.

The Cessation and Early Recovery Training and Therapy Sessions

In order to provide the amount of support needed to break from a drug as powerful as cocaine, the cessation program must be relatively intensive. It consists of three 90-minute drug-free group meetings a week for 4 weeks. There is a half-hour orientation session for newly entering clients. Each group meeting is structured around a topic of importance to early recovery. The topics themselves are described in detail in subsequent chapters. Here, we provide a brief overview of their basic conception and design.

The session formats were designed and arranged to meet the newly abstinent client's needs for structure, for clear, basic information, and for maximum social learning and support. We concluded that these needs could be met most cogently and efficiently by groups focused on issues specific to early recovery. In the concreteness of its focus and in the "scripted" spelling out of recovery-specific objectives, our approach differs from traditional psychotherapy. Sessions structured around specific topics of immediate relevance to all members help to prevent the group from skipping about inefficiently. Instead, issues can be covered in depth in the limited time available. This provides members with much intensive learning, and it gives them a needed sense of accomplishment and progress. The systematic arrangement of topics also allows us to demonstrate in each session the theoretical unity of our approach. Clients not only learn specific strategies, but in learning repeatedly the principles that integrate those strategies, they become increasingly able to adapt them to varying circumstances.

Maintaining focus on a topic requires a directive leadership style. Leaders must guide the group through the logical progression of segments in each session. Without step-by-step guidance, early recovery can be a chaotic experience for leaders as well as clients. At the same time, the exercises must be imaginative enough to involve clients actively in the learning process. A recovery group is not a class, nor should its leader be a lecturer. It is a form of behavioral group therapy in which the leaders, the program, and the group itself help each member to adopt behavior patterns that will end drug use, extinguish addiction, and begin the process of lifestyle change. Group cohesiveness is an essential part of this process.

The format we chose to meet these ends was adapted for early recovery from the proven RTSH format (McAuliffe & Ch'ien, 1986; Zackon et al., 1985, 1992). Recovery Training (RT) consists of two group meetings and a group social–recreational activity each week. The first weekly meeting is the RT session, a topic-based workshop that addresses common recovery issues such as intimate relationships and drug-free recreation. Through a series of connected exercises and structured discussions, the group learns the "whys and hows" of good planning, of using social support, and of attaining the healthy rewards that produce full, long-term recoveries. The second weekly RTSH session is the somewhat less structured "self-help fellowship" (SH) session. In the SH sessions, the principles set forth in the RT sessions are applied to the recoveries of individual members in more extended discussions. The SH sessions also encourage active peer support, and they reserve a segment to plan for the third weekly session, the weekend social–recreational activity. Although the SH session allows opportunity to air feelings and personal concerns, the emphasis is on identifying and supporting practical steps.

Unlike the clients in the RTSH group, who have achieved stable abstinence, a foundation for recovery, and a reasonably secure commitment to recovery, the clients in Clean Start (CS) sessions need intensive structure and support for these primary care issues. CS modifies RTSH accordingly. We feel that two weeknight CS sessions, instead of the single weekly RT session of RTSH, meet the needs of clients in initial recovery for intensive structure and for considerable information and foundation-building compressed into a brief period. These twice-weekly CS sessions are similar to the very structured RT sessions of RTSH, although they have been modified to allow for more individualized support to "shaky" members. The opening check-in was borrowed from the self-help fellowship format partly to allow the leaders to stay abreast of individuals' immediate issues. In addition, provision was made for using frequent "live case studies" to illustrate the importance of fore-thought and to commend positive examples of commitment.

In order to provide extra structure, we adopted a formal weekend Problems and Progress session instead of the weekend social–recreational activity of RTSH. The format of the Problems and Progress session is patterned after that of the self-help component of RTSH. Like the leader-facilitated self-help sessions, the Problems and Progress sessions allow for extended discussion of personal concerns in recovery while identifying and supporting practical steps. "The Daily Chart" (see below, p. 142) is used to demonstrate that "you feel better when you do better."

In our project, the Problems and Progress session was scheduled for late Saturday afternoons, a time when many clients are feeling vulnerable and need immediate support and planning for the evening. We met these needs, in part, by reserving a final segment for planning the evening's activities. The planning segment was so successful that it resulted in a tradition of informal social outings after the session. Many clients went to dinner together and then to a designated NA or CA meeting, followed by coffee and snacks. Whereas many cessation clients would be vulnerable in a "party" atmosphere such as a dance, a barbecue, or a restaurant where there is a lot of drinking, most clients find attending NA meetings en masse and eating in a deli-style restaurant tolerable and often extremely valuable. The outings help to introduce clients to the recovering community, and they create within the larger cessation group a core of committed, cohesive members who help to draw in others. Like the social–recreational activity of RTSH, the CS version is led by the recovering peer leader. However, its activities are restricted to a centrally located Saturday 12-step fellowship meeting and a nearby delicatessen.

Scheduling

Since the cessation program is designed for clients who are either already employed or for whom employment is a critical goal in recovery, the sessions are scheduled for times that are least likely to conflict with normal work hours. Our Clean Start sessions were scheduled Tuesday and Thursday evenings from 7:00 P.M. to 8:30 P.M., and the Problems and Progress sessions were on Saturday afternoons from 4:00 P.M. to 5:30 P.M. Less ideally, sessions could be scheduled on Monday, Wednesday, and Friday evenings. (Monday evening sessions conflict with many national holidays.) An appropriate schedule conflicts as little as possible with normal working hours; it distributes treatment contacts evenly throughout the week in order to ensure that clients will spend minimal periods without intensive support; and it provides for a session on Friday night or Saturday afternoon or night — times that are most associated with cocaine use for many addicts and that are therefore logical times to provide immediate planning and support. We scheduled the weekend session immediately before Saturday night, one of the most dangerous times of the week. This allows the leaders to demonstrate with practical relevance sound planning and the use of social support.

On weekends, the strengthening pull of the addict lifestyle is often reflected in poor attendance. The leaders must emphasize repeatedly that failure to attend weekend sessions is a fairly reliable indicator of insufficient commitment to recovery. Clients who miss weekend sessions should be assigned appropriate commitment steps to increase recovery activities on weekends.

Cocaine Anonymous Meeting

In addition to the three weekly cessation sessions, clients in our program are required to attend a Friday night CA meeting that is held at our site in the same room. (A concurrent Co-Anon meeting is also held at our site for spouses and family members.) This requirement not only ensures an additional weekly treatment contact but is also an auspicious means of introducing clients to the wider recovering community. Clients who might have hesitated to attend a strange meeting alone are reassured by the company of other group members. Attending a meeting in a familiar place en masse overcomes much of the typical resistance to 12-step fellowship meetings and provides a base from which to branch out to other CA or NA meetings. "Veteran" cessation members who have attended two or three CA meetings are encouraged to tout them to new members. Because members of the long-term group and its recovering group leader also attend this meeting and invite new clients out afterward for refreshments, Friday night attendance is a key to creating familiarity and continuity between the phases of our program.

Although attendance at the CA meeting is required, an attendance list is not kept, nor is one necessary. The events and speakers at the meeting are frequently topics of enthusiastic discussion in the cessation sessions, and it quickly becomes clear who is attending and who is not. Frequently, the peer leader encourages one of the former members to invite one of the latter to attend. But just as often, the level of enthusiasm of the attenders is itself enough to pull in many nonattenders. Many who miss the CA meeting feel left out and are sure to attend the next one.

Although it may not be feasible for every program to host a CA or NA meeting at the program site, an alternative strategy is to designate one centrally located weekend 12-step fellowship meeting that may be familiar to members who already attended it and/or to the leaders. In any case, there are clear advantages to the peer leader's regularly attending a meeting that is convenient to members.

Although only one weekly 12-step fellowship meeting is *required* in our program, it is made clear that every client is expected to have a minimum of one daily therapeutic contact (either one of our group meetings, individual counseling, or a 12-step fellowship meeting). Clients who do not meet that minimum standard through concurrent counseling or some other form of strong support are urged even more strongly than the others to attend additional CA, NA, and AA meetings. Although cessation from cocaine use may not require the total immersion of inpatient treatment or the intensity of day-care treatment or a halfway house, it does require at least some therapeutic support for an hour or more each day. Self-help groups can provide a majority of that support for no cost.

Membership

Enrollment in the group is "open" each week with new members allowed to enter at the beginning of the week when the orientation session is held. Initially, we allowed new members to enter at any session, but that did not allow for sufficient orientation and it led to an inefficient use of the leaders' time. Persons eager to enter treatment immediately are referred to 12-step fellowship meetings or may be seen by an individual counselor. Clients who call to inquire about the program and who are deemed eligible for it by their responses to a telephone questionnaire are directed to attend a half-hour orientation session, which immediately precedes the first group meeting of each week. To review, the major eligibility requirements are that clients: (1) be primarily addicted to cocaine; (2) be recent users or recently discharged from inpatient treatment—that is, persons for whom cessation and early recovery issues are appropriate; (3) be willing to commit themselves to complete abstinence (including alcohol and prescribed psychoactive drugs such as methadone or tranquilizers) and full attendance for the length of the program; (4) be free of severe physical or psychiatric conditions that require hospitalization; (5) be willing and able to begin to build a foundation for recovery and to resolve any potential conflicts with or obstacles to attending treatment sessions; and (6) are not applying to treatment because of legal coercion.

Difficult decisions occasionally arise around "borderline cases." For example, because almost all cocaine addicts use alcohol and other drugs as well, they are likely to be polyaddicted. The leaders must determine whether the alcohol, opiate, or other drug problem is or should be perceived by the client as the *primary* problem. If so, then the proper clinical decision may be a referral to treatment elsewhere. The leaders should explain to the client that, although all addictions are similar, cocaine addiction has some unique aspects that our program is tailored to address. Extended discussion of these issues might not seem wholly relevant to someone who needs to deal with other issues. For example, the early strategy of avoiding dealers, cash, and users might be irrelevant to a primary alcoholic. Conversely, the primary alcoholic may want to address a host of medical issues that have little relevance to cocaine programming. Similarly, whereas many cocaine addicts must struggle against denial to accept the reality of their problem, most long-term heroin addicts have been forced by withdrawal symptoms to accept that they are addicted. Extended discussions of whether one is an addict will seem beside the point to such clients, and their impatience can undermine the group intervention. Leaders are well advised to refer some clients elsewhere for the good of the group, even if they want to remain in the program after learning of the group's focus.

Leaders may sometimes have difficulty determining whether paranoid, schizoid, or depressive symptoms merit referrals to appropriate psychiatric treatment. Such symptoms are often temporary artifacts of cocaine toxicity or withdrawal. Our practice was to hold questionable clients who were not suicidal or violent for up to 2 months in the cessation program and to seek psychiatric consultation when appropriate. The obverse problem, clients who were in need of a mental health intervention but were not really addicted, was more difficult to detect but, fortunately, it was also much rarer.

The "no-coercion" requirement seems particularly important for successful outpatient treatment. Clients who enter treatment under pressure from a probation officer, to impress a judge, or to avoid losing custody of a child tend to relapse. Too often, they are motivated to make no lifestyle changes other than attending the sessions. The program presented in this manual is not primarily designed to instill motivation for recovery where little exists. Although most acceptable clients are under pressure to change, a wide range of drug-related adversities and failures produces more effective motivation than overwhelming pressure from a single source. In order to succeed in outpatient treatment, the addict must have had a fairly comprehensive self-demonstration that the drug life is no longer viable.

Although the program presented here is supplemented with printed handouts for the clients, literacy is not an absolute requirement. In groups with high rates of illiteracy, leaders can ask for volunteers to read aloud the printed materials, and written exercises can be converted to spoken ones. Nevertheless, leaders should be sensitive to the embarrassment illiteracy can cause and to the possibility of undetected illiteracy.

Finally, a special caution about couples who come seeking treatment together. Among the hazards of admitting both partners of a couple to the same recovery group is the tendency of the couple to form a negative alliance. Clinicians have long noted the power of such alliances to withstand the group pressure that is otherwise one of the great advantages of a group approach to behavior change. In addition, each partner of a couple is vulnerable to the other's relapse; each partner may feel inhibited from honest expression by the presence of the other; and each partner may become distracted by the recovery issues of the other. The experience of the HCRP eventually led us to adopt a policy of admitting to treatment only one partner of a couple and referring the other partner elsewhere. For the same and other reasons, a program rule forbids sexual liaisons between group members.

Leadership

Both the professional group leader and the recovering peer leader should be warm and open individuals who are experienced in working with addicts in groups. The Masters level professional leader must be organized and capable of applying the concepts of the sessions systematically to the diverse experiences of the members. Because many of the newly abstinent members will be unused to therapeutic group settings, the professional leader must be able to direct and contain the discussion firmly without appearing to lecture or preach. The leader must be disciplined in front of a group and able to hold to the theme of a session and to cover its main points within the allotted time.

The peer leader should be an active and committed member of the recovering community with at least 3 years of sobriety. He or she must also have made significant strides in most of the major areas of recovery. The recovering group leader must be a role model, a concrete embodiment of what the program hopes its graduates will achieve. He or she should have the cognitive skills to understand the points and the structure of each session. And he or she should be willing and able to be an active friend and confidant of members outside the sessions as well as in them. Although the peer leader should be involved in 12-step programs, the better to assist clients' entry into the recovering community, he or she must not be doctrinaire or rigid and must be able to integrate without difficulty the sociobehavioral principles of recovery with 12-step fellowship philosophy. The ideal leadership team includes opposite genders with a complementary balance of skills and personal styles.

Leading a cessation group can be a difficult job. It requires energy, dedication, preparation, and consistency. Leaders who cannot command respect, prioritize quickly, and respond flexibly without sacrificing structure can become overwhelmed. The professional leader, particularly, must be able to project to a large group, inspire confidence, set clear limits, and elicit and organize the relevant clinical information from a large number of clients. He or she must keep abreast of clients' living situations, their drug-use patterns, current crises or potential crises, individuals who may need extra encouragement or extra urine monitoring, and so forth. In order to stay in contact with the needs of a rapidly changing group, the leaders must work as a team and trade information before and after every session.

Depending on the size of the cessation group, it may be desirable to supplement the leadership team with recovering volunteers. These should be individuals of at least a year of strong recovery who can help with paperwork and urines, and who can offer individual clients extra support. Some of these volunteers can be recruited from among the program's graduates. This has the additional clinical advantages of providing a positive service activity for the volunteers and relevant role models for the group.

Finally, the importance of thorough preparation for each session cannot be overemphasized. Especially until a session has been led often enough for the material to have become second nature, the leader who is worrying about "what comes next" or how to cover all of the key points will be unable to respond attentively and flexibly to clients. Leaders should *never* have to look at the manual while conducting a session. Doing so results in a wooden and disjointed presentation, and it indicates that one has not sufficiently mastered the ideas and the continuity of the session. The best preparation consists of several readings of the material, followed by ample time to reflect on the purpose of each segment and its relation to the whole. The leader's notes should consist of no more than a short list of key words. Leaders will bring their own styles and their own illustrative anecdotes and metaphors to the material; however, they should not improvise too freely, because the interrelated content and formats of the sessions have been proven effective after much trial and error. We recommend resisting the temptation to revise the sessions until they have been used as designed at least once.

Individual Counseling

Clients are assigned to an individual counselor for weekly hour-long sessions after 2 full weeks of perfect attendance in the cessation group. The reason for the delay is to avoid wasting program resources on early dropouts and nonattenders. It is well known that cocaine addicts have a high rate of attrition in most outpatient programs. Indeed, as indicated, this group was conceived partly to counteract the adverse effects of this attrition rate on the long-term group. We determined therefore that attending six consecutive sessions demonstrates sufficiently that the client is likely to benefit from the additional counseling. However, clients may be assigned individual counselors from the outset if they ask for them and/or if the leaders decide that individual counseling is clinically indicated. For example, individual counseling may be indicated earlier if a client needs coaching to be able to speak in groups; has pressing shame-producing issues such as sexual or physical abuse; is in special need of containment, comforting, and trust; or if a more thorough assessment than the leaders have time for is needed. Early individual counseling may also be needed to determine the need for psychiatric or medical referrals; to address severe crises that would distract other group members; or to address and make referrals for withdrawal symptoms caused by dependencies on alcohol or other drugs.

Normally, the individual counselor conducts intake assessments and formulates treatment plans. He or she is a confidant for issues that a client is unwilling or unable to discuss in the group, and addresses in depth personal issues that may not be relevant to the entire group and that may predate the addiction or require more extensive attention than the group format allows. The individual counselor discusses attendance problems and individual problems with group participation, and acts as case manager, keeping abreast of the major areas of a client's recovery— for example, work, family life, legal and medical issues—and helping to coordinate diverse services. The individual counselor works closely with the group leaders to make full assessments of clients, to set appropriate treatment goals, to facilitate clients' participation in group, to help individuals overcome specific obstacles to change, and to determine if and when a client is ready to advance to long-term treatment.

Rules and Requirements for Advancement

The Cessation and Early Recovery regimen is designed so that it can be completed in 1 month, but the requirements for advancement include much more than mere attendance. The rationales for these requirements were developed and refined through the experience of running the program.

1. *Clients must remain abstinent from all mood-altering substances for the minimum 1-month period of the cessation program.* A single instance of drug or alcohol use will necessitate reapplying to the program and reattending the full sequence of sessions (with the exception of Orientation). In order to be allowed to reapply to the cessation program, clients who have used mood-altering substances also will have to demonstrate a willingness to take additional steps that will increase their commitment to recovery and their likelihood of remaining abstinent. A second instance of drug use will usually result in a referral to treatment modalities that offer more intensive support, such as day care, a halfway house, or residential treatment. (The rationale for this requirement is explained under the program goal of "Abstinence" in Chapter Four.)

2. *Clients must attend all sessions.* Full attendance preserves the continuity of treatment, allows the leaders to assess the clients properly, and indicates appropriate levels of commitment and stability for outpatient treatment. An unexcused absence or a second absence of any sort requires restarting the sequence of sessions (with the exception of Orientation). A second unexcused absence usually results in referral to treatment elsewhere. An excused absence must be made up by staying in the program long enough to make up the missed session.

Family or medical emergencies are counted as valid excuses, but having to work overtime or to care for a child is generally treated as a weak excuse because it indicates possible ongoing sources of conflict with long-term treatment, which need to be resolved early.

3. *Clients must attend sessions on time.* Lateness is disruptive to a structured group, results in missing important parts of an intensive treatment process, and indicates an unstable or uncommitted recovery. Being on time, like full attendance, must become a quickly and clearly enforced group norm. If it does not, lateness will increase and spread (in the manner of poor attendance). Two unexcused latenesses of more

than 10 minutes will be treated like an unexcused absence; three such latenesses will be treated like two unexcused absences.

4. *Clients must participate actively and appropriately in group.* If a client is not "group-worthy," he or she will be unable properly to utilize group treatment. Moreover, as we told our clients, "We can't help you if we don't know you." "Appropriate participation" can be an elusive and subjective category, in theory. In practice, however, it often means the willingness of clients who have said virtually nothing to say something about how they understand and are implementing the program. Alternatively, clients given to disruptive outbursts, to glorifying the addict lifestyle, or to irrelevant rambling must show some willingness and ability to contain themselves. Some addicts are not good candidates for group membership and should be referred to individual treatment.

5. *Clients must demonstrate a willingness to take the initial steps that build a foundation for recovery* (see Chapter Four). Satisfactory implementation of the principles of cessation and early recovery is the program's goal.

6. *Clients must adhere to the other program rules and regulations,* including demonstrating respect for the recoveries of other group members, complying with the urine policy (see "Urine Testing," below), and completing "Ownwork" (see p. 61).

Willingness to Graduate

Joining a new group is usually difficult. It can be especially difficult for people whose addictions have alienated them radically from normal social memberships. Having overcome the initial difficulty once in joining the cessation group, new clients often quickly form intense attachments to it. The group and its leaders are seen as a safe and welcoming harbor – perhaps as uniquely safe and welcoming. A common result is that clients become unwilling to move on to long-term treatment. Some client express their reluctance openly, petitioning the program to let them remain in the cessation group for up to 6 months. Others try to sabotage graduation by poor attendance or other rule-breaking.

Leaders must be alert to this sort of resistance to termination and change. They must also avoid complicity in the client's resistance. It is easy for leaders to feel flattered by clients' attachment to the group or to form overprotective attachments of their own. However, when clients are allowed to stay in the group beyond their fulfilling the requirements for graduation, the group's primary focus on cessation and initial recovery issues is diluted and its mission of fostering progress is compromised. Like the condition of stable abstinence, completing the other cessation-group requirements must be perceived by members not just as ends but as necessary means to other ends. Completion is significant in that it enables other achievements.

One way to counteract reluctance to graduate is to make graduation an attractive occasion. In some cases, certificates of graduation and ceremonies that publicly recognize achievements can be powerful incentives to move on. In others, the most effective strategy is to familiarize resistant clients with the members and leaders of a long-term group to which the client will advance. The leaders can arrange for a reluctant graduate to be invited to an outing of that group. A brief personal overture by one of the leaders of the long-term group can also work wonders. Where long-term group membership is an option, leaders regularly should emphasize its advantages, including the expanded opportunities it offers for close and cohesive belonging.

Urine Testing

At least two supervised urines should be taken from each client, one in each 2-week period, on a random basis as a prerequisite for advancing from the cessation program. If possible, the urine testing should be supervised. The capability to supervise urine testing is another advantage of having both genders represented among the group leaders and volunteers. Clients who are to give urines should be notified at the beginning of a session that the urine will be taken immediately after the session and that coffee is available if desired. Refusal or inability to urinate must be counted as a "dirty" urine (positive for substances of abuse).

In our project, we tested routinely for the presence of cocaine and alcohol, and due to cost constraints, we tested selected clients for marijuana and/or opiates, tranquilizers, and amphetamines based on their drug-use histories. Urines should be taken early enough to leave time for laboratory processing before clients are due to advance to long-term treatment.

We found it helpful to explain that urines are tested not only to determine whether clients may be too severely addicted for the present to remain abstinent but also to provide clients with extra support for abstinence during a difficult period. We found that the therapeutic relationship was best preserved (and the laboratory fee often saved) by asking each client directly before taking his or her urine whether the result might be substance-positive.

Sometimes a client's behavior and/or appearance and/or the reports of others will arouse a leader's suspicions that psychoactive substances have been used. In our project, for example, a member who had missed a weekend session was reported to be hanging out with known users. The leaders conferred to confirm their suspicions and decided to approach the client together immediately before the Tuesday meeting. The leaders discreetly and respectfully gave the reasons for their suspicions. Then, explaining that the program regulations are to protect the recoveries of all members, the leaders requested a urine. The client denied the suspected use, and the leaders explained as nonjudgmentally as possible that the urine test could "clear the air" and that it was "nothing personal." Finally, it was necessary to explain that a refusal or failure to supply a urine must be treated as a substance-positive urine.

It is tempting to avoid this sort of confrontation altogether or to accept a convincing denial. But giving in to that temptation is an invitation to wider drug use in an outpatient group modality. It also colludes in clients' denial, and it undermines the integrity of the group. Just as drug-free group members can help one another to remain drug free, members who are actively using can cause other members to relapse. In addition, secret users often become known to other members, thereby damaging the credibility of the group discussion. Drug use must therefore be monitored and confronted immediately.

"Ownwork" and "The Daily Chart"

In the early days of the Cessation and Early Recovery Program, we sometimes assigned homework that we called "ownwork." We originated the term when some clients objected to homework as being treated like "school kids." The criticism seemed fair enough because our clients were adults who had already taken an important step toward becoming responsible adults. Everyone preferred the label "ownwork," which honors the idea that recovery is ultimately one's own responsibility, and which refers to the individualization of some of the assignments.

One sort of ownwork assignment, standardized for all literate clients, was to complete "The Daily Chart" (see the Erecting the Walls session) at the end of each day and to bring it to each session. Charts are used mainly for daily self-monitoring and planning. Clients also use them during the check-in to jog their memories about relevant activities since the previous session. However, if they are at all shaky or unsure of their daily routines, the chart is also a useful adjunct to consultations with the group leaders after the session. All charts are to be turned in to the group leaders each Saturday as a condition of advancement. (Clients are responsible for making copies of the blank charts as well as of the completed ones.)

Completing the chart should take about 5 or 10 minutes. At the end of each day, the client checks off each positive activity that applies, assigning one point to each—for example, attending work or school, avoiding triggers, exercising, and attending 12-step fellowship meetings—and two points for the completion of a commitment step. Below the instructions for the chart is a list of common valuable commitment steps. After scoring for the day past, the client plans the next day's activities, penciling in treatment appointments, meeting times, people to call, situations to be avoided, situations requiring support, and ways of filling idle time. Finally, before bringing the chart to each session, the client completes the following two sentences at the bottom of the chart:

"I'm doing well at _____ ."
"I need to work on _____ ."

The chart is intended to help clients concretely apply the principles of the program to daily life. It offers a quick profile of their understanding of and commitment to recovery while highlighting precisely those areas where work is needed. Is the client spending too much time idle? Is the client exposing himself or herself unnecessarily to dangerous situations? Is the client actively pursuing a recovering lifestyle outside of our program? At a time of great potential confusion, the chart is a clearly marked "map" that also provides concrete indications of progress. Many of the clients who successfully completed our program reported that the chart was a great source of clarity and security. However, many clients will not stick with the chart unless the leaders take it very seriously and consistently monitor clients' completion of charts.

In addition to completing the chart, some clients are asked to keep daily journals of the times and circumstances of drug cravings. Others document the completion of assigned tasks such as making appointments for physical or dental examinations or getting information about appropriate residences. Again, information provided by the chart helps leaders to individualize these assignments.

Instead of completing the chart, illiterate clients are allowed to offer oral reports of their daily activities.

CHAPTER SIX

Session Topics

What needs to be accomplished in cessation and early recovery sessions? One way to approach this question is through a broader model of acute health care. The new patient in the initial stage of any sort of treatment needs (1) administrative information: the "wheres," the "whens," and the regulations; (2) patient education: a description and explanation of the diagnosis and treatment, why it is necessary, and how best to comply with it; and (3) therapy: implementing the primary steps of treatment. Because we believe that cocaine addiction is like any disease in this regard, we have adopted the three categories as guides to the content, selection, and ordering of the Clean Start topics. The sessions, in order, are:

Orientation (30 minutes)
Erecting the Walls
Closing the Doors to Addiction
Problems and Progress
Addiction and Denial
Making the Most of Treatment
Problems and Progress
Coping with Dangerous Situations
Family and Partners in Early Recovery
Problems and Progress
Making Changes
A Road Map to Recovery
Problems and Progress

Orientation

Although the primary emphasis of the Orientation session (which immediately precedes the first weeknight session) is administrative, it also has elements of patient education and therapy. The new client learns the times and places of treatment, the program rules, and the requirements for moving on to long-term treatment. He or she receives an overview of the nature of addiction and its treatment, emphasizing that major commitments of time and energy are involved. And he or she is given a condensed version of relapse-prevention techniques, a sort of "survival kit."

The administrative information must be repeated several times slowly and clearly at the end as well as at the beginning of this introductory session. Many clients have attention difficulties stemming from or predating cocaine use, and many are simply too preoccupied or distracted to read the printed handouts containing program information. Consequently, the handouts should be carefully reviewed as they are mentioned in the session. The leaders should pause frequently to invite questions while explaining the program, and they should continually scan the members' faces for signs of lack of understanding, inattention, intoxication, or agitation. The "Don't Come High" rule and the reasoning behind it must be explained with particular emphasis. The recovering peer leader should ask any member who appears obviously high to accompany him or her out of the room. Once outside, the peer leader should politely explain the reason for the rule and invite the individual to return sober to the next week's Orientation. The recovering peer leader should also give the prospective client the Orientation handouts, including the leaders' telephone numbers, "The Foundation and the Walls," and the "Invitation to Loved Ones," and NA and CA meeting lists with some of the more accessible meetings marked.

The overview of addiction and treatment which is the patient education component of this session also helps to weed out members who are not ready for treatment. When the leader is finished explaining the extent and length of the required commitment and the scope of the necessary lifestyle changes, members who do not want to enter the program should be cordially invited to leave. In our experience, most of those who either leave right away or stay only until the end of the session had no idea of what intensive treatment entailed and were hoping to find a painless way to escape residential treatment.

The relapse-prevention training segment of Orientation consists of a summary of what to avoid, how and why to avoid it, and what to do instead (the "walls"). Leaders also distribute and discuss NA and CA meeting lists and an easy-to-remember acronym of techniques for dealing with unavoidable temptations. The other therapeutic functions of this session are to instill hope, an effort that is aided by clear information about the treatability of addiction, and to make the newcomer feel welcome and understood. In Chapter Three, we discussed at some length the new client's need for safety, order, hope, and belonging. Because the Orientation session is the client's first contact with a new way of life and, in a sense, an initial entry or reentry to society itself, the importance of a warm and understanding welcome cannot be overemphasized. A formal welcome praising clients' decisions to seek help and acknowledging the difficulty of those decisions is the session's first order of business. The second order of business is to describe the program and its purpose. Then each member introduces himself or herself to the group. Depending on the size of the group, all members should be allowed a minute or two to identify themselves and to comment on what brought them to treatment. (These introductions are also vital to leaders' getting an early sense of the most immediate needs in a particular group of newcomers.) After the introductions, the program rules and administrative procedures should be described, always taking care to explain the clinical rationale for the rules and procedures.

Orientation should conclude as it opens – on a personal note. After all of the potentially overwhelming information that occupies the middle of the session, leaders should ultimately reassure clients that recovery proceeds one step at a time, that "returning here clean" is a sufficient next step for anyone, and that everyone should feel free to ask the leaders for help.

Erecting the Walls

This session responds to the newly abstinent person's immediate need for direction. Even before addiction and treatment can be discussed at length, the new client typically wants the clinician to "tell me what to do." Clients need a therapeutic regimen to secure their abstinence on a day-to-day basis.

The first segment of the session offers a brief rationale for the regimen and a preview of the extended discussion of addiction and conditioning contained in Addiction and Denial. Explaining the "whys" of a safe daily routine lays the groundwork for the rest of the session. The earliest days of recovery are the most vulnerable to relapse. Just as drug use is not the same as addiction, cessation is not the same as extinction. Because cessation has just begun, the client is still highly addicted and thus highly vulnerable to both internal and external triggers. Newly recovering addicts may still be in withdrawal from cocaine and other drugs, and because they have not yet developed alternative responses to the full range of temptations, they are likely to feel frightened, confused, and defenseless.

Thus, special restrictions are in order. We call these self-restrictions, which resemble the supports of inpatient treatment, the outpatient "walls." The walls were briefly introduced in Orientation and referred to throughout the week, but here they are elaborated on. They are an organizing metaphor for the session. The walls, in brief, are:

- staying away from drugs, drug users, and all avoidable situations associated with drug use;
- planning days carefully;
- keeping busy with safe activities;
- surrounding oneself with supportive people; and
- making access to drugs and money as limited as possible.

Clients are not likely to accept the necessity of these measures unless they first accept the need for abstinence from all mood-altering substances. The rationale for abstinence from all mood-altering drugs is discussed in this session using a simplified model of conditioning theory. As with all of the discussions, leaders draw heavily on the relevant experiences of clients in order to avoid slipping into a dry, abstract lecture. The clients' experiences can be clearly interpreted to demonstrate why stopping all drug and alcohol use is a necessary first step in recovery.

Because every drug-free day reduces addiction and makes possible new learning and long-term recovery, the newly recovering addict must plan for each day. Thus, this session demonstrates in detail the proper use of our planning and assessment guide, "The Daily Chart." The Chart "operationalizes" the concept of the walls. Each day clients can check off their successes in keeping busy at work, school, or child care, attending self-help meetings, associating with other abstinent and recovering people, exercising and taking care of their health, avoiding idle time, trying drug-free recreation, avoiding drugs and dangerous situations, and taking care of family responsibilities. It allows clients (or clients in consultation with the leaders) to answer such questions as: "Am I doing enough?" "Am I doing anything foolish?" "Am I sufficiently committed?" "How can I arrange my daily routine to support my recovery more effectively?"

The "Avoided Triggers" category of the chart is explained, in part, by a "Brainstorming" exercise during which the group generates a long list of common and personal triggers and dangerous situations. This is an energetic and often a humorous segment. It is liberating for clients to realize that the craving, which can seem ubiquitous, has a pattern; that they are not alone with it; and that it can be reduced.

Closing the Doors to Addiction

Of course, knowing what to do every day does not ensure that the client will do it. Most new clients are ambivalent about putting in place the daily regimen described in Erecting the Walls. They are still attached to familiar rewards, and they have not yet experienced alternative rewards. This session explains that ambivalence can be resolved by taking action, and it presents a special sort of pivotal action that we call the commitment step (for a more extended discussion, see Chapter Two). Like the steps discussed in Making Changes (below), commitment steps bring one the new rewards of recovery, but at the same time, they make it harder for clients to backslide. For example, if clients take the important commitment step of disclosing their recovery to their families, then they are likely to receive new support that is contingent on continuing to recover. When they are "watched" by those whose approval they care about and who have a stake in their progress, they have more to lose by relapsing. They cannot slide back into drug use without a confrontation. This sort of action is particularly critical in the cessation phase, when recovery is just "getting off the ground," so to speak. To use an analogy of rock-climbing, at this stage, each step upward makes turning back a less viable option. Thus, the client is progressively locked into a healthy course. Each social and financial investment is a barrier against relapse and a spur to further investments. Each step makes other steps more likely, progressively resolving the natural ambivalence of early recovery and building momentum when it is most needed. There are natural incentives to relapse and natural disincentives to making difficult changes. This session is intended to help clients counteract them by creating disincentives to relapse and incentives to recovery.

By way of introduction, the session considers the nature and effectiveness of commitment steps. Members are asked to supply examples of leaving "doors open" to readdiction. Leaders then ask why recovering people would leave such doors open unnecessarily and how one closes doors. This is followed by members giving examples from their own lives of the effects of closing doors. Most groups will have a fund of relevant experience. Entering treatment is a commitment step. How well it closes doors may depend, in part, on how many key people in the client's life know about it, how long the client stays, and how open the client is with leaders and other members. A group "brainstorm" generates a list of the ways the client can make drug use harder for himself or herself (e.g., having someone hold one's money). Clients are invited to voice objections challenging the necessity of any of these measures. Then these objections are examined in light of members' personal experiences.

The second half of the session is devoted to identifying and supporting key personal commitment steps in the major "foundation areas" of early recovery: that is, establishing a drug-free living situation, working situation, leisure activities, and social support. The group is encouraged to select from a menu of commonly productive commitment steps or add a relevant next step to the menu. Because members can be exquisitely sensitive to one another's vulnerabilities, the whole group can help members to select and refine an appropriate step.

Some clients will use this session to make more binding a change initiated in the previous session. For example, if as a result of that session some clients have discontinued telephoning active users, the next logical step might be to destroy their address books, to change their telephone numbers, or to ask their spouses or parents to screen their calls. If they have successfully turned down an offer of a beer by pleading an upset stomach, they can decide to turn down the next offer by disclosing their recovery. In other words, having taken a tentative step ahead as a result of a previous session, they use the present session to shut the door behind them.

Problems and Progress

The weekend Problems and Progress session is a practical therapy group intended to maximize individual participation, allow for the venting of feelings, and mobilize the group's support for individual actions. The session provides clients with the opportunity to take stock, consolidate gains, and practice in-depth individual application of the program's principles. Some members may be rewarded with the group's approval for steps already achieved, while others receive the group's support for examining obstacles more closely.

The format of the session is designed to enhance the group's sense of active "ownership" of the mutual help process. Thus, the sheer *amount* of directive leadership is less than in the other sessions; yet the leaders must nonetheless actively facilitate the group's problem-solving and mutual support. Because in this session members are encouraged to express personal concerns at more length than in the weekday sessions, leaders may need to be especially adept at extracting relevant points from member contributions. Ideally, this session should present many opportunities to integrate and illustrate the principles set forth in the weeknight sessions. Leaders must use those opportunities when members do not.

The dominant theme of this session is that there is always a next step, a small, concrete action that will facilitate feeling better in the long run. Continual reference to the daily planning and assessment chart is central to the format. Clients should be encouraged to ask of one another, "What on your chart applies to your problem? What else or what more can you do?"

The final segment of this session utilizes another principle from the chart—that of careful planning. Since Saturday night is a particularly dangerous time for recovering cocaine addicts, a Saturday afternoon group offers a special opportunity to make this principle immediately relevant. It also allows members to extend the session's emphasis on mutual support to planning group drug-free social activities. Often a member who has gained a "toehold" at a Saturday night NA meeting will extend an open invitation to the group. (Alternatively, members from the same general neighborhood may settle on a mutually convenient meeting to attend for the first time.) At the same time, arrangements can be made for refreshments or a movie after the meeting. The recovering peer leader should take an active part in these plans, and both leaders should ensure that enough time is left to finalize arrangements before the end of the session.

If properly managed, the closing of the weekend session can be a time of spirited pulling together. Clients sometimes set off together with the excitement of new friends on an adventure. Those who participate return to the next weekday session still discussing the NA meeting and perhaps the movie or late dinner that followed it. Very often they are visibly changed in their attitudes toward recovery.

Addiction and Denial

Addiction and Denial is primarily a therapy session. Its main purpose is to help members fully accept that they have the condition that the program is designed to treat. This may sound like a cognitive task, and indeed it involves considerable patient information about the nature of the disease. But it is also much more than that. It can entail a change in one's entire psychosocial orientation. It is not surprising that people who are still conditioned to regard the powerfully reinforcing drug experience as The Solution, the source of all pleasure and protection, are deeply reluctant to see it as the problem. Indeed, a central dilemma of early recovery is that until one actually begins to experience the *rewards* of change, the pull of addiction can warp the recovering person's perception of the *need* for change.

Yet some degree of fundamental change is often feasible, even in the short span of the cessation program, because many clients come to treatment precisely because they are ready, or almost ready, for change. Their self-deception has begun to break down, and they may have had a terrible glimpse of the dimensions of the problem. They need to have that glimpse validated and explained in treatment and, above all, they need to know that the consequences of accepting the problem are hopeful. Explicitly or implicitly, clients say to the clinician, "Prove to us that we need you"; and they say, most desperately, "Give us a hopeful alternative to addiction."

This session must demonstrate that alternative. Most clients are ready for such a demonstration, because denial is so exhausting and isolating. At some level, they long for release. As members show one another the way to release, this can become a most intense and exhilarating session. The process of letting in the truth can take on a life of its own. Clinicians and those clients who have already overcome much denial can assist at the birth of this new life. Through them, members sample the relief, support, and hope that can come with accepting the *recovering* addict identity.

One obstacle to accepting the truth is probably the easiest to understand and to overcome. People naturally resist a stigmatizing label. As we suggested earlier, many cocaine addicts take particular exception to the label "addict" because of its association with the street addict stereotype. Many of them have not been addicted long enough to experience the most severe adverse consequences of addiction. Because they may still have good jobs, intact families, and so forth, and because they may be able to stop using for regular periods, it is easy for them to tell themselves that they are not *real* addicts. They do not fully realize that they themselves hold a flawed stereotype. It derives partly from its associations with heroin addicts of 30 or 40 years ago, a time when competent treatment and self-help organizations were almost unknown. More important, it is based on a "physical dependence" model of addiction rather than the conditioning model, which is now widely accepted by scientists and clinicians.

Patient education, then, is the first job of this session. If a mistaken notion of the diagnosis feeds clients' denial, then that notion should be corrected by accurate information. This session presents a model of addiction as a continuously conditioned response to the reinforcement produced by drug use (see Chapter Two). Drug use causes addiction;

more drug use increases addiction; and when drug use stops, addiction does not. An implication of the model is that the ability of cocaine addicts to stop using cocaine for limited periods represents a typical stage and pattern of addiction to stimulants rather than a capacity for control. The conditioning model also explains why severe physiological withdrawal is not an essential component of addiction and why trying to use any mood-altering substance in a controlled manner is likely to lead to rapid renewal of the strength of addiction. The self-assessment instrument presented in this session pointedly asks not whether the client is or is not an addict, but "how addicted" he or she is.

It also follows from the conditioning model that virtually anyone can be severely addicted, regardless of appearance, class, or admirable personal qualities. Yet in the earlier stages of the disease, virtually no one feels like an addict. In fact, drug use feels like such a positive experience to early-stage addicts that they can see no reason to give it up. They do not feel out of control. On the contrary, they feel more in control of their lives. As attachment to the drug grows, objective evidence of the loss of control over cocaine use mounts. A common response to this dilemma is to ignore, minimize, or rationalize the threatening evidence. The newly recovering addict's greatest obstacle to accepting the truth of his or her disease is a reluctance to accept the logical first prescription: Stop using drugs. Instead the person becomes blind to the consequences of his or her use. If a man punches his wife, she "deserved it." If a woman is arrested for speeding, "The cop was making his quota." If someone spent the family nest egg, it will be replaced twofold. Denial enables the progression of addiction by masking a growing loss of control with a persistent delusion of control.

The further addicts become alienated from mainstream social supports and rewards, the more desperately they need to cling to their use as a solution. Yet most clients new to treatment are in the uncomfortable position of having had their walls of self-deception cracked. They may have tentatively accepted that there is a problem that they haven't been able to solve alone. However, in the early days of treatment, when the reality of necessary, painful changes begins to sink in, they may be most tempted to slip back out. They may accept that they have a problem with cocaine but continue to defend their ability to drink safely. Or they may admit the extent of their problem, but insist that they can now deal with it on their own. One of the purposes of this session is to familiarize members with the common forms of denial. By listening critically to their own and other members' versions of these forms, each member can learn to identify the characteristic "sounds" of denial, which are alternately defensive, contentious, whining, and vague.

As indicated, clients at different stages of addiction constitute a kind of living demonstration of the progression of the disease. Where one client is headed, others have been. The same is true of denial and acceptance. What one client now tells himself or herself to justify addiction, others once told themselves. The experience of peers can be of incomparable value in overcoming denial. However, the leader must model a caring style of offering his or her experience to others, for clients who are not yet secure in their own recoveries can become hostile toward reflections of their own too-recent attitudes. The essential experience of this session should not be one of a group pitted against its recalcitrant members but rather of a group united against addiction.

To sum up, clients in this session must become aware of the common tendency of addicts to deceive themselves into rejecting the correct diagnosis or its full implications. They must further understand that this rejection is a way of avoiding the prescribed changes. This session must present a clear and up-to-date model of addiction; it must show that this model fits the facts of individual cases; it must demonstrate the ways that addicts typically try to escape the fit; and, most important, it must demonstrate the advantages to individual clients of accepting the fit.

Making the Most of Treatment

Addiction and Denial is logically followed by Making the Most of Treatment because a key advantage of accepting the diagnosis of addiction is that it lets the client accept competent help. This session addresses the kinds and the extent of that help as well as the client's role in using it most effectively. Thus, its main mission is one of patient education. However, the very fact that effective help *exists* is inherently therapeutic, for many new clients share the myth of the untreatable addict ("Once an addict, always an addict"). This self-fulfilling pessimism was a product of the 1950s and 1960s, when the typical addict was addicted to heroin and lacked the social and economic foundation for recovery. Moreover, would-be treatment providers lacked the conceptual framework necessary for behavioral retraining, and there were no widely available peer-support organizations.

Advances in research, increasingly sophisticated aftercare programs, and the spread of EAPs and self-help fellowships have all contributed to a relative age of enlightenment in addiction treatment. It is now possible to assure clients new to treatment that they "are in the right place" and that addiction is indeed treatable (McAuliffe, 1990; Sells, 1979; Stanton et al., 1982). However, being treated for addiction is not a passive process. Most chronic medical conditions require patient compliance and behavioral change. Perhaps even more than with other medical conditions, successful treatment of addiction depends upon the patient's actively embracing the prescribed regimen. That regimen can be difficult. It involves separation from many habitual sources of pleasure. It is not only an intensive undertaking, but also an extensive one, affecting virtually every aspect of one's life. What is more, it requires a long-term commitment. Therefore, clients should know what to expect from the outset.

Although new clients need a particularly clear idea of how the cessation program works and what its relationship is to long-term treatment, they also must become familiar with other treatment resources. Most clients need some sort of concurrent and/or subsequent involvement in self-help organizations, various modes of counseling and family therapy, and/or psychiatric and medical treatment. Issues of particular relevance are:

How long does treatment take?
What are its effective mechanisms—that is, how will attending treatment groups help to reverse one's addiction?
What does the client have to do to make treatment work?
How can one make it quicker, more certain, or easier?
What is the likelihood of recovery?
Are there costs or possible harms?
When is outpatient treatment appropriate?
What is the relationship between group and individual treatments?
What are the differences between early and more long-term treatment concerns?

Because group members will have differing levels of experience and knowledge of all of these matters, the leaders should encourage the more experienced members to become resources for those with less experience.

Knowing *about* treatment does not ensure that the client will know how to use it most effectively. Thus a major therapeutic objective of this session is to create in the group an *example* of effective treatment. Each client should have the opportunity to participate and consciously to rehearse appropriate group skills such as good listening, coming to the point, reaching out to others, and asking for help in areas of immediate need. Leaders must take special care in this session to encourage and praise even small efforts at participation because many clients are initially afraid to speak in groups. Finally, all members should leave this session understanding that if they take some small step to implement the treatment regimen more wholeheartedly than before, then they will have effectively advanced their chances of recovery.

Coping with Dangerous Situations

Just as Erecting the Walls addresses avoidable or temporarily avoidable dangers, this session addresses those unavoidable triggers that one must learn to escape or cope with immediately. Among the unavoidable triggers of early recovery are the withdrawal syndrome; many "bad feelings" such as anxiety, depression, boredom, and anger; unforeseeable chance encounters with users; paydays, weekends, and holidays; pain and sickness; the death of loved ones; casual drug and alcohol offers; and some stressful legal, financial, and family situations. In addition, many addicts in early recovery are powerfully affected by any talk of drug use at recovery meetings.

This session must first stress that it is the client's responsibility to determine (and to seek help in determining) whether a given danger is truly unavoidable. For example, many clients assume that they "must" go to weddings, funerals, or family parties that are, in fact, avoidable. Indeed, from the perspective of many clinicians or senior recovering people, many such functions are "relapses waiting to happen." Avoiding these events for many members requires only the group's support and, perhaps, a few examples of tactful refusals. (Sometimes the true source of the perceived unavoidability is the client's reluctance to disclose recovery to family members. That issue is more closely addressed in the Closing the Doors to Addiction and Family and Partners in Early Recovery sessions.) Similarly, some negative feelings result from arguments that could have been avoided or major decisions that should have been put off. Whereas payday may be unavoidable, handling cash may be avoidable. Whereas painful injuries may be unavoidable, prescriptions or unsupervised access to pain medication may be avoidable. Finally, newly recovering addicts' old drug-using friends are much harder to avoid if clients hang out in the old places, if they keep to their old routines, and so forth.

Truly unavoidable dangers include both internal cues and external situations. An example of the former is withdrawal-aggravated anxiety. An example of the latter is an unexpected offer of drugs from a new friend the recovering addict met at an NA meeting. This session devotes segments to coping with each category, for the coping strategies are rather different. For example, whereas the proper initial response to the drug offer would be to "escape" – that is, to leave the scene quickly – the proper initial response to the anxiety might be to breathe deeply and recite a prayer. However, the follow-up responses in both situations would be to contact a supportive person. Thus, this session gives special emphasis to building and using a support network. If the individual is unavoidably in a situation where there is alcohol, one tactic is to seek out support from nondrinkers in that setting. The session includes role-plays of refusing casual alcohol and drug offers, brainstorming successful techniques members use to cope with stressful situations, exercises in prioritizing, and techniques for coping with some common withdrawal symptoms such as sleep disturbance, depression, and restlessness. One internal trigger that receives special emphasis is distress from psychological disturbances that may have predated and influenced drug use. Guidelines are generated for deciding whether the recovering addict needs additional counseling, evaluation, or therapy.

Family and Partners in Early Recovery

This session is both for clients, who are responsible for bringing their loved ones into the recovery process if possible, and for their family members, who should have been issued written invitations shortly after the Orientation session. We found it necessary and useful to define "family" loosely to include anyone in the client's immediate support system. Thus, a lover, a close friend, a roommate, or a 12-step fellowship sponsor—the people most directly involved in the client's recovery—should be invited to this session. Including partners in recovery as well as actual family members is especially important because some clients are without supportive family members. The broader definition allows leaders to insist that virtually every client bring *someone* to the session.

In a sense, family members may be thought of as one of the unavoidable dangers in early recovery, for even supportive loved ones trigger powerful feelings and the need for major readjustments, whereas clients without family support are in special need of developing other sources of support. For too many clients, either during the course of addiction or predating it, loved ones became "part of the problem." The essential task of this session is to assess whether and how they can be made part of the solution. Some clients must reconcile themselves to avoiding family members who wittingly or unwittingly feed their addictions. But others, including some who may have entered treatment because of the threatened loss of support from a parent or a spouse, must take more initiative to bring in family members. Still others leave themselves room to back out by not disclosing or incompletely disclosing their recoveries to family members.

The first business of the session is to welcome the family members and close friends who have been invited, to praise the clients who have invited them, and to explain once again the importance of bringing loved ones into the recovery process. Making recovery a team effort requires that clients and their loved ones understand one another's needs from the outset. First, family members must learn that recovery is a major effort, that the walls are vital and reasonable, and that clients *and* their family members need extensive treatment and support. Clients are not "cured" because they have managed to stop using drugs. Cocaine addiction is particularly manifested by the individual being unable to *remain* abstinent. Stopping drug use and entering treatment take courage, but they are only beginnings.

At the same time, both clients and key family members should recognize the difference between cooperation and caretaking. The client's recovery is the client's responsibility. Recovery presents many opportunities for shared activities and responsibilities and for building and rebuilding bridges to loved ones; but ultimately, the part of the family that the client can best change is himself or herself.

Just as family members can most effectively support recovery, unsupportive or addicted family members can powerfully sabotage recovery. Many clients who have overcome considerable denial about their own addictions remain in denial about their abilities to deal with drug-using loved ones. Both clients and their family members need to understand the dangers of living or closely associating with loved ones who use drugs. Clients may need special support for separating from users, and they may need to become involved intensively in the social life of recovery groups.

This session begins by summarizing some of the patient education that has already been supplied to clients and by introducing new information about family issues and resources. This sets the stage for discussions on the complementary roles of clients and their family members in recovery. These discussions, in turn, prepare members for a final "family communication." Clients and their family members are given opportunities to deliver significant communications to one another such as, "I love you," "I forgive you," "I need your help," "I'm sorry," and "Thank you." (Clients without family members present are also encouraged to deliver communications to absent family members.) The groundwork must be laid carefully for this final segment so that clients understand that they have earned distrust and must be patient in regaining full trust. Family members should understand that completing the cessation program represents an important step in a new direction. With that accomplished, the conclusion of this session can offer intense moments of reconciliation, reaffirmed bonds, and new hope. The spirit of openness and hope is often contagious, as the separate families within the group start to feel membership in a larger "family" of recovery.

The CS session on the family addresses initial recovery issues. In a comprehensive recovery program, family issues should also be addressed in a long-term recovery group and/or in individual counseling. Advanced groups and counseling deal with later recovery issues such as ongoing conflicts, family members needing to become more involved in or supportive of a client's expanded participation in the recovering community, family members recovering at different rates, and the delayed surfacing of buried resentments. Some of the issues overlap, but with differing emphases. For example, whereas a relapse in the first days of recovery might reasonably make a loved one question whether outpatient treatment is sufficient, 4 months later a brief relapse might signal the necessity for the client to intensify his or her recovery routine and for the loved one to stand by preset limits.

We recommend that family members also be invited to meet with the client's individual counselor during the client's first month of treatment in the CS program. (Information about this session is included in the Orientation session.) This session gives the individual counselor a more rounded picture of the client's family situation, offers the opportunity for conflict resolution, and allows loved ones to express personal concerns—for example, regarding sexual matters or AIDS. If a family member or sexual partner appears guarded in the presence of a client, the counselor may suggest a separate session with the loved one. At this time, the individual counselor may also address a loved one's drug use and make the appropriate referrals. For serious family problems that predate treatment, the individual counselor may refer the client and the loved ones to more extensive family services.

Making Changes

The more clearly clients understand what changes are necessary, the more they are confronted by their resistance to making some of those changes. For some clients, the previous sessions merely validate and explain what they already know. Clients may know, for example, that they must separate from a sex partner who is using drugs or from a career in the liquor or pharmaceutical industry; yet they may have come to treatment precisely because they have been unable to initiate or follow through with the necessary steps on their own. Other clients may be hoping that they can get away with half-measures or shortcuts. Thus, they throw away their stash but not their paraphernalia. Or they tell their best friends but not their spouses about their recovery. Or they hang on to a single, cherished relationship with an active user, or continue to visit a nightclub just on Saturdays, or withhold critical information from their recovery group and counselor, or harbor a secret hope that they can become controlled users, or attend recovery meetings without speaking or getting to know anyone.

Whether the client is "stuck" despite knowledge of what needs to be done, or is hoping to be able to circumvent some difficult areas of the regimen, the basic problem is the same. People resist making major changes. Although resistance to change is hardly peculiar to addicts, the nature of drug addiction adds a particular urgency to the need for *thorough* change. As we indicated earlier, the "old ways" are not only powerfully reinforcing, they are woven into a pervasive fabric of norms and behaviors that we refer to as the addict lifestyle. Any resistance, inertia, or reservation can help to unravel the thin fabric of recovery. Conversely, the only way to overcome the fear of changes is to take the actions that will lead to experiencing new rewards. The rewards of a lifestyle of getting high must be fully replaced by the rewards of a lifestyle of recovery. Like a rock-climber, the recovering person becomes secure in a new foothold only as the balance of his or her weight is shifted there from the old foothold. The desire to be in a higher place is not enough. One must move. In this session the essential message is, "Now is the time to shift the balance of your weight, for now you can use the group's ropes and leverage for support."

The heart of this session is a series of exercises designed, first, to help members understand the necessity of making thorough changes; second, to identify an area in which members have failed to make a difficult but critical change and to analyze what is holding them back; and third, to define an appropriate next step to initiate that change. In many cases, the targeted step will be small enough not to be overwhelming. Clients can get better in incremental steps, just as they became addicted. There is always a manageable next step that can improve their outlook and increase their commitment to recovery.

Although the session is designed to result in some group-supported concrete actions, members who are not ready to act should not be pressured excessively to do so. Thus, a distinction is made between members' publicly committing to take action, on the one hand, and members' publicly defining an action as a future goal. Both tasks are acceptable, and both are made easier by a group atmosphere in which members are committing themselves to take actions, telling how they took successful actions in the past, and encouraging one another to act.

A Road Map to Recovery

Having addressed unfinished present business in the previous session, A Road Map to Recovery takes a realistic and hopeful look ahead. Its therapeutic objectives are to reduce anxiety about the course and nature of recovery, to provide clients with incentives to persevere at a difficult time, to reassure them that difficulty at this time is normal, and to define more clearly each client's current priorities. The metaphor of a map underlines the fact that recovery is now a known, chartable territory. One can learn from those who have gone before. Clients occasionally object that they are having too difficult a time staying abstinent *today* to think about the future. While reaffirming that remaining abstinent today should be the client's first priority, leaders also should point out that recovering people sometimes relapse because of unrealistic expectations or poor preparation. That is, the bigger picture can help the client see more clearly *how* and *why* to stay abstinent today.

For most of this session clients fill out individually and then analyze together a chart of the phases of recovery. The chart helps them to identify and take credit for what they have already accomplished while locating logical next steps. For example, a client may note that he or she no longer associates with users but still feels awkward around recovering people. The chart underlines that such awkwardness is normal as one begins to make new friends. It also makes clear that a new phase is reached by becoming active in the recovering community.

The session is also an opportunity for the client to begin to construct a recovery story. Members specify where they have come from, where they are, and where they are headed. They also integrate relevant morals, the principles of recovery that will guide next steps. Like any story, recovery stories attempt to fit the meaning of individual experience to larger cultural patterns, myths, and values. An individual's recovery takes its shape from those likely patterns of recovery that the chart tries to articulate. The chart helps to give members a sense of the *shape* of recoveries, of what sorts of events go together. Ambivalence about drinking, ambivalence about hanging out with drinkers, and an undeveloped drug-free social life are likely to coexist in the same phase. Conversely, progress in one area of recovery is likely to lead to progress in other areas. For example, becoming financially responsible may promote better family relationships, which in turn may lead to more support for financial progress.

The chart clarifies that, as uncomfortable new responses are rewarded and become habitual, the walls are gradually lowered, and one's recovery becomes more full. Thus, it allows clients to connect small steps, such as having money automatically deposited to pay debts, with long-term outcomes such as home ownership. An overview of the territory shows that recovery proceeds one step at a time toward a worthwhile destination. However, leaders must emphasize that individuals move forward at different rates, that making deliberate progress is the key, and that scrupulous self-honesty on the part of the clients about their current position will best serve their progress.

The Order of the Sessions

The order of the sessions as well as the structure of each session reflect a movement from problem to solution. To begin, clients must understand and accept the need to make changes; then they must learn what initial changes need to be made and, with help, begin to make them. Thus, each session is designed to examine a need and a resource of early recovery and to result in a specific action. The topics of the weekday sessions are ordered according to two additional principles. First, a session that contains basic, early-recovery "survival" strategies should occur each week. Thus, the session Erecting the Walls contains the "nuts and bolts" of initial safety, and similar segments occur in Making the Most of Treatment, Coping with Dangerous Situations, and Making Changes.

Second, maximum continuity should exist between the weeknight topics—that is, there should be a sense of the steps emphasized in the first session leading logically to the steps emphasized in the second session. Erecting the Walls gives the client a regimen of immediate necessary steps, whereas the Closing the Doors session offers techniques for making those steps binding. Overcoming denial (Addiction and Denial) makes the client eligible for the structured help described in Making the Most of Treatment. For many clients, the unavoidable stresses and temptations of early recovery are best faced with the support of loved ones, whereas for others the feelings triggered by absent or unsupportive family members are an unavoidable source of danger. Finally, completing the foundation by overcoming resistance to change (Making Changes) allows the client to take a more confident look ahead (A Road Map to Recovery).

The weekend Problems and Progress sessions ensure that the week's issues will be grounded in personal realities, they reward progress, and they exemplify the value of belonging to a recovering community.

A central message, articulated in various ways in the content of all of the sessions, must also be reinforced by their form: In early recovery, people need structure and direction. The importance of systematically structured sessions is the subject of the next chapter.

Session Format

Although the formats of individual sessions vary somewhat according to the requirements of specific topics, the formats of all of the sessions reflect the underlying unity of our model of addiction and behavioral change. All of the Clean Start sessions, like the Recovery Training sessions on which their formats are based, are structured according to a logical sequence of learning. Clients must first understand and identify with the issue—the common problem in recovery that the session addresses. Then they must assess how well they have dealt with the issue in the past and how well they are dealing with it at present. Next they consider optimum coping strategies. Finally, these strategies are translated into specific individual plans and manageable steps.

One advantage of well-structured formats is that they allow the form of a session to express important elements of its content. Well-planned sessions illustrate the value of planning in recovery. Sessions in which each segment is clearly related to an overall goal illustrate the value of stepwise progress and goals. Sessions that consistently proceed from careful group considerations of shared experiences to principles of recovery illustrate the advantages of drawing on the experiences of others and using support. All of these values are reflected in the formats of the Clean Start sessions.

Format of the Weeknight Sessions

The following plan underlies the formats:

1. Administrative business and individual communications.
2. Check-in: 1- or 2-minute report (depending on the size of the

81

group) from each member on current concerns and progress, including those relevant to the topic of the session.

3. Leader presents topic and states goal of session.
4. Discussion of members' experience of the topic—what has and has not worked for them—ensuring that each client understands the issues and their personal relevance and that each client assesses his or her current situation.
5. Distill general strategies consistent with principles of recovery.
6. Review strategies and principles in handouts or chalkboard lists.
7. Apply handouts or lists to individual situations.
8. Sum up key points.
9. Define and support individual next steps.
10. Half-hour postsession for individual conferences and administrative business.

Administrative Business and Individual Communications

Leaders who do not deal systematically and promptly with administrative details will be distracted from clinical work. This is partly because of the brisk turnover of clientele in the cessation program, partly because there is much to accomplish in a limited period of time, and partly because many clients are disorganized in the wake of addiction. Leaders must be prepared for many questions in the moments before and after sessions: When is Client A due to advance to long-term treatment? Does Client B have to make up a missed session? What about Client C's emergency at work that conflicts with treatment? Can Client D attend a "super important" wedding that conflicts with treatment this weekend? What if a prescription medication shows up in Client E's urine? When and where does individual counseling begin?

Leaders also have many questions and communications for individual clients. A client may have missed a scheduled individual conference; have failed to pass in his or her ownwork; need to sign a consent to release information form; be suspected of using or dealing drugs; have shown evidence of redoubled commitment and need a few words of recognition; or seem unusually shaky and need extra encouragement. Ownwork must be collected (see "Ownwork" in Chapter Five), and clients who are due to give urines after the session must be notified of this before the session begins (see "Urine Testing" in Chapter Five). It is futile to try to keep all of this information only in "mental files." Leaders must confer well in advance of each session to write out a checklist of members needing any sort of individual attention. The recovering peer leader would normally offer the bulk of this attention in order to leave the professional leader free to concentrate on the session and on communicating with the group at large.

Check-In

The leader opens the check-in by asking members to go around the room introducing themselves and answering very briefly (a minute or two) a question relevant to the evening's topic. For example:

- "How do you feel about the label 'recovering addict'?" (Addiction and Denial);
- "Have you been in treatment before? Did you use it well?" (Making the Most of Treatment);
- "What is a primary source of craving for you now, and what are you doing about it?" (Erecting the Walls);
- "What might be an obstacle to your recovery? Are you still 'on the fence' about anything?" (Closing the Doors to Addiction); or
- "Is your family helping or hurting your efforts to stay clean?" (Family and Partners in Early Recovery).

The relevant question may be repeated after each client introduces himself or herself. The recovering peer leader may introduce himself or herself first to model the check-in. ("Hi, I'm Todd, a recovering addict. My family is helping my recovery today. We have a good time, and they give me a lot of encouragement. But for a long time they didn't trust me, and for an even longer time I couldn't see my brother until he got into recovery.") Then the recovering peer leader might provide a brief example of family progress from the week's events.

In addition, the leader might ask of selected clients, "How are you staying clean today?" or "What is working for you now?" or simply "How are you doing?" Most clients can think of some small accomplishments, and these are worth eliciting to avoid excessive complaining or dwelling on failure. In this setting, "accentuating the positive" means always using the available examples to emphasize that staying clean is both possible and desirable. The ideal check-in might stimulate fence-sitting members to think, "If he or she can do it, I can do it."

The check-in has a number of other related functions. First, it "breaks the ice," allowing relative strangers to get to know one another. Many members are intensely uncomfortable in drug-free social situations, and this discomfort is increased by feelings that their problems are unique or by not knowing what to expect of a room full of addicts. The check-in usually allays these fears by demonstrating common concerns and backgrounds. Moreover, having been obliged publicly to introduce themselves, many members become more willing to speak voluntarily in the group.

The check-in also gives leaders a chance to assess individual clients, to identify problems that may require immediate individual attention, and to gauge members' level of knowledge about the evening's topic while determining what aspects might be especially relevant. As clients situate themselves with respect to the topic, leaders can note examples that illustrate key points of the sessions. Some of these examples might lead later to "live case studies."

The clients' introductory remarks also give the leaders a chance to insert brief questions or responses that indicate priorities of recovery and that model helpful problem-solving. Signs of progress should be immediately commended, and problems, or indications of problems, should be "flagged" for further discussion. In their preparation for the session, the leaders should note for follow-up during the check-in individuals who have been struggling with an issue or a step. However, the check-in is not the occasion for extended discussion. The 60-second limit on clients' initial contributions must be strictly enforced. Once the time limit becomes a group norm, infractions will be rare; but if rambling is not dealt with immediately, check-ins will start to consume ever-increasing proportions of the sessions. The leader will sometimes need gently to defer further discussion to later in the session, to another, more appropriate session, or to individual conferences.

Finally, the check-in, like the closing next step exercise, can be used to recognize publicly the completion of ownwork assignments and the completion of the requirements for moving on to long-term treatment. Members who are moving on should be encouraged at this time to sum up for the group what they have learned and what steps they have taken.

Topic and Goals

The purpose of this segment is to make clear what problem in recovery is to be addressed, why it is important, what is to be gained by learning more about it, and what sorts of practical action should result. The Topic and Goals segment of the session is one of the few occasions for the leader to make "a little speech" without trying to elicit most of the participation from the members. However, the segment should take no more than 5 minutes, and the leader should avoid a long, classroom-style lecture. The brief suggested "scripts" (included below in the individual sessions) may be supplemented by leaders' own anecdotes illustrating the importance of the topic.

The leader should remind the group at the outset that because each session points toward a next step for each member, "You should be thinking throughout the session about practically applying what you learn. Near the end of the session you will be asked to think of a specific action that would strengthen your recovery." During this brief introduction, members also should be encouraged to consider how their own experiences might illustrate the main points to be made in the session. Emphasize that sharing such information is likely to benefit the whole group.

Open Sharing of Experience

The Open Sharing of relevant personal experience makes the material come alive. Concrete and immediate examples involve the group in the topic and demonstrate the commonality of issues. As group members realize that their problems are shared by others, they feel freer to speak, and they begin to see the value of pulling together. Members can begin to trade strategies that have worked and draw on their collective experiences to generate guidelines for recovery. The leader underlines each notable contribution, periodically reviews the points, and ensures that participation is as widespread as possible. If a client does not participate, leaders cannot be sure that he or she understands the issues and their personal relevance. Before this segment ends, leaders and members should have some idea of the particular issues and the degree of progress of each client. In Erecting the Walls, for example, the discussion may reveal that one client needs to get rid of a stash, whereas another needs to plan more carefully for paydays and weekends or to look for a new job.

Another function of the Open Sharing is to continue to define the scope of the topic. Thus, although the sharing must be "open" in order to tap the group's energies and to establish a range of relevant problems and issues, it can not be "wide open." Without suppressing individuals' efforts to contribute, the leaders will need to defer some issues to different sessions or to individual counseling. The leaders can best ensure appropriate participation by containing and paraphrasing contributions and explaining how each relates or does not relate sufficiently to the topic. For example, a client who keeps challenging the necessity of the safety measures discussed in Erecting the Walls may need to be assured that fuller discussion of his or her issues will be possible in the Addiction and Denial session and that in the meantime the client might benefit from listening carefully to the experiences of others.

Although formal definition of strategies and steps should be deferred to later in the session, members should be commended for offering one another experience-based tips. For example, a client who has learned to have his or her paycheck directly deposited might suggest the same procedure for another client who is having trouble handling cash. The leader might encourage further discussion of this suggestion in the "next step" segment. The application of one member's solutions to another member's problems begins to establish an atmosphere of mutual help and group cohesiveness.

General Strategies and Principles

In segments usually labeled "Open Discussion," the group extracts from its collective experience of an issue some general strategies for recovery. For example, in the Open Sharing segment of the Addiction and Denial session, several members may have reported having relapsed to cocaine use consequent to trying to "prove" their control over alcohol in bars or clubs. The leader could then ask the group whether foolish self-testing might not disguise a desire to get high. Other principles that the leader could extract or summarize are that minimizing past problems is a hallmark of denial, that denial is frequently displaced from cocaine to a more socially acceptable substance, and that stimulating a craving with any mood- and judgment-altering substance is likely to cause a relapse. An example from the session on treatment might follow from members sharing experiences of having left treatment too early in the past. The Open Discussion could then generate the following guidelines: (1) It is better to overestimate than underestimate the need for continuing treatment; (2) being tired of attending groups and meetings all week is not a reliable indicator of readiness to cut back; (3) the best criteria for a client deciding whether to lower his or her walls are whether alternative responses have become second nature, whether craving is significantly reduced, and whether the key members of his or her support network agree that the client is ready.

Open discussions of general strategies usually precede the review of a chalkboard list or a printed handout that summarizes the relevant principles and strategies. During the discussion, the leader's questions should help the group to anticipate as many of the items on the list or handout as possible. People internalize most readily principles that they have arrived at by active reasoning.

Review of List or Handout

This review is intended to summarize and complete the previous discussion. It imprints the main points in memory, and supplements group-generated lists of "recovery ingredients" with any principles or strategies that had not been discussed earlier. Having members take turns reading aloud from the list or handout facilitates group participation, and ensures that illiterate members will be exposed to all of the items.

The leader should point out any items on the list or handout that correspond to points generated in the previous discussion. The leader should also ask periodically, "Is there some item that doesn't seem to apply to you? If so, you are probably not alone and would be doing the group as well as yourself a service by speaking up." The leader may also invite alterations and additions, pointing out that, although the principles and guidelines represent the scientifically explained experience of many addicts, no list is complete or perfect.

The leader should periodically remind the group that the handouts are a way of "taking the session home." They are also a reminder that treatment is useless unless one takes it home. Therefore, the handouts should be bound in a personal notebook and prominently displayed at home. Reading the handouts can be particularly useful to fill idle time or time alone.

Application of Principles to Members' Individual Situations

The individual application of the strategies and principles should take at least 20 minutes. The leader can ask for volunteer "live case studies" or probe situations generated in the open sharings and check-ins. It is important to prevent infrequently participating members from "playing possum." Members should be asked how the earlier discussion and the handouts apply to their current situation.

During this segment, the leader must encourage team spirit. This can be done, in part, by comments such as, "How can we help Harry?" or "Who has faced a situation like Sue's? What have we discussed here tonight that might help?" However, before allowing a rush to make suggestions, the leader should set a good example by carefully eliciting the facts and sorting out what is relevant from what is not. The leader might ask frequently, "What else do we need to know in order to help [Harry/Sue]?" It is important to commend the honesty of those who volunteer case material and remind the group that the ultimate purpose of this exercise is to define next steps.

Summary of Key Points

The leader's brief summary of the key points reviews and highlights the essence of the session. This is also an appropriate preparation for integrating the content of the session in the final Next Step segment, when clients will apply what they have learned to defining an appropriate action.

Next Step

The Next Step exercise closes the session in a spirited, upbeat manner. Members are encouraged to commit publicly to perform their next step because public commitment and the prospect of reporting success to the group can give members the extra support they need to follow through. However, realism and self-honesty must remain first priorities. The leaders should point out that it is easy to get carried away in the enthusiasm of the moment and to overreach. Thus, members should feel free to set *goals* for action rather than premature commitments that could be set-ups for failure.

Thus, although the Next Step segment should be presented as an opportunity to use the group's support to move forward, leaders must emphasize that it is equally an occasion for clients' honest assessment of where they stand currently. When clients propose steps that sound either too general or too ambitious, leaders must demonstrate the advantages of specificity and realism. A "can-do" spirit is best maintained by breaking down vague or wishful steps into their manageable components. For example, the leader can point out that "Regain my spiritual center" is not a step but a goal that can be approached by specific actions such as "Attend church this Sunday." For a member who has not yet spoken at recovery meetings, a proposal such as "Speak more at CA meetings" might be usefully narrowed to "Identify myself as a newcomer Friday night."

Each session presents a menu of commonly productive steps related to its topic. For example, a suggested step in Addiction and Denial is "Admit to the group a deep reservation about whether you are badly enough addicted to take all of the suggestions of treatment." One of the suggested steps in Making the Most of Treatment is "Attend an NA meeting every day that Clean Start sessions are not scheduled." A step for Closing Doors to Addiction is "Change my phone number." And so forth.

Members may also use this segment in addition to the check-in to report on steps already completed. Applause and cheering should be encouraged; however, an indiscriminately "rah-rah" atmosphere should be avoided. Reserve the group's fullest acclaim for achievements and commitments that seem especially "on the mark" and productive. Members who wish to do so may commit themselves publicly to returning clean to the next session.

At the close of each session, announce once more the names of members who need to be seen after the session for administrative business or extra clinical attention, offering extra attention to any client who feels shaky. Finally, remind members that their primary commitment now is to stay clean and that each day clean is itself a significant achievement.

Half-Hour Postsession

The postsession period, like the immediate presession period, can be an extremely busy time for which careful preparation is required. Advancing clients may need to complete forms for the long-term treatment counselors. Forms may also be available certifying that they understand and are committed to observing the requirements and regulations of the program. In addition, those moving on might need to be given appointment sheets that include the times and places of scheduled group and individual counseling meetings. These tasks must be predivided among leaders.

Individual conferences are held during the postsession period. Some conferences may be scheduled in advance, either at the request of clients or of leaders; others will be requested or held informally during the postsession period itself. These conferences serve the double purpose of client evaluation and crisis support. Both functions are vital in Clean Start programming. Leaders need to learn as quickly as possible whether individual clients pose any immediate risk to themselves or to the group. They must determine who needs referrals to alternative or concurrent therapies. They also must provide support for clients who need to resolve situations of immediate danger to recovery. Some clients may need to discuss personal problems that they are reluctant to bring up in the group. And, finally, some clients just need extra individual encouragement or reassurance.

Because the average conference takes about 10 minutes, each leader may hold two or three conferences during the postsession period.

Leaders should also confer with each other at the end of the postsession in order to stay abreast of individual problems and proposed interventions.

Format of Problems and Progress

Although the weekend Problems and Progress session is less rigorously structured than the other sessions, it nonetheless follows a standard agenda, and it is actively facilitated by both leaders. Consistent adherence to the agenda prevents the discussion from becoming an unfocused free-for-all or a series of disjointed crisis interventions. Both alternatives are unproductive and frustrating for most members. The agenda follows:

Check-In (10–15 minutes)

This consists of brief reports on each member's problems and progress during the week. The recovering peer leader can check in first to demonstrate how to balance reports of success with constructive self-criticism. Special attention should be given to significant steps members have taken or have had trouble taking. Either clients or leaders can "flag" issues raised in the check-in for fuller discussion later in the session. Although clients will have more opportunity in this session than in the others to ventilate feelings about recovery, the check-ins themselves must be brief. Whereas leaders can accept for further discussion even general statements such as, "I just can't take the pain," they should attempt to have clients describe the difficulties behaviorally. For example, "I'm depressed about the whole thing" may be traced, through a question or two, to spending a lot of time alone and bored—a situation for which the program has specific prescriptions. At the same time, leaders must be alert to the possibility of emotional disorders that require alternative or concurrent therapies.

Leaders' questions should probe taciturn clients about their progress in the key foundation areas.

Extended Discussion of Issues Raised during Check-In and Defining Next Steps (45–50 minutes)

Issues that have been "flagged" for further discussion either by clients themselves or by the leaders should be addressed in order of their urgency. Generally, issues of greater urgency require more extended discussion. When pressing issues do not take up the available time, infrequent participators should be encouraged to speak about what has stood out for them in the week's previous sessions. When time seems short for adequately covering all issues, members should be reminded that the leaders are available after the session; alternatively, some of the less urgent issues can be put on the agenda for the following Problems and Progress session.

Throughout this segment, leaders should encourage members to share their successful strategies in areas where others are having problems. The leaders should also continually ask members to recall key points from the weeknight sessions that might suggest a course of action. For example, "Does anything from Tuesday's Erecting the Walls session apply to Sally's situation? Would things be easier for her if she avoided some trigger? What improvement on the daily chart would improve her situation?"

Summary of Issues and Steps in Terms of Program Principles (about 5 minutes)

The leaders ask for volunteers to give a brief summary of the foregoing discussion. What were the problems? What solutions were suggested? How do the suggested solutions illustrate program principles? The leaders should paraphrase and repeat the main points.

Weekend Social-Recreational Planning (20-30 minutes)

It usually becomes clear in the foregoing discussion that the weekends are the most difficult time for many clients and that some clients have learned better than others how to fill them productively. The wide range of coping levels is confirmed in this segment as each client describes his or her plans for Saturday night. Some have no plans at all. More commonly, members have plans too vague to be useful. When vague plans are presented, leaders must show clients how to probe them carefully. For example, "You are visiting your ex-wife and child? How is that likely to make you feel? Are you ready for this? Will anyone else be there? What are your plans for afterward?" Then members should be encouraged to constructively criticize one another's plans. This not only helps to firm up individual plans; it also demonstrates good planning to the whole group.

A central aim of this segment is to allow members who have been coping well on weekends to show the way to others. Members serve as powerful examples when they have made some headway in the recovering community and/or have learned to make detailed plans and to surround themselves with supportive people. Moreover, they can provide direct suggestions and invitations to 12-step fellowship meetings and social outings. Leaders should explicitly encourage members to reach out to one another and to plan group activities. The recovering peer leader can announce his or her plans and ask, "Who else needs someplace to go?" and "Who *has* someplace to go and would like extra company?" In order to prevent negative pairings, leaders should try to ensure that at least three members are in each planned subgroup. A *minimum* of 20 minutes should be allowed for this segment so that members may make firm arrangements.

Processes

Many of the structures and processes derive from RTSH (Zackon et al., 1992). Leaders should understand the terms defined below which appear throughout the formats to designate various segments and exercises:

Brainstorming

The purpose of this exercise is to generate from the whole group a list of practical suggestions and possible steps. Responses should be listed visibly on a chalkboard or a large sheet of paper and then refined in open discussion.

Discussion Questions

These are questions that the leader poses to the group to help focus its attention and clarify some aspect of the topic.

Handouts

Written handouts summarize a session's key points, provide fictional case studies (see below), and offer practical suggestions and self-assessment checklists. Handouts are not replacements for the discussion; rather, they supplement it. The more thorough the discussion, the less time need be spent on a handout. Pay the most attention to the points on a handout that have not been raised by the group in the previous discussion.

Fictional Case Studies

Among the handouts are some fictional example situations. Their purpose is to allow for more straightforward comments when the discussion of sensitive issues seems likely to hurt members' feelings or to interfere with rational discussion and analysis. The Comments sections offer leaders guidelines for interpreting the relevant points of the fictional cases.

Live Case Studies

This is an open analysis of a personal situation volunteered by a member for its relevance to an issue at hand. Where Fictional Case Studies are indicated, Live Case Studies may be substituted for or supplement them. The leaders must elicit the relevant facts of the case and sum them up concisely. The questioning of the volunteer should be nonconfrontational and respectful.

Open Sharing

Open Sharing gives members a chance to offer personal experience of an issue and to make related practical suggestions. Volunteers should contribute in turn, going around the room. Leaders should ensure that members come to the point within reasonable time limits. Open Sharing is useful for starting and summing up a discussion.

Open Discussion

Open Discussion designates segments of the session when members share views and ask and answer questions freely, with the leader maintaining focus on the topic and stimulating broad participation. The purpose of the Open Discussion is to generate strategies, principles, and practical suggestions from clients' experiences of the topic's issues.

Partners' Communications

In Partners' Communications, all members pair off to discuss an assigned issue. The leader instructs each person in the group to find a partner. If someone does not have a partner, the recovering peer leader should serve as a partner. In some cases, the group leader will want to select the partners so that one member with more experience in recovery is paired with one with less.

Each pair should sit far enough away from other partners so that conversations remain private. The leader announces the topic of the communication (e.g., "How do you feel about being called a 'recovering addict'?") and instructs partners to decide who will go first and to talk about 2 minutes each. Members should be instructed to listen carefully and respectfully when the other is speaking. Then members should be given about 1 minute each to respond constructively to what their partners said.

Partner communications are optional in our format; however, they are especially useful in large groups. Reducing the group to smaller units alleviates some members' fears of speaking in large groups; it builds trust; it helps clients to feel at home; it stimulates participation in the wider discussion; and it encourages identification with other recovering addicts.

However, these exercises require consistent direction from the group leaders. The two principal pitfalls of undirected partner discussions are the formation of negative alliances and the degeneration of the discussion into an unfocused chat. Both tendencies can be prevented if the leader makes very clear the purpose of the exercise and the importance of sticking to the topic. The leaders should circulate separately from subgroup to subgroup, intervening and redirecting the discussion when necessary.

Sample Session: Family and Partners in Early Recovery

Background

This chapter is intended to illustrate the workings of a Clean Start session. Almost all of the dialogue is transcribed from a tape recording of one actual family session. However, we have added a small vignette from a second session in order to ensure that a broad cross-section of issues is represented. Readers may wish to review the Family and Partners in Early Recovery Clean Start session prior to or in conjunction with this chapter. We have provided an outline of the session (Session at a Glance) below.

Although the session that we chose went well, it also presented some common perils. At several points, the leaders might easily have become sidetracked from the session format. Instead, they adapted the format, without substantial changes, to the immediate concerns of the members. Occasionally, some of the operations intended for one segment of the session were included in another. But rather than insisting that every segment of the session receive equal attention, the leaders concentrated on covering all of the key points and ensuring that members could apply them to concrete situations and steps. The leaders' thorough familiarity with the purpose of the exercises and with their interconnection allowed them to respond sensitively to the concerns of group members without compromising the flow from one segment of the session to another.

Session at a Glance

1. **Welcome.**
2. **Introductions.**
3. **Topic and Goals.** The client and family member's or companion's new roles in recovery.
4. **Check-In.** Members' family situations/questions. Assessing concerns.
5. **Brainstorming and Discussion of Problems.** Other family problems. Eliciting more participation and perspective.
6. **Brainstorming and Discussion of Suggestions.** Suggestions for clients and for family members—sharing what has worked and what has not.
7. **Optional Fictional Case Study.** "Robert." Applying the suggestions.
8. **Review Handout.** "Suggestions for the Family in Early Recovery." Summarizing the suggestions.
9. **Open Discussion.** Applying the suggestions to members' problems and/or to the problems of Robert's family.
10. **Closing Communication.** ("I love you; I need your help; Forgive me; Thank you"; etc.) Creating a sense of solidarity among family members and partners and with the group.

The remainder of this chapter provides the reader with what was actually said by the group members and leaders in each segment of a session. For most of the segments, we have added italicized commentary that explains how the excerpts illustrate major points and goals of the session. The commentary also analyzes the leaders' uses of the session format to meet the specific needs of the group.

Welcome to Family Members

LEADER: Welcome to the [names program]. Clients who have invited loved ones deserve credit, and the loved ones here deserve credit for accepting the invitation. You are expressing your support and love for one another. We understand that addiction is painful for family members and companions. We hope to show that recovery can be a new beginning.

Introductions of Leaders and Members

The leader and recovering peer leader introduce themselves. Then family members and companions go around the room introducing themselves by name and relation to the client.

Topic and Goals

> LEADER: Addiction affects whole families, not just addicts, and recovery is most effective when family members and clients are on the same team. Teams share priorities and assign roles. Yet addiction badly disrupts normal family roles, and in recovery these roles must be redefined. Family members often ask, "How can I help?" And just as important, "How can I avoid doing harm?" And clients often are uncertain what *they* can do with and for their family members. Tonight we will examine these questions: What is helpful? What is harmful? What is the loved one's responsibility? And what is the client's? We hope to arrive at some practical suggestions for some common family problems in early recovery, and we hope to bring everyone a bit closer in the larger "family of recovery."

[The leader closely follows the sample script from the session.]

Check-In

Of the 12 client-members, 6 are accompanied by at least one family member or companion, resulting in a combined group of 20 persons. The size of the group requires leaders to expedite check-in by paraphrasing many issues and deferring further discussion to later in the session. In several cases, the professional leader contains a rambling presentation by pointing out that the issue is "important enough to be given fuller attention later." Frequently, clients and their loved ones enter this session guardedly, with great hopes, but also fearful of what will be said, of whether they will be blamed, and of whether their positions will be understood and respected. Mindful that clients and family members can be taking a great risk by opening up in front of one another, the leader invites members to "open up at any time during the session." He adds, "You are likely to find that you are not alone in your concerns, and you will be helping the whole group as well as yourself by speaking."

Mack leads off, complaining in a surly tone about his lack of supportive family members: "I've got no family issues, because I've got no family." He is alluding to his father's alcoholism and his brothers' addictions of which he has spoken in previous sessions.

Stu expresses frustration about a court order allowing him only an hour per week to visit his 4-year-old son. The visits must be supervised by his estranged wife. In passing, Stu remarks to Mack, "At least you're living with your wife." Mack responds, "I'll let *you* live with her for a few weeks; then you'll feel better about living alone." The laughter that follows seems to ease some tension in the group. The leader commends Mack's ability to lighten the tone, but adds teasingly that if Mack had invited his wife to the session the group could have decided for itself which spouse was harder to live with.

Joe's fiancee, Ellen, expresses her anxiety about Joe's relapsing again. In the event of another relapse, she doesn't know whether it would be more supportive to leave him or stick with him. She is afraid that if he feels he has nothing to lose, he will just keep relapsing. The leader promises that the group will return later in the session to useful and nonuseful responses to relapse. Ellen and her mother-in-law say that they want to trust Joe, but that it is difficult. Joe himself complains that there seems to be no way to gain his wife's trust: "She's always looking at my eyes, always making me account for my money."

Ray's mother says that she can identify with Ellen: "Does he understand what he put you through for so long? Then you're supposed to trust him overnight because he's in treatment?" She says that she's glad someone else feels this way because she didn't know whether she would have the courage to say it herself. She wants to know whether she should drive her son to treatment to make sure that he gets there. Ray's wife, who looks troubled while her mother-in-law is speaking, says that it was difficult for her to come to this meeting "because for the last three years everything has revolved around Ray and his problem." She asks, "What about me? He's gone five, six nights for *his* treatment. Ma [mother-in-law] says 'Don't argue with him, don't get him upset, but make sure he goes to treatment.' She gives him money so he won't want to get high from worrying about bills. What about me?" Again, the leader promises to return to the issues, which he labels: "Trust, helping, and support for family members and companions."

Sherri speaks next. During her 3½ weeks in the program, she has used the group to help resolve a crisis. She had been living with an addicted boyfriend who beat her. She revealed this fact in her second group session after the leader asked her (before group) about a facial bruise. Subsequently, with the group's intensive support, she disclosed her situation to her widowed father from whom she had been estranged. The father responded by inviting Sherri to move in with him temporarily. Sherri also obtained a restraining order against the boyfriend. She says, "Everybody here knows my situation. I feel like I'm introducing my first family [her father] to my second family [the group]. I just want to express my gratitude to both families." Several group members warmly welcome the father, and one remarks, "I feel like I know you, I've heard so much about you." The leader jokes, "It's all been positive. Don't look so worried." (*laughter*) The father also expresses gratitude "to have my daughter back" and says he hopes he'll learn more tonight about what he can do for her.

While Sherri and her father speak, Carol, Sherri's closest friend in the group, keeps staring at the floor. She says that she can't speak "right now." The leader invites her to speak when she is able. He adds again, "This is a very emotional time for many of you, clients and loved ones. But if you can bring yourself to speak, you will probably be relieved and find that you aren't alone."

Commentary

During the check-in the leader jots down a list of the major issues mentioned or implied, including the need for a drug-free living situation, dealing with feelings of grief and aloneness, dealing with impatience and resentment, the difference between "enabling" addiction and supporting recovery, overprotectiveness, difficulties in earning and giving trust, responding to relapse, the need for loved ones to obtain outside support, and the need to bring supportive loved ones into the group members' recovery. As Mack speaks, the leader writes, "No supportive family?" This is a question because resistant clients commonly defend themselves by scapegoating absent family members. Especially because Mack had mentioned in earlier sessions that he has a drug-free wife and that he still "occasionally" plays in a softball league with his drug-using brothers, the leader senses that Mack's stance during the check-in should not go unchallenged. Indeed, a principal reason for the family and partner session is to help foster commitment from "chameleon" clients who try to keep their home lives separate from treatment. In order to avoid pressure to change, they lead double lives that reflect their ambivalence about recovery. Bringing family members and companions to a treatment session represents an opportunity for such clients to increase their investment in recovery. For this reason, the leader amiably confronts Mack during the check-in about failing to invite his wife to the session, and he decides to probe Mack further during the ensuing discussion. Such probes, although direct, will remain friendly, for like most clients, Mack responds best to a welcoming approach that gives him full credit for his strengths and for the steps he has taken. The leader plays to Mack's sense of humor (as he uses gentle humor throughout the session to bring the group together, to ease its initial awkwardness, and to maintain an optimistic tone). Aside from helping Mack to take an important step, the leader is hoping that Mack's situation will become a live case study illustrating the importance of clients taking active responsibility for family changes.

Brainstorming and Discussion of Problems

The leader reads aloud the list of issues and writes them on a chalkboard. Then he invites members to add other current or likely issues. None are offered immediately. The leader invites members to add new problems at any time and asks members to respond to the issues already mentioned. Again, no one speaks immediately. The leader remarks that Mack seemed to feel alone, and he asks whether anyone else feels that way. The recovering peer leader says that she had felt lonely in early recovery. She had moved away from her home town, which was fairly small and where "all the wrong people knew" her. She says, "I still can't go back there for long periods, and when I do visit I make sure my [stable and supportive] sister is around and knows my needs." The leader asks the recovering peer leader how she overcame the initial loneliness. She tells of finding sponsors and new friends: "I made my groups my family. My sister also visited me a lot and came to meetings with me." At this point, Jason breaks in with great animation:

> JASON: That's what I was wondering when you (*indicates Mack*) were talking, man. Are you using what you've got? I mean I had to swallow a lot of pride to ask Uncle Will [his uncle] to come here. He called me an asshole more times than I can remember when I was out there (*laughter*), and he was always right, but I never admitted it or listened. So I took a chance and asked him. I mean, he's like the *freak* of our family being clean and sober. (*laughter*) Besides inviting him here, I'm always going out with this group for coffee. But I don't see you there, man (*addressing Mack*). Also, you say you've got nobody to invite here, but what about your wife?

> MACK: It wouldn't do any good to ask. She doesn't want to hear about this shit. She sees it as just more of *my* problem. It used to be bars and broads; now it's groups and meetings. That's how she sees it.

ROD: She doesn't see that as progress? Have you shown her any program handouts or NA stuff?

MACK: She wouldn't read it.

JASON: Have you tried?

MACK: What's the point?

LEADER: I think Jason and Rod are wondering how you could read her mind.

JASON: Yep. She *definitely* isn't going to come here if she doesn't know that she is invited.

LEADER: Interesting point. Mack, you are someone who seems to have a lot to offer this group. You explain things well, and you can make people laugh, which we all need. So I think some of the members are saying, "It would be nice if Mack would jump in here with both feet." Am I wrong about that? Jason?

JASON: No. I like Mack. I've been where he is, and I know that it's hard. It's why he's always fighting with himself about seeing his brothers [as he was in the previous Problems and Progress session]. He's on the fence. Maybe your old lady would come and maybe she wouldn't, but I think you've got to ask yourself why you're not asking her. I mean I had second thoughts about inviting Uncle Will. I knew if he got *wised* up, he'd make it harder for me to get *screwed* up. (*laughter*)

LEADER: How about that, Mack?

MACK: Busted. (*laughter*) I'll ask her to the Co-Anon meeting Friday and out to coffee with the group. But I still don't think that she'll come.

LEADER: But it's great that you're going to ask. So we can hope to see her at [names the deli], but we can *count* on seeing you there?

MACK: Right.

Commentary

Having the members themselves make the key points taps into the group's power to motivate change and at the same time enhances group cohesiveness and autonomy. It helps to establish norms such as active participation and initiative, member-to-member helpfulness, and group problem-solving. However, the group's identity and sense of its purpose are fragile at this early stage and can be undermined if healthy support and advice are allowed to become scapegoating of an ambivalent member such as Mack. Sensing that Mack is ready to make a move toward the group, the leader tries to encourage him while creating an atmosphere in which reluctance can be expressed. Thus, he models for Jason a way of emphasizing Mack's strengths and welcoming their addition to the group. Jason takes the cue. The leader makes clear that he is aware of Mack's shaky commitment, but also that the group is willing to reach out to ambivalent members. The exchange culminates in a suggested step for Mack that underlines the group's expectations of its members.

Feeling that Mack still has reservations about inviting his wife to recovery activities and that other members may be struggling with similar resistance, the leader asks, "What else besides the desire to keep open one's escape routes might prevent someone from inviting loved ones?" Members mention shame, pride, and fear of rejection as other obstacles.

LEADER: Has anyone taken the chance of asking and been surprised by the results?

Sherri points to her father, who is smiling sheepishly. Sherri tells how her father's supportive response quickly dispelled her fears and made her recovery feel more solid.

LEADER: How about the family members and companions of clients? What was it like for you to be invited?

Several family members tell of being relieved and proud to have been asked.

JOE'S WIFE: It made me think he might be serious this time. I also felt he cared enough to let me in on this and ask me for help. Also, I was glad he realized how bad the problem was. It was no news to me that he needed help. But it was good news to me that *he* knew that he needed it.
LEADER: Well said.

Commentary

Because fears of being rejected by prospective guests seem to be widespread in this group, the leader tries to elicit models of fears overcome and examples of invitations accepted. Many clients anticipate rejection from others because of their lingering shame about addiction or uncertainty about recovery. Later in the session, the group will examine in more detail the example of those who have overcome such obstacles.

Carol looks increasingly dejected during the discussion, and the leader tries to draw her out.

LEADER: You look deep in thought, Carol.

CAROL: I feel like people here have been saying, "If you're living with someone who can't come or won't come, then move out and find someone who will. Or you can't be part of this group. Fuck you." I feel like you're forcing me to choose. Leave Damon [Carol's drug-dealing addict boyfriend] or leave the group. I mean, I think it's wonderful what Sherri did, and that she's here with her father. I love Sherri [Carol's closest friend in the group], but I can't do what she did. Damon's provided for me. He's been good to me, and he's using less now too. If I left him, he'd just get worse again. We've been through so much. And if I left him, how much is this group going to be there for me? For how long?

SHERRI: There's this group. Then there's other groups. There's your family, your mother if you'd let her help. Maybe the question shouldn't be how long *we'll* be there for you. Maybe it should be how long you'll stay clean living with Damon. I know that James [Sherri's boyfriend] *is* my addiction. Going back to him is the same as picking up.

ROD: Carol, I think you are afraid of being alone. I don't blame you. That's why I didn't leave Mandy [who has since gone into treatment] earlier. Now I realize that I was more alone living *with* her. And now she says that she's grateful—that my walking out woke her up.

CAROL: But Damon is *not* my addiction. My addiction is drugs. Isn't it enough that I'm clean now?

LEADER: That counts for a lot, and you deserve credit. It's what is getting you here. But it must be very hard to stay clean in your circumstances.

CAROL: Yes, that much is true.

LEADER: I think that is why Sherri was wondering how long you could hang on. Based on experience with a lot of people, we have to say that your odds aren't good. There's no addiction trigger stronger than having someone close to you whom you used to use with using under the same roof. Why do you think that would be?

Members discuss how the pull of a relationship can combine with the presence of the drug and associated triggers such as resentment, loneliness, and bitterness. The recovering peer leader summarizes, "One weak moment, one bad day at work, one wish to celebrate, and you're gone, because it's right there."

JASON: I think it's great that you're asking this group for help, Carol. You're someone I admire a lot, and I'm glad I've been able to give you something—even if it's only a ride. [Jason has been Carol's regular ride to treatment.] But to tell you the truth, I don't know how long I can hang in with you. Just knowing that you're living with a dealer messes with my head. I'm not that strong yet. I drop you off and I'm down thinking, "It's up there. Right up the stairs." I pick you up and I'm checking out your eyes to see if you're high. I can relate to [indicates Joe's wife and mother]. I *hear* that shit about having trouble trusting. (*laughter*)

RECOVERING PEER LEADER: Good point. Most people here are still too new and shaky in their own recoveries to deal with some situations even second-hand.

LEADER: Yes, but from Carol's point of view, I know that nothing is harder than separating from someone you love like she loves Damon—someone you've relied on so much and shared a lot with. No one here can say, "You've got to leave this guy. You've got to choose." That isn't our decision. All we can do is to help you examine your choices. What is likely to happen if you do this or that? You came here in the first place because your own thinking wasn't working out for you. It was warped by your addiction. We can also tell you what effect your situation has on us, as Jason did. We can tell you what has worked for others. And if you do decide you need to make a change, we can help you. If you're ready to make a move, we'll stand behind it as much as we can.

SHERRI: For me, it worked to ask my father for help. Also to go to counseling [for battered women]. I told my father what I needed and he was there. Now when I feel lonely for James, I've got people who understand to talk to.

CAROL: (*smiling*) You got an extra father? (*laughter*)

RECOVERING PEER LEADER: Carol, remember what some of the family members here said about being told about recovery? It sounds like now may be the time to open up to your mother. I know you've been struggling with that.

CAROL: Yes. (*She starts to cry. Sherri hugs her. Ellen touches her shoulder.*)

LEADER: (*after a pause*) I think Carol is working to use this group well. The group is working to help her, too. We have already started to get into some suggestions for her and for others. Now we are going to be doing more of that.

Commentary

The leader here restates the group's mission (as leaders should do periodically) and explains its mechanisms—such as helping members understand the consequences of choices and supporting productive changes. Because the first priority is to "be here clean," members must be commended for achieving that, as the leader commends Carol. At the same time, by expressing his and the group's concern that Carol will not remain clean for long in her current situation, the leader underlines the necessity for lifestyle change. The idea is made more acceptable by emphasizing the difficulty of Carol's situation than it would be, say, by suggesting that Carol is kidding herself. At the prospect of making a difficult change, Carol is besieged by several natural anxieties. The unreasonableness or irrelevance of some of her fears (e.g., that Damon will get worse if she leaves) can be best examined after Carol is helped to focus on the single paramount threat to her recovery.

To a limited extent during the check-in and to a greater extent during the foregoing segment, the leader allows a prolonged discussion of Mack's and Carol's situations. Longer discussion is justified both by the urgency of the issues and their relevance to wider group concerns. The problems of relationships with active users, of failing to utilize available support, and of taking unrealistic responsibility for the recoveries of others are shared by several clients and their loved ones. Carol's ability to use the group's help and the group's willingness to pull together for her exemplify a group process that should not be cut off too quickly. Mutual problem-solving and support gives the group a concrete experience of the extended "family" of recovering people and their loved ones.

The limited suggestions generated at this point anticipate and provide a transition to the next segment (Brainstorming and Discussion of Suggestions). The leader is mindful that a preview of the suggestions can save time in the later segments where some points will require only summaries or brief reviews. This sort of flexibility, which is possible only because of the leader's deep familiarity with the purposes of the individual segments and their sequence, helps the session to flow naturally.

Brainstorming and Discussion of Suggestions

LEADER: We've already arrived at a few rules of thumb about what works or doesn't work for people. For instance, we've spoken about the need to keep the house drug free, and the group suggested that Carol and Mack might have people in their families that they haven't asked for support—that they would have a lot to gain and nothing to lose by trying. Also, people seem to agree that it is a good idea to use this group as much as possible without endangering it, and to have separate systems of support for clients and loved ones. [The discussion of the latter point was not included in the vignettes.] What other useful suggestions can we come up with? (*silence*) How about some guidelines on getting and giving trust? Several people have mentioned that as a problem.

ROD: After I got out of the detox last time, I always resented being watched. I couldn't understand why Deb [Rod's wife] didn't trust me and I would blame her for making me want to use. What I learned is that I was getting so angry because I didn't trust myself. I was angry that I couldn't do it my way—and angry that I couldn't get high. I hadn't really accepted how bad it had been and what I'd put Deb through. So I thought, "Why doesn't she get off my goddamn back?"

RECOVERING PEER LEADER: Were you keeping anything behind your "goddamn back" that you didn't want her to see? I know I always used to yell loudest when I had a guilty conscience.

ROD: I was blowing off aftercare meetings fairly often, and I told myself it was because she was pushing me to go.

LEADER: But now you see it as your lack of commitment back then?

ROD: Right. The pushing doesn't help, but it's no excuse for me to screw up.

LEADER: Well put. The pushing doesn't help but it's no excuse to screw up. That gives us another guideline. (*Writes on chalkboard, "It is the client's responsibility to stay clean and get to treatment."*) What about knowing that someone who basically wants the best for you is *there*? That she can't help watching to some degree. That if you screw up too much she'll know.

ROD: That still helps. Especially in weak moments. Now I'm *grateful* to have that.

JOE'S MOTHER: But it's exactly this "weak moments" stuff that worries me. This makes me feel I *have* to push. I mean, I thought he'd be in treatment and things would be different. But I'm hearing today about this one wanting to use and that one wanting to use. What's the point of treatment if everyone still wants to use?

LEADER: Two important issues, Mrs. J. Let me address the first one. Have you pushed Joe in the past? Tried to make him stay clean and meet his responsibilities?

JOE'S MOTHER: Well, I suppose . . . I know he'd say so.

JOE: Is the Pope Catholic? (*laughter*)

LEADER: And has it ever worked?

JOE'S MOTHER: No.

LEADER: How about anyone else? Has anyone else had any luck forcing an addict to stay drug free?

Rod's wife confirms that forcing doesn't work. The leader acknowledges that the desire to control the addicted person is natural but counterproductive, as is the desire to take on his or her responsibilities. A discussion of the difference between supporting recovery and "enabling" addiction follows. The group makes a distinction between "what the recovering addict wants" (e.g., money, which should not always be supplied) and "what the recovering addict needs" (sometimes saying no can meet the needs of recovery). Then Rod's wife, who attends Al-Anon, underlines the importance of loved ones seeking their own separate support.

> LEADER: Now what about Joe's mother's other concern? Based on what the clients here have learned so far, can any of you explain to Joe's mother why someone who is in treatment and doing well might still want to use?
>
> JASON: That's addiction. That's how it works. It's the disease. It can be triggered by things. Your nervous system learns a certain way and it takes a while to teach it a new way. It's automatic. We fed addiction a lot of years, but we've only fed recovery a few weeks.

Jason's essential points are contained in the "Addiction: Myths and Facts" handout from the Addiction and Denial session. The leader indicates that the recovering peer leader should supply Joe's mother with a copy of the handout.

> ROD: Also, I think we've got to keep clear the difference between wanting to use and using. (*turning to Joe's mother*) A lot of things make me *want* to use. Nothing makes me use.
>
> LEADER: True. And one of the things our clients learn—Jason's point—is that craving for drugs is reduced gradually by learning new responses to craving. That means making major lifestyle changes. You have to separate from more than just drugs, especially in the beginning. Does someone who hasn't spoken yet want to explain some of the changes to the family members? What we call the "Walls."

Jason and Sherri explain. The leaders complete the explanation. Then there is some discussion of productive and counterproductive responses to a client's relapse. Loved ones are urged to stick by clear self-protective limits, to understand that relapse in early recovery often indicates the need for more structure and stronger "walls" (sometimes including those of residential treatment, a halfway house, or day care), and to take care of their own lives and seek their own support.

> LEADER: We have talked about clients having to be patient with their loved ones' lack of trust. Trust is not established overnight. You have to build up a track record. And we've also talked about loved ones having to be patient with all the treatment and the time it takes to get better. Now can we add a suggestion (*turns to the chalkboard*) that clients and loved ones *both* need to be patient?

There is general agreement. The leader reviews on the chalkboard the suggestions generated up to this point.

Commentary

The leader allows clients such as Jason and Rod (who has been in treatment before and whose spouse is now educated about recovery) to make key points. In the foregoing segment especially, the leader relies heavily on these more advanced members to share experiences and knowledge with the group. Such "leader-assistants" exemplify and model what they explain. The leader frequently needs only to clarify, supplement, and summarize their contributions. At the same time, leaders must beware of relying too much on too few members. In a group of such short duration, it is likely that accomplishments will be modest. In the excerpt above, the leader tries to achieve more balanced participation by directly addressing nonpartici-pators (calling on them to explain the "walls"). Often a single participation by a reticent member can break the ice, and wider participation creates cohesion and energy in the group. It also ensures that clients and issues will not "slip through the cracks."

The leader's summaries here of suggestions generated throughout the session (not merely in this segment) expedite the Brainstorm and provide an introduction to the "Suggestions" handout. Although leaders should always summarize key points toward the end of a session, partial periodic summaries throughout the session are also very useful.

Distribute and Review Fictional Case Study (Optional)

The leader chooses to omit the Optional Fictional Case Study because many of the problem cases and issues that it emphasizes were antici-pated in the previous discussions. Omitting the case study in this instance saved time and avoided too much redundancy.

Distribute and Review the Handout

The leader reads the handout ("Suggestions for the Family in Early Recovery") aloud and asks whether everyone "understands and agrees with the suggestions."

Open Discussion

LEADER: What points stand out for anyone, especially any point that we may not have discussed?

STU: Point number one for the recovering addict rings a bell for me. ["You've earned distrust, and you must re-earn trust."] I need to remember to be patient and to work on my own recovery – not expect others to change right away.

LEADER: Can you be more specific?

STU: Just what I said before. Going easier with my wife and the visiting with my son. I can't let myself get upset making demands. It was me that gave away a lot of my fatherhood privileges. Now I'm doing all I can for my son just by working on me. I can't be a father if I'm out there using.

LEADER: Well said. Anyone else? How about the viewpoint of a family member or companion?

JOE'S MOTHER: Point number two for the family strikes home. ["The client is not 'cured' by stopping drug use."] We've already covered it, I guess. But also the last point – that you can't make someone else recover. That's hard to accept – that I've just got to say, "It's his responsibility," when I'm not used to his taking *any* responsibility.

SHERRI'S FATHER: Well, you've got to give him the chance. He won't learn to do it if you do it for him. People rise to the challenge. I used to lean on my crew at work all the time, but it got me nowhere. Now I give them room to make mistakes, and I get burned once in a while, but I also get better production. Just be there for him, like it says. And take care of yourself. I admit, it's easier for me to say some of this than do it.

LEADER: For a lot of us, I'm sure. How about a suggestion from the family column that would help make it easier to do?

Several members refer to point five, obtaining "outside support." The leader, once again, refers to the Al-Anon and Co-Anon meeting lists. Rod's wife, who is experienced in Al-Anon, invites Joe's wife and mother to accompany her to a meeting.

Commentary

Most of the points from the handout are covered and summarized during earlier segments, so it is not necessary to spend much time on the handout during this segment. However, the ways of thinking that underlie this session are new to many members and bear repeating. This segment allows the leader to ascertain that members have digested the main points well enough to be able to apply them to concrete situations. He asks Stu to be more "specific," because if members are allowed to speak vaguely, they sometimes manage to "sound good" without truly coming to grips with the material and without making a useful contribution to the group.

The leader also tries to elicit a balance of participation from the clients and their loved ones. Alternating between questions about clients' new roles in recovery and questions about the roles of companions or family members underlines how well these changed roles can complement one another.

Closing Communication

LEADER: We've spoken about reopening lines of communication tonight, and a lot of you already are making great strides. Now you will get another chance to practice what we've preached. Communications such as "I love you, Thank you, I forgive you, I'm sorry, I need your help" will help your personal situations as well as the whole group. You can also address yourself to absent or dead loved ones. The message should be something that *you* need to say, even if someone absent is not ready or able to hear it. Some of you (*smiles encouragingly at Carol*) may want to use this occasion to rehearse making an actual communication. That would be most useful. Does everyone understand? Make a simple communication (*repeats examples*) to someone here or someone not here—or a rehearsal for an actual communication. Let's go around the table.

RECOVERING PEER LEADER: Let me start. This session got me thinking about my ex-fiance and my sister, the one who's still using. First, to John [her ex-fiance]: Thanks for leaving me, babe. (*laughter*) It helped. To my sister: I miss you [names the sister, who is still a drug user]. I still care. Get into recovery. I hope we can share that with each other some day.

SHERRI: I want to say thank you to my father. Thank you for being here for me. I'm sorry I didn't do this sooner. I love you.

SHERRI'S FATHER: I love you, too. What you're doing, what all of you here are doing is wonderful. I feel like you're all giving me my daughter back. To be part of this and to help any of you if I can is a privilege.

Jason, addressing his uncle, echoes Sherri's communication to her father.

JASON'S UNCLE: I was surprised when Jason said he was afraid to ask me. It was a gift to be asked. I've no kids of my own, and I've always had a special feeling about Jason. I've always known that there was something great under all the bullshit. (*laughter*) But I haven't been good at expressing it. And I always thought that he thought of me as sort of a heavy. That he would think enough of me to invite me here means a lot. Thanks, kid.

SHERRI'S FATHER: It's hard for men, isn't it? What you want to say is "I love you."

JASON'S UNCLE: I love you. (*Jason and his uncle embrace. Everyone applauds.*)

JOE: I just want to say that I'm glad my family is here. I get pissed at them, but some people don't even have someone to get pissed at. (*laughter*) Also: I'm sorry for what I put you through.

JOE'S MOTHER: We are proud of you.

JOE'S WIFE: We love you.

MACK: I want to say something to my [absent, drug-using] brothers. I miss you, but I can't see you. It's nothing personal, but I can't help you now. I'd like to say something nice to my father too, but I can't. I mean, I hate to bring down this love fest here, but that son of a bitch fucked over my mother and the rest of us too many times. My communication to you, Dad, is "Fuck you." Excuse my Irish, ladies, but it's all that Dad understands. (*laughter*)

SHERRI'S FATHER: But don't keep screwing yourself, young man. There's nothing you can do about the past. If you can't forgive your father, at least don't let it eat you up. Get on with your life.

Several members agree.

LEADER: You needed to say that, Mack, and you deserve credit for your honesty. We know that you are hurting about this. At the same time, people are saying it's time to take care of yourself. Maybe you can start with those commitment steps. Remember them?

MACK: Bring the wife. Go out with the group. Will do. (*applause*)

RECOVERING PEER LEADER: Carol looks like she's about to do something desperate.

CAROL: This is hard to say. I miss you, Mama. I need your help.

The leader commends Carol for making a difficult communication and for her honesty. He ascertains that Carol hasn't spoken to her mother for a year. He asks what would be the worst outcome if Carol were to call to say hello and disclose her recovery.

CAROL: She could call me a whore and hang up — like the last time.

LEADER: You were in recovery?

CAROL: No. I wanted to see my son and borrow some money for drugs. (*She smiles, understanding the irony. Members point out that things might be different now.*)

SHERRI: And suppose she calls you a whore and hangs up again. Are you any worse off?

CAROL: No. Nothing to lose.

The leader agrees and summarizes some of the reasons why "things might be different now." Carol agrees to make the call, and the leader promises that the group will check back on the outcome of the step.

Commentary

The recovering peer leader leads off the closing communication. This had not been planned explicitly, but it reflects a working rapport between the leaders. The recovering peer leader here senses that her sentiment will set a productive tone of acceptance, reconciliation, and present-orientation for the group. As frequently happens during this segment, a chain reaction is established — what Mack aptly calls a "love fest." Each member's communication facilitates a similar communication from a member in a parallel situation. An intense communal experience of this sort helps to give momentum to early recovery. However, in order to prevent the "love fest" from glossing over enduring difficulties, leaders must be alert to reticent members who may be cowed by the positive atmosphere. During this session, Mack's and Carol's honesty grounds the general hopefulness, and the leader commends them for it and acknowledges their pain. At the same time, the leader is able to focus the group's support (and its applause) on the concrete steps defined earlier in the session.

In sum, this Closing Communication dramatizes the value of reestablishing supportive connections on a new basis and of letting go of harmful attachments. It also underlines the importance of actively taking appropriate steps. By the same token, it provides an uplifting ending for the session. Each member who opens up and reaches out is expressing the potential for new solidarity not only within the family or couple but also with the group and its larger enterprise of recovery.

Note

Al-Anon and Co-Anon meeting lists should be available on a table for family members. All of the Clean Start program handouts should also be available. The leaders should plan to remain about 20 minutes after the session ends to answer family members' questions.

Relapse and Other Problems

Formats may not go as smoothly as they look on paper. Turbulence and disruption, although infrequent in a well-run group, nonetheless occur. A client bent on taking over the group may seem impossible to shut up. Another may start to act abusively or aggressively. An otherwise inoffensive client may show up reeking of alcohol. But relapses, however inevitable, are the greatest threat to the group, for they challenge the group's claim to efficacy, and they can become epidemic.

Dealing effectively with relapses is essential to successful group leadership. Reacting belatedly, underreacting, or overreacting to the crises of early recovery can distract a group from the business of a session. However, prompt, judicious responses can contain crises and make them instructive. Indeed, immediate problems squarely acknowledged can dramatize the main points of a session. A rational, "up-front" approach to adversity is a reassuring and useful example to the whole group. Leaders may be naturally resistant to taking time away from a carefully prepared topic. They also may be understandably reluctant to confront awkward situations or those that remind everyone of clients' vulnerabilities in a group that is generally doing well. Yet we cannot reasonably expect clients to face difficult problems if the leaders do not. Moreover, like addictions, unaddressed problems in the group tend to spread and to snowball.

Conversely, addressing problems quickly and fully usually results in keeping them minimal. In fact, one of the main advantages of group treatment is that once positive and productive behaviors modeled by the leaders become group norms, then many problems, including major distractions and relapses, are markedly reduced. We have previously discussed at length how these positive norms are established. But how are they maintained in the face of periodic challenges? Even experienced leaders used to "thinking on their feet" are aware that crises can warp reason and compromise balance. This is true of leaders and clients alike. In emergencies, leaders must not rely on wit and instinct alone. They must be guided by reliable principles. "Gut responses" must be firmly grounded in an understanding of the rationale of program policies. The group's response to a member's relapse should illustrate the value of planning and serve as a model for members' responses to their own relapses.

A leader who is overinvested in the success of a client might overlook a degree of addiction that indicates a need for inpatient treatment. Conversely, a leader who feels betrayed by a relapsing client may react judgmentally and with unwarranted "clinical force." Similarly, a group that is insecure in its own abstinence may react punitively or with hostility to the threat posed by another's relapse. Alternatively, the group may unwittingly conspire with a member's denial of the seriousness of the event—perhaps hoping at some level to receive similar leniency should the roles be reversed.

In responding clinically to relapse, and in guiding the group's response, leaders must learn automatically to consult the principles that underlie the program's relapse policy. What is the client trying to accomplish? What does a relapse mean in terms of the program's broader view of addiction and initial recovery? These questions are central to the next section. The principles and guidelines that they generate, such as keeping the group's safety a first priority and responding promptly and forthrightly, apply to other problem areas as well and provide a foundation for the remainder of the chapter.

Relapse: The Problem and the Policy

Relapses are "facts of life" in an outpatient cessation group. However, to recognize the reality of relapses is not to encourage them or to say that they are inevitable or permissible. As we made clear in the discussion of conditioning theory (Chapter Two), acute vulnerability to relapse is partly a result of the unextinguished cravings of early recovery. The problem for the clinician treating outpatients is that the relapses that result from this vulnerability also increase it. Any cocaine use increases the probability of subsequent use and of an eventual full-blown relapse. On the one hand, single episodes of drug use can be viewed as symptoms of the very disease that a cessation program is designed to treat; on the other hand, any drug use may indicate or cause a level of addiction too severe for current outpatient treatment.

Beyond the danger to the recovery of the relapsing individual, a primary policy consideration in a program based upon outpatient group treatment must be the safety and integrity of the entire group. Even if the relapser does not actively "pull down" another member, the mere presence of intoxicated individuals can erode group morale and stimulate the general level of craving. The very knowledge that other members have relapsed can undermine a norm of abstinence. "If them, why not me?" wonders the insecurely abstinent client. At the very least, relapses are dramatic events that can commandeer disproportionate amounts of the group's time and attention and shift the group's central focus from success to failure. Shaky members might find using "one more time" appealing if its consequences seem to be merely getting the whole group to help them learn how not to use again.

A productive relapse policy must balance the interests of the individual and the group; it must reflect an understanding that relapses are dangerous setbacks to recovery that appropriate responses can nevertheless convert to important learning experiences; and it must indicate the nature of an appropriate response. Our policy of requiring clients to repeat the sequence of sessions and demonstrate an increased commitment to recovery in the event of a single relapse underlines the seriousness of any drug use. The policy indicates the need to relearn intensively and reapply the fundamental principles of the program, and suggests that the appropriate response is to "do more" (to become more active in recovery, to make changes that had been resisted, to shore up one's walls). The purpose of referring clients to a more intensive level of treatment in the event of a second relapse is to protect both the individual's recovery and those of other members. Once the more intensive level of care is completed successfully, the client is encouraged to return to the group to complete his or her treatment.

The experience of our project substantiates the wisdom of this policy. Not infrequently, clients learn from limited relapses. In some cases, the responses to relapse are watershed events whereby clients overcome previous reservations and embrace the program wholeheartedly. Some clients seem to need to prove to themselves that they couldn't drink in safety. Others need to experience the consequences of "one last party" before fully accepting the recovering addict identity and beginning to participate fully in the recovering community. However, when a client's response to relapse is not immediate and open to guidance, extensive further drug use follows.

Detection and Response

Relapses may be detected by a client's self-report, by the report of others, by a client's behavior or appearance, or by a urine that tests positive for a substance of abuse. Because self-report is clearly the most desirable means of detection, group leaders must continually honor and reward honesty. Self-reported second relapses should be especially commended. Leaders can point out that there is "no disgrace in getting more help when one needs it." By contrast, refusing to acknowledge the need for more treatment, insisting on one more try without it, and continuing to resist making essential changes are viewed as self-defeating responses.

Leaders should make direct questions about current drug use a standard feature of the check-in. This is especially important when members appear shaky, when they admit to having been tempted or having put themselves in a dangerous situation, when in the previous session a client had seemed besieged by cravings and dangerous situations but now claims to be doing fine, when attendance has been spotty, when thoughts seem disconnected, when pupils are dilated, and so forth. When there is reason for suspicion, clients should be asked forthrightly, but respectfully, whether they have used drugs or alcohol. Those who acknowledge such use should be asked the details: What was used? How often? When? Where? With whom? An appropriate clinical and group response to relapse must be based upon the facts. However, the denial that accompanies readdiction can lead the one who has used to obscure or soft-pedal the facts.

If leaders are suspicious of a client who denies using, they should request a "spot" urine (in addition to the minimal two urines that are asked of each client before advancement). They should also encourage clients who suspect others of drug use to express their concerns in the group or privately to the leaders. Reporting suspicions should be viewed as necessary self-defense (and defense of the group). Silence about known or suspected drug use or dealing defeats the purpose of treatment. It stimulates craving and resentment, damages self-esteem, reinforces the habits of deceit, and undermines group cohesion by creating schisms between those who know and those who do not. The authenticity of the group discussion and the entire treatment effort can be undermined when members know that others in the group are secretly using drugs. Under such circumstances, secrecy is a burden best shared with the patient's supporters, especially the leaders.

Someone who freely reports a relapse deserves the group's full attention. The relapsed client needs help in assessing the extent of the drug use and craving, in identifying what is triggering the craving, and in determining how best to use the group and other resources to reduce the current danger. The client may need to vent some feelings, but the leaders should not allow the group to become a confessional; it is better to keep the focus on the concrete task of reestablishing abstinence. Among the questions that the group can bring to bear on this task might be: Are drugs at home or easily accessible? Is the client in touch with other active users? How seriously have the client's job, key family relationships, or finances been affected? Who else knows about the relapse, and whom might it be helpful to tell? What help does the client think that he or she needs? If a more intensive level of treatment (e.g., day care, halfway house, or full residential inpatient care) is indicated, what arrangements should be made immediately?

The initial discussion of a relapse should focus on the practical issues of whether and how safety can be established. It is necessary to limit the damage before extensively analyzing its development and long-term prevention. The relevant principles and strategies that should guide the discussion are contained in the Erecting the Walls session. Initial measures might include the client's making a commitment to avoid the setting where the relapse occurred (even if it is the workplace or home), severing a relationship with a drug source (e.g., a friend, family member, or dealer), giving cash to a loved one to hold, being accompanied while throwing out a stash or destroying drug paraphernalia, and making a commitment to attend designated NA or CA meetings at dangerous times. (Because being alone with someone who may be actively using drugs is dangerous for cessation group members, two or more members should accompany a recently relapsed peer.) Also in the initial discussion, a schedule of telephone contacts with the leaders can be agreed on.

Simple priorities should be emphasized in the session at which a "fresh" relapse is reported. For example, beyond taking steps to separate from temptation, a client may need to focus mainly on returning "clean" to the next session. In *that* session, if a client has remained abstinent, leaders should follow up on the primary steps agreed upon in the previous session. In the following Problems and Progress session, leaders can initiate a more reflective analysis of the gaps in the client's walls that contributed to the relapse. Did the client neglect to limit access to drugs? Did the client cut off contacts with drug users? Did the client keep all treatment appointments? Did the key people in the client's life know about his or her recovery? Did the client have a busy daily schedule including recovery activities? Was the client in contact with supportive drug-free and recovering people? Did the client have a sufficient list of telephone numbers that he or she called habitually? When there is an outbreak of several crises, the follow-up on a given individual's crisis may have to be deferred, foreshortened, or referred to individual counselors. *Note: Dwelling too much on relapses without a balancing emphasis on members who are making progress can foster "epidemics."*

Doing More

The extended group analysis of a relapse and how to respond to it should be guided by the principles discussed in the sessions on Erecting the Walls, Coping with Dangerous Situations, Making Changes, and Closing the Doors to Addiction. To the degree that relapse rekindles the client's level of addiction, he or she must become more committed to recovery. The recovering addict must not merely apologize for failing or vow to try harder. He or she must *do* more. The client should take concrete steps to fill free time more carefully and more bindingly. More people must know about the client's recovery so that incentives to stay abstinent will be maximized and escape hatches will be closed off. The client must attend more recovery meetings, speak more, and participate more actively in group social and recreational activities. The client might need to ask for a sponsor or for an individual counselor. Moreover, a significant sacrifice might be in order. To give up some ordinary convenience or pleasure—such as an individual checking account, a Friday night card game that might expose the recovering addict to users, windfalls of cash, or offers of beer—signifies an increased level of commitment. How much more the client must do depends, of course, on the severity of the relapse, how much is already being done and the unique problems recovery presents to him or her.

Commitment steps are particularly useful responses to relapse. Too often, a resolution made in group to "attend more NA meetings" or to "start using the telephone" is forgotten as soon as the group "spotlight" is turned elsewhere. One way to ensure that the client will *continue* to do more is to close some doors against backsliding. For example, one of our clients whose relapse was precipitated, in part, by seeing drug users in his workplace cafeteria told his supervisor about his recovery and requested an extra half hour at lunchtime in order to attend a nearby NA meeting. The request was granted. Then the client took the additional step of signing up to be the "greeter" for 3 months at that meeting. Sanctions against backsliding and support for progress were thus set up on two connected fronts—work and the recovering community.

Another client, who had been unable to break away from an abusive, drug-using sex partner, used the group's support to make the break after she relapsed. This step freed her to reestablish contact with some drug-free family members whom she invited to the cessation family session. There, it became clear to the family members that returning to the boyfriend would constitute a virtual relapse. Their new knowledge helped them to support the client effectively and became an additional barrier against slippage. This client also committed herself to use group members' help in finding a new residence.

Clients who return to the cessation program after a period of inpatient treatment or halfway house residence necessitated by relapses can become models for the group. Their stories are examples of the need to do more. There is a sense of full *presentness* about such clients when they return that underlines their earlier reservations and tentativeness. As one client put it:

> "Before I was always struggling about how much of the program to follow. It felt like a sacrifice. Now the struggle is over. I do what others tell me, because we share the same goal. It's like being a shareholder in a company that you work for. You'll probably work harder and not be wasteful. I realized I'm a shareholder."

"Clean" Sessions

It is especially important to keep the sessions themselves free of drugs, intoxicated members, and dealing. Clients should be notified when they first call seeking treatment that they should not come to a session on a day when they have used any mood-altering substance or when they possess such substances. Callers should be encouraged to begin the process of recovery immediately by getting rid of their drugs and going to 12-step fellowship meetings during free time. The intoxication and drug-possession rules should be prominently posted, and the leader should explain the reasons for them regularly:

> "Members who are high or 'holding' endanger the whole group. They trigger craving in others, and they often bring negativity and confusion to the discussion. Each of you who has committed yourself to recovery has earned the right to a safe, drug-free treatment space."

The priority of making the group a safe place justifies a policy of expelling from the group anyone who sells or gives drugs to another member.

The leaders must act quickly when they suspect that a member is intoxicated. After consulting with the group leader to confirm the suspicion, the peer leader should take the member in question out of the session room, indicate the leaders' suspicions, and respectfully explain the policy:

> "It's nothing personal, but it makes it more difficult for everyone to stay drug free when anyone here is not drug free. Being even a little high also makes it much harder to learn from or contribute to the group discussion."

The member should be encouraged to return "clean" to the next session and should be offered the option of extra conference time with the leaders.

Intoxicated members who go unnoticed by busy group leaders and who are not reported because of the group's lingering "street code" or its reluctance to take responsibility can quickly undermine the program's credibility and the group's morale. While leaders must be as observant as possible, they should also periodically ask members to report any suspicions of other members to the leaders:

> "We have a lot to think about here, and we can't always notice everything. This is your group. Rather than allowing another's addiction to threaten your recovery and take your attention away from the purpose of the session, you will be doing everyone a favor—including the person who is high—by speaking up."

Attendance and Punctuality

Spotty attendance and poor punctuality are behaviors that become contagious in an early recovery group. They distract leaders as well as clients from the purpose of the sessions, and they demoralize the group. The attendance policy and its rationale were discussed in Chapter Five, and here we need mainly to reemphasize that the policy must be enforced promptly and consistently. The level of commitment evidenced by regular compliance with the policy should be regularly rewarded; leaders should publicly commend individual clients for "being here every time on time." But public praise for compliance must be coupled with quick public sanctions for noncompliance. Otherwise, the credibility of the rules and of the program will suffer, and absences will spread along with a general erosion of commitment. Indeed, in their enforcement of the attendance policy, leaders must exemplify the program's principles of commitment, of consistency, and of prompt attention to backsliding. Failure to act for fear of losing one weak member will likely result in losing many strong members.

The attendance policy should be prominently posted along with slogans such as "Showing up is half the battle!" and "Every time, on time!" If feasible, it is useful to lock the door of the session room 10 minutes after the starting time. In the first two sessions that we tried locking the door during our project (after announcing that it would be locked), the recovering peer leader was obliged to leave the room twice in response to members who had been shouting and banging on the door. In the corridor, he reexplained the new measure; after that, punctuality improved dramatically.

Violent or Threatening Behavior

Socially inappropriate behavior that threatens the physical safety or emotional security of any member is prohibited, and it must be grounds for expulsion. Since the cessation group is a "little society" embodying standards of social civility, reasonableness, and respect, the boundary between it and "the street" must remain well defined.

During the entire course of our project, there were only two instances of aggressive behavior which required the leaders' intervention. In one case, a member experienced a paranoid episode and became verbally threatening to the group at large. In another case, the addicted boyfriend of a client attempted to drag her out of a session. In both instances, the leader politely but firmly reminded the agitated individuals of the purpose and the rules of the program and invited them to share their grievances personally with the recovering peer leader in a separate room. ("Here we are trying to help each other, stick together, and reason things out. We'd like to hear your viewpoint and your experience when you calm down.")

The next step in such situations would have been to call the building security or the police, but that was not necessary. Nonetheless, we recommend opening lines of communication with security personnel and police and keeping their numbers handy.

Uncontrolled Talking and Objections to the Topic

"Don't hog the floor" can be usefully stated as a rule of conduct, but the leader must also demonstrate in practice the value of getting to the point and giving everyone a chance. Sometimes this can be accomplished by quickly summarizing and redirecting rambling contributions. Sometimes the leader must ask that urgent concerns be deferred to a more appropriate time. (Times for venting feelings extensively and pursuing unrelated personal concerns are made available after the session and during the weekend session.) Often the leader can good-naturedly convince the "enthusiastic" talker to be more self-contained, but sometimes leaders must directly ask for shorter or more relevant contributions.

In any case, it is important to keep the discussion on track. Otherwise, maintaining the focus can become an ongoing struggle. But if leaders consistently contain excessive digressions, show enthusiasm for the topic at hand, and defer unrelated issues to appropriate occasions, then most members are quick to learn how to participate.

Although the topics of the sessions have been selected based on their relevance to virtually all cocaine addicts in early recovery, some members may object that the topic of a session is not a problem for them. Though objections may merely arise from denial, they may also stem from other considerations. These claims should therefore be heard out respectfully, even if there is reason to doubt them. Sometimes an open-minded atmosphere will lead such clients to reconsider their positions as the session proceeds. Alternatively, the leader can make allies of those who have already dealt successfully with an issue by drawing on their experience to help other members.

Care in the admissions process can prevent many of these problems. If a member who is not merely in denial repeatedly objects to a topic, the leader should consider the possibility that the program is not appropriate treatment for that individual. For example, because many topics are important to individuals primarily addicted to cocaine rather than heroin, primary heroin addicts are likely to become restless or disruptive if they slip through the admissions process. If a primary heroin addict is admitted (one who may occasionally use cocaine in a "speedball") because a friend in the group can provide transportation, the reward is likely to be complaints, poor attendance, and dropping out.

Discussion, Not Debates

Whereas leaders should respectfully consider all opinions, they should not hesitate to endorse positions consistent with the program. A little controversy can stimulate clients to think actively about the issues, but extended arguments become counterproductive. Members come seeking guidance from those with special knowledge and experience. It should be pointed out to contentious clients how easily arguments can sidetrack them from the difficult business of making changes. Sometimes members are well advised simply to listen carefully for a period.

A useful discussion may be generated, for example, from a member's claim that controlled drinking is not a problem. The leader may ask members to examine their actual experience more carefully with regard to drinking. The benefits and risks of intoxicant use can be viewed in relation to the needs of recovery. And the group can productively consider how social attitudes about drinking have an impact on its opinions. At some point, however, the leader might have to close the discussion by pointing out that the program's rule of abstinence is the product of much experience and study, and that members who object vehemently to it might reflect on why this particular rule is so important to them.

Another frequent source of controversy is tobacco smoking. Argumentative clients will insist that it is inconsistent to prohibit the use of other addictive substances but to allow cigarette smoking (in the parking lot). Leaders can easily get drawn into the medical and political intricacies of this question. The more productive course is to point out that although "we support your desire and efforts to stop smoking, we have been trained to help you stop using other drugs, and you came to us seeking that help." If an individual feels that tobacco smoking triggers his or her craving for other drugs or alcohol, then smoking should indeed be stopped, and a concurrent smoking cessation program might be indicated. At the same time, it is important that the group does not support smoking by allowing smoking in the meetings or scheduling a break to allow members to smoke.

PART II

THE INDIVIDUAL CLEAN START SESSIONS

Orientation

Background

The 30-minute Orientation session, scheduled immediately before the first session of each week, is the client's first substantial contact with the cessation program and perhaps with recovery itself. The session should inspire realistic confidence. Leaders should convey their understanding of clients' distress; and, at the same time, they should indicate how distress can be eased gradually with hard work in treatment. The promise is for a better way of life, but not one that is easily or instantly attained.

The various requirements of administrative information, patient education, and therapy ensure that the half hour will be a full one. Because the time should not be hectic, leaders will need to prepare carefully in advance. Handouts and materials should be organized in advance and distributed at the session's beginning. (Leaders must fill in Handouts 1.2 and 1.6 prior to duplication.) Leaders should also survey program records in advance in order to estimate how many new clients are expected, how many have been in treatment before, and how long they have been abstinent, if at all. This information will help leaders determine which points in the short overview presented below require special emphasis. The introduction and overview should *not* be memorized or read verbatim. However, the professional leader should rehearse a version that covers all of the main points and borrows some of the language.

The essential message of the session is that recovery is a long and difficult journey that nonetheless proceeds by manageable steps. The cessation program will provide guidance and support for the initial steps. The first step is to "be here and be clean."

Materials

Handouts: "The Cessation and Early Recovery Program"
"Days, Times, Places, and Leaders of Sessions"
"The Foundation and the Walls"
"Client Information Form"
"Getting into 12-Step Fellowships"
"Invitation to Loved Ones"
"The Daily Chart" (*only for weeks when Orientation is not followed immediately by Erecting the Walls*)
Pencils
NA and CA meeting lists

Key Points

1. The decision to enter treatment is difficult and should be commended. It can be the beginning of turning one's life around.

2. Intensive outpatient treatment and recovery require commitment to making difficult long-term changes and to faithful, punctual attendance. Many suitable clients may have doubts, but if they are truly unwilling or unable to undertake such commitments, they should not be in an intensive outpatient program.

3. Outpatient cessation requires having a "foundation" for recovery and building "walls" against addiction (see below). Treatment professionals can guide and support this building, but the execution is ultimately up to the client.

4. If the client can begin to put the minimal structures in place during the cessation and early recovery period, then he or she probably will be ready to advance to long-term treatment. The initial period of recovery is the most self-restrictive one. The walls are gradually lowered in the months ahead as craving diminishes and the recovering addict learns new responses.

5. The program rules exist to protect and further the recoveries of all group members. A key rule requires abstinence from all psychoactive substances.

6. Although recovery is a big job, it is undertaken with help and in small steps. Right now, the client's primary focus should be on attending treatment faithfully and remaining abstinent.

7. The client should not "pick and choose" among the parts of our regimen. Too often the parts that the client rejects are the parts that he or she needs most.

Session at a Glance

1. Welcome the clients and commend them for taking an important first step in recovery.
2. Identify the program and **introduce** leaders and members.
3. Give **times and places** of the cessation sessions, including length and number of sessions and duration of the program.
4. Explain **purpose** of and **eligibility** for the program.
5. Review program **rules**: Violence, intoxication, weapons, and drug dealing will result in expulsion. The group must be safe. Continued drug use will necessitate reapplication or referral to more intensive treatment. Emphasize full attendance and punctuality.
6. Summarize **how it works** (learning about the problem we have in common, establishing new priorities, supporting necessary changes) and how well it works (e.g., cite completion rate, frequency of lifestyle change, many examples of long-term recovery).
7. Emphasize the **client's role**: Show up faithfully, participate, be open, work hard, take *all* of the suggestions, support one another's recoveries.
8. Explain **cost and paperwork.**
9. Indicate supplemental or alternative **resources** (medical, social work, psychiatric, inpatient detoxification, 12-step fellowships).
10. Explain the **invitation to family members.**
11. Discuss **what comes next**: long-term treatment and the requirements for advancing to it.
12. Explain **"The Daily Chart"** (on weeks when Orientation is not immediately followed by Erecting the Walls).

Format

Distribute All Handouts and Materials

Welcome

The leader welcomes the clients and commends them for "being here and being clean" and for taking "an important first step toward a better way of life." "This 30-minute orientation session is for new members only. We will briefly describe the program, goals, structure, and rules.

We will give you handouts to review at home, and you will fill out a brief intake form."

Program, Leader, and Member Introductions

The leader identifies the program and its affiliations and explains that it is an "outpatient group program designed to help cocaine addicts stop drug use and remain drug free during early recovery."

The leader and peer leader briefly introduce themselves including information about formal training and recovery experience.

Ask for first-name introductions around the room.

Review the Handouts

"The Cessation and Early Recovery Program"
"Days, Times, Places, and Leaders of Sessions"

Indicate that all handouts should be studied carefully at home.

Purpose and Eligibility

"The main goals of the Cessation and Early Recovery Program are to help you stay drug-free during a difficult period, to help you make the changes that build a foundation for long-term recovery, and to prepare you for long-term treatment. We will also help you decide whether outpatient treatment is currently right for you.

"This program is for cocaine addicts who want to stop using and to find a better way of life. To be eligible you must be willing and able to attend all of the sessions; you must be free of serious medical problems or conflicting obligations that would interfere with your attendance; and you must be willing to make the changes that the program prescribes, including complete abstinence from cocaine, alcohol, and all other mood-altering drugs."

Briefly summarize the main points of "About the Program" and the specifics of when, where, and with whom the group will meet.

Program Rules

Review the rules, giving special emphasis to the importance of having a "safe and drug-free group for everyone." "People who are struggling in the early days of recovery deserve no less." Therefore, "violence (to yourself or others) and threats, intoxication, drug dealing, and possessing alcohol, drugs or weapons will result in immediate expulsion and loss of group membership."

Explain the reason for the "Don't Come High" rule: "This rule protects the whole group, since an intoxicated member can trigger everyone's cravings for drugs. In addition, you won't be able to get much out of these sessions if you are high, and you can provide no real support for others."

Emphasize the importance of complete abstinence as a necessary first step in recovery as well as an essential part of protecting the recoveries of others. Stress full attendance and punctuality at the sessions. Explain the urine-testing system and the contingencies for drug use and for unexcused absences (see Chapter Five).

"We request that you take care of your bathroom needs, cigarette smoking, food, and so on, before the session begins. The group meets for an hour and a half with no breaks. Since people who walk out of the session miss important points and distract the attention of the whole group, we ask you to remain in the room throughout the session."

Review the Handout

"The Foundation and the Walls"

How the Program Works

"The people here have a problem in common: addiction. In these group meetings we learn about that problem, and we learn to use some well-tested solutions. Applying this knowledge well requires setting new priorities and supporting one another. It also requires some difficult but rewarding changes. Many of the people who have taken *all* of the suggestions and who have completed treatment have made solid and satisfying changes in the way that they live.

"Addiction is like a fire that grows out of control and consumes more and more of your life. Once you stop using, the fire may be contained, but it still smolders. In these groups you learn how to avoid a flare-up and how to plug into new sources of heat. You accomplish these things with the program's guidance and with one another's support.

"The basic strategy of the program is to help you cut yourself off from the risks and opportunities to use while you gradually learn to live a satisfying drug-free life. To employ this method, you must begin with a solid foundation, and then erect strong walls around you. The essence of the foundation is to clean out your living, working and recreational spaces and to get social support. The walls are all of the daily habits and routines that protect you from the drug world and make it harder to use drugs. Although we will devote a meeting to these concepts, you should study them in the handout, 'The Foundation and the Walls,' as soon as possible."

The Client's Part

"The client's role is to show up faithfully, participate, be open and honest, take all of the program's suggestions (don't 'pick and choose'), and support one another's recoveries. You can use the leaders' experience and training for guidance, but the ultimate responsibility for making the treatment work is yours. You get out of this group what you put into it. Since groups benefit from the efforts of all of their members, you must all pull together.

"We emphasize taking *all* of the suggestions because in our experience the suggestions that you resist taking are the very ones that would have prevented backsliding and relapse. Doing your part in treatment does not mean merely coming here and speaking in the groups. That is important, but to recover *you* have to put the principles we offer into action. You must take our program home and put it to work in your daily lives. That is the key ingredient. Since your drug-taking was deeply attached to a whole way of life, any part of that way of life can lead back to the drug-taking, just as any part of a spider's web leads to the spider. Therefore, you must make difficult changes in your way of life. At first, some of these changes will feel like big sacrifices. For example, we will tell you to cut off all association with drug users, to stop hanging out at bars and nightclubs, to change your job or residence if either endangers your recovery, to avoid easy access to cash, and to fill up all possible free time, especially on weekends, with recovery meetings and other healthy activities."

At this point, leaders may invite those who feel that the program is not for them to leave "with no hard feelings." Those who choose to leave should be given the program's phone number in case other referrals are appropriate.

Program Costs and Paperwork

Have clients fill out and turn in the "Client Information Form." If relevant, describe program costs and payment methods.

Other Resources

Explain the uses of supplemental or alternative resources including physicians, social workers, psychiatrists, family services, residential treatments, and 12-step fellowships.

Review the Handout and Materials

"Getting into 12-Step Fellowships"

"This program is fully compatible with fellowship participation, and we strongly encourage full use of this most important resource. Cocaine Anonymous and Narcotics Anonymous meetings help to strengthen your commitment to drug-free living, to broaden your social support network, and to fill idle time productively. For your convenience, we have included NA and CA meeting lists in the materials we distributed at the beginning of this session."

Review the Handout

"Invitation to Loved Ones"

"One of the group sessions concerns the role of the family in recovery, and we ask that you sign the invitation and give it to your family members as soon as possible so that they will attend."
    Participation of family members and spouses in the Clean Start session designed for them is critical. Some time should be given to the importance of participation if full attendance appears unlikely.

Moving On

"Coming here clean is an important step. Completing the cessation program is another. Completion allows you to advance to long-term treatment, where you will learn to cope with the common problems of recovery that occur well after drug use stops. In order to advance to that stage, you must abide by all of the rules of the cessation and early recovery group, you must participate actively, and you must show some willingness to make necessary changes.
    "Most of you have not kept commitments or completed anything for

a long time. By completing the cessation program, you will have begun to turn things around."

Reassure clients that they needn't be overwhelmed by all of the new information. It will all be repeated, and it is contained in the handouts. Urge the members to study the handouts, and emphasize the importance of the invitation to family members. Invite clients to approach the leaders individually for clarification or extra help.

Review the Handout

"The Daily Chart" (*only for weeks when Orientation is not followed immediately by Erecting the Walls*)

Briefly explain "The Daily Chart," and indicate that the leaders will be available to answer individual questions about the Chart. Also announce that the Chart will be explained more thoroughly during the Weekend Problems and Progress session.

Comments

The leaders should pause frequently to invite questions while explaining the program, but this is not the time to become involved in extended discussions. Both leaders must continually scan members' faces for signs of inattention, intoxication, or agitation. The "Don't Come High" rule and the reasoning behind it must be explained with particular emphasis. The peer leader should ask any member who appears obviously high to accompany him or her out of the room. Once outside, politely explain the reason for the rule and invite the member to return sober to the next week's Orientation. Advise the member that following the suggestions in "The Foundation and the Walls" handout will help him or her to avoid using.

HANDOUT 1.1: The Cessation and Early Recovery Program

About the Program:

The Cessation and Early Recovery Program is an intensive outpatient program for the initial treatment of cocaine addiction. It is for people who are trying to stop using cocaine or who have recently stopped but need help staying drug free and achieving solid recovery. The program consists of two 90-minute group Clean Start sessions on weeknights and a 90-minute Problems and Progress meeting on weekends. In the Clean Start meetings, clients learn about addiction and treatment, they identify and overcome the major obstacles to early recovery, they discuss the whys and hows of making the lifestyle changes necessary to achieve long-term recovery, and they support one another in beginning to make those changes. In the Problems and Progress session, individual concerns are discussed at greater length, clients help one another take small steps toward building a foundation for recovery, and safe weekend plans are made.

After 4 weeks of perfect attendance, of staying drug free, of participating actively in group, and of beginning to make suggested changes, clients are eligible to advance to long-term treatment.

Program Rules:

1. A client must not attend a session on a day when he or she has used any mood-altering drug (including alcohol).
2. Completion of the program requires that clients must remain free of mood-altering drugs and alcohol for 4 consecutive weeks. A single use of drugs or alcohol will result in a client's being held back from graduating to long-term outpatient treatment. A second use will result in referral to more intensive treatment — usually day care, a halfway house, or residential care.
3. Clients must give urines upon leaders' request. Each client will be asked to provide urine samples in accordance with program requirements.
4. Clients must attend all sessions on time unless excused in advance by the leaders. One unexcused absence or two excused absences will result in a client's being held back from advancing to long-term treatment. A second unexcused absence or excessive lateness will result in referral to treatment elsewhere. Clients who arrive more than 10 minutes late for a session will be turned away and referred to an NA meeting.
5. Clients must behave respectfully, nonviolently, and nonthreateningly toward one another and toward the leaders.
6. Vacations are not allowed for the duration of the program.
7. Clients must respect the recoveries of others. Disrespecting the recoveries of others includes making drug offers, dwelling on or glorifying the drug high, becoming sexually involved with another client, or attending with another a dangerous or inappropriate place.
8. Clients must respect the confidentiality of all members. What is said here stays here.

HANDOUT 1.2: Days, Times, Places, and Leaders of Sessions

Day	Starts	Ends	Location
1. _____	___ : ___	___ : ___	_____
2. _____	___ : ___	___ : ___	_____
3. _____	___ : ___	___ : ___	_____

Group Leaders	Phone Numbers
_____	( ) ___ - _____
_____	( ) ___ - _____

HANDOUT 1.3: The Foundation and the Walls

Successful recovery requires much more than willpower. The real strength of early recovery lies in recognizing your limitations, in accepting help wholeheartedly, and in constructing solid structures of support — including a *foundation* and *walls*.

The *foundation* for long-term recovery consists of **a drug-free residence, a drug-free place to spend leisure time, a drug-free source of income, a drug-free immediate support group** (family, spouse, or closest friend), and **guidance in recovery.** You cannot live with active users, your job must be safe, and the person or persons you will depend upon most for support must be clean. If you cannot arrange for these conditions, then you may need residential treatment, a recovery or halfway house or day care.

The foundation supports the *walls*, which protect you during the vulnerable time of early recovery. The walls can be gradually lowered as recovery progresses. Like the walls of a residential "detox," outpatient walls reduce your exposure to drug use to a minimum. You build your outpatient *walls* by **avoiding "craving triggers," surrounding yourself with supportive people, making it harder for you to obtain and use drugs, keeping busy** with safe activities, and **attending recovery activities regularly.** Here are some "blueprints":

1. **Eliminate and avoid all unnecessary "craving triggers"** — that is, all avoidable dangerous situations such as exposure to dealers and users, excess cash, places where you used to use, emotional extremes (arguments, major decisions, intense occasions), casual sexual encounters, parties, rock concerts, celebrations, and anything that reminds you of getting high or makes you want to use. Throw away records you got high to, posters, books, and videos. By putting them in the trash, **not just putting them away,** you show that you are serious about never needing them again.
2. **Surround yourself with clean, supportive people.** Get in the habit of asking yourself, "Should I be accompanied? Whom can I call? Whom will I be with tomorrow?" Planning cements your walls.
3. **Make it harder for you to get drugs.** Have someone hold your money and have your paycheck deposited; destroy your 24-hour cash card; get rid of paraphernalia; destroy your address book; change your telephone number; move, if necessary; tell people clearly about your recovery in order to shut the door on future drug offers and to have more to lose from those you care about.
4. **Keep busy every waking hour.** Minimize time idle and alone. Plan for where you are going after work, especially on paydays, weeknights, holidays, and weekends.
5. **Attend recovery activities regularly.** These include our group sessions and NA and CA meetings — any place where you are accompanied by other people in recovery and where you can learn more about recovery. You must show up even when you don't feel like it. Recovery is hard but rewarding work.

HANDOUT 1.4: Client Information Form

Name _____

Address _____ Phone _____

Age ___ Sex ___ Married? ___ # of Children ___ Occupation _____

When did you last use cocaine? _____
On how many days did you use during the last month you were not in a facility? _____

When did you last use another drug (including alcohol)? _____
On how many days did you use during the last month you were not in a facility? _____

Have you been in treatment before? Yes ___ No ___
When was the last time? _____

Are there drugs or drug users in your residence? (Check)
Drugs _____
Drug users _____
Neither _____

Are there drugs or drug users where you work? (Check)
Drugs _____
Drug users _____
Neither _____

Do you have supportive friends or family who don't use drugs?
Yes ___ No ___

What situations make you want to use? _____

Do you have outstanding criminal court cases? Yes ___ No ___

Do you have acute psychiatric or medical conditions other than addiction that need treatment?
Yes ___ No ___

Are you on any psychoactive medication? Yes ___ No ___
What medication? _____

Do you have any obligations (e.g., work or child care) that could cause conflicts with treatment times? Yes ___ No ___
What are they? _____

Do you currently have a legitimate, reliable source of financial support?
Yes ___ No ___

138

HANDOUT 1.5: Getting into 12-Step Fellowships

AA (Alcoholics Anonymous), NA (Narcotics Anonymous), and CA (Cocaine Anonymous) are all valuable, free, widely available sources of support. Attending their self-help meetings regularly will help you to learn more about recovery, to socialize drug free, and to expand your social circle. If you have any free mornings, lunch hours, or evenings, filling them with meetings will probably speed and strengthen your recovery. Here are some tips:

- Show up and keep showing up. Soon enough your face will become known, and the language of the fellowships will feel more comfortable.
- Meetings vary widely in style and size. If you sample a lot of them, you will find some where you feel comfortable.
- Listen with an open mind. Focus on similarities instead of differences.
- Say *something*, even if it is only that you are new. Taking such risks will open doors. Invite a friend from our program to support you.
- Practice what you will say, including that you are a recovering addict in the Clean Start group.
- Look for people with strong recoveries — the "winners" who do the group's business. Join groups going out for coffee after the meeting and volunteer to do group jobs, such as helping to clean up. This is how you start to feel like an insider.
- Ask people for their telephone numbers and write them in an appointment book. *Use* the phone.
- Ask for a sponsor. A sponsor is someone more experienced in recovery who is willing to show you the ropes and give you a word of encouragement. People are usually flattered to be asked. Don't wait for the "perfect" sponsor. You can always find another one.
- Sign up to join a group. Your "home group" is a base for your recovery.

HANDOUT 1.6: Invitation to Loved Ones

Dear _____ ,

You are cordially invited to attend a group session about family concerns in recovery. The session will be held at

Time: _____

Date: _____

Address: _____

This invitation was prepared by our program, but it was extended to you by your loved one. We feel that extending the invitation is an important step and that your accepting it would effectively express your support for your loved one's recovery.

We also feel that attending would be a valuable experience for you. Family members, spouses, and intimates have often been deeply hurt by a loved one's addiction. When the addicted one enters treatment, the others are in special need of education and support. Some of that will be provided at the meeting. We will try to answer some common questions, such as, "How can loved ones help?" "How can they hurt?" "How much treatment is needed?" "What is the recovering person's responsibility?" "Can trust grow again?" and "What about relapse?"

We look forward to meeting you and hope that you can become part of a healing process.

Sincerely,

_____
Recovering Addict

_____
Group Leader

HANDOUT 1.7: The Daily Chart for a Clean Routine

This chart will help you to answer the most common questions in early recovery: "What should I be doing?" and "How am I doing?" The *more* that you do, the better you are doing. The chart is a daily planning and record keeping guide for constructing your "walls" — for keeping busy, for staying away from avoidable craving triggers, for surrounding yourself with supportive people, for learning more about recovery, and for making it harder for you to use drugs.

Begin by setting out the times for your schedule of activities for tomorrow. Include work or school, treatment (professional or self-help), networking (face to face or by phone support), self-improvement (e.g., hobbies, reading), recreation and relaxation, and physical activities. Then use the Commitment Step and Common Triggers Keys below to identify any commitment steps you plan to take and common triggers you will take positive steps to avoid. At the end of each day give yourself one point for each item accomplished and two points for each commitment step. (You probably know whether you did well enough on a given item to merit a point, but if you have doubts, ask the group leaders.) After scoring your day, pencil in the next day's plans. You are responsible for copying this chart each week.

Use the chart to measure your progress. At week's end, total your points for the week, and complete the sentences on your progress and problems.

Commitment Step Key
A. Get rid of drugs and paraphernalia.
B. Stop dealing/drinking/smoking pot.
C. Deposit paycheck.
D. Destroy 24-hour card/dealer's #.
E. Tell recovery to loved ones, friends, boss.
F. Change phone #, move.
G. Plan new weekend activities.
H. Make new friends/ask for sponsor.
I. Others.

Common Triggers Key
1. Using drugs, alcohol.
2. Seeing drugs.
3. Old "hot" spots, such as bars, clubs, street corners.
4. Extra cash.
5. Weekends, holidays, vacation time.
6. Loneliness, boredom, anger.
7. Rock music, concerts.
8. Some sexual encounters.

The Daily Chart

ACTIVITY (Points)	SUN.	MON.	TUES.	WED.	THURS.	FRI.	SAT.	Weekly Total
Work/school (1)								
Treatment; Meetings/CA/NA/ AA (1)								
Phone/support (1)								
Self-improvement (1)								
Fun/quiet time (1)								
Workout/sports (1)								
Commitment steps (2)								
Avoided triggers (1)								
Others (1)								
DAILY POINT TOTAL								

I'm doing well at _____   I need to work on _____

142

Erecting the Walls

Background

The client new to recovery is adrift in time and space. Self-direction ("willpower") has failed. Cut off from old coping strategies, the new client is buffeted by fears, by feelings of loss, and, from every direction it seems, by cravings. In initial recovery, many clients report feeling safe only when in a group session. The client's goal is to occupy safely all of the time when he or she is not in a session and to keep "clean" all of the spaces in his or her life other than the program site. The two principal objectives of this session are (1) to explain in terms of conditioning principles the "whys" of structuring time and space outside of treatment and (2) to offer guidance in the "hows," including a model regimen of daily activities and of "dos and don'ts." Each client should leave this session with concrete answers to the questions "Why should remaining abstinent be my top priority now?" and "What sort of daily activity schedule would best support that priority? What does a model day look like in initial recovery?"

Materials

Handouts: "The Foundation and the Walls II"
            "The Daily Chart"

Key Points

1. The first step in recovery is to stop using all mood-altering chemicals. Every drug-free day reduces addiction, makes new learning possible, and makes long-term recovery more likely.

2. Newly recovering clients should make it as difficult as possible for themselves to return to drug use. All substances must be removed from the home and work environments. Obtaining drugs must be made maximally inconvenient, time and energy consuming, and socially embarrassing.

3. Addiction is not extinguished when drug use stops. Because clients in initial recovery have not yet learned new responses to a wide range of craving triggers, they must restrict their exposure to those triggers whenever possible. At first they must stay in places such as home, work, and program and self-help meetings where they can be certain of being able to avoid drugs.

4. Newly recovering clients must keep busy with positive activities and they must surround themselves with abstinent, supportive people.

5. Newly recovering clients must develop the habit of carefully planning their days in advance.

Session at a Glance

1. **Check-In:** A current trigger.
2. **Topic and Goals:** Explanation of addiction and craving.
3. **Brainstorming:** More examples of triggers, divided into "avoid for good," "avoid for now," and "unavoidable."
4. **Open Discussion:** The need for abstinence from all drugs. Alcohol and marijuana are among the most dangerous triggers.
5. **Open Discussion:** Inpatient and outpatient "walls."
6. **Handouts:** "The Foundation and the Walls II" and "The Daily Chart."
7. **Next Step:** A wall that needs strengthening—a chart item that applies.

Format

Check-In

"Mention something—other people, feelings, pressures, places, sights and sounds, and so forth—that makes you want to get high no matter how hard you are trying to stay clean. If nothing is making you want to use now, what *could* make you want to use?"

Comments

Point out to the group that drugs, paraphernalia, and other drug users are among the most threatening triggers. Underline that craving is automatic. It can begin "even when you have good intentions and know better."

Topic and Goals

"There are no easy ways to become drug free. There are no magic pills. You have been unable to stop using drugs on your own, and if you want to stop using and *stay* stopped, you will have to take difficult steps to change your life. You will have to cut yourself off from drugs and everything associated with them. At first, this will mean going to very few places and doing very few things. You will be focused on one thing: becoming free of drugs. Once you have established some stability, you can learn gradually to live the fuller life of a recovering person.

"But remember, addiction does not stop when you stop using drugs. In the first weeks of recovery, you are extremely vulnerable to craving from many sources. Until you can learn new responses to craving and its triggers, you must take special precautions. Tonight you will learn why these precautions, which we call the 'outpatient walls,' are necessary and how you can put them in place. Many of you have asked, 'How do I stay clean? Tell me what to do, and I will do it.' Tonight you will get your instructions. Those of you who are willing to follow *all* of them will stay clean.

"First, a few words about addiction, because once you understand what you have done to yourself, you can become responsible for changing it. Addiction is a powerfully conditioned attachment to drug use. By using drugs over and over, you have trained your nervous system to desire the drug high. Your willingness to do whatever is necessary to obtain drugs has grown. Each time that you used, you made this training a little stronger. Whatever else was going on when you used—where you were, the time of day or week, how you were feeling, whom you were with, what kind of music was playing—now has the power to stimulate that desire. Your craving for drugs can be activated by *associations* with past drug use. This response can occur long after you have stopped using, and occurs automatically, without any need for thought. As we mentioned in Orientation, your addiction is still 'smoldering.' The sight of a dealer, a nightclub, the smell of a match, good feelings and bad feelings—all of them and much more can act like gasoline on the embers. When your nervous system is reminded of the drug high, you suddenly find yourself wanting to use. We call anything that stimulates craving in this way a 'craving trigger.'

"In the early weeks of recovery, you are most vulnerable to a host of craving triggers, because you have not yet learned to deactivate them by responding to them in a new way—that is, without using. We will help you learn some new ways, but until they become second nature, you must avoid as many triggers as possible and make drugs harder to obtain. Your 'fire' almost burned down the house (you). Until you learn to use a safer 'heating system,' you need to stay away from matches and remove everything flammable."

Note

The foregoing explanation of addiction should not be read aloud. The leader must prepare sufficiently to be able to deliver it naturally. The key ideas and analogies should be retained, but word-for-word delivery is not necessary.

Brainstorming

"The first steps in getting and staying clean are to rid your daily life of the most threatening triggers. Let's think of what they are." Have the group generate a large list of common and personal triggers in addition to the examples already mentioned. Write the list on a chalkboard or newsprint. Then have the group divide the list of triggers into (1) those that should always be avoided, (2) those that cannot be avoided, and (3) those that should be avoided for now but eventually should be faced.

Comments

The list should include: (1) drugs and alcohol, (2) paraphernalia, (3) active drug users, (4) a dealer's residence, (5) bars and nightclubs, (6) excess cash, (7) stress, (8) casual sex, and (9) unpleasant feelings. The leaders can prompt the group if a broad cross-section of triggers is not forthcoming. For example, "What about holidays or birthdays? What about money? What about the death of a loved one? What about feeling lonely or angry?" When someone mentions a very common trigger such as old drugging partners or paydays, the leader should ask whether "anyone else has problems with that." This can be a lively and good-humored exercise which helps to break the ice for many members who find that their cravings are far from unique.

Point out that people are often overconfident about being able to deal with triggers. Problems occur partly because the triggers are themselves attractive, naturally or by association. Eventually, clients can determine their readiness to cope with once-avoided triggers by considering three questions: (1) Has craving produced by limited exposures been reduced? (2) Is support available? and (3) Are all other aspects of recovery being managed at this time?

Open Discussion

"Why would the use of alcohol, marijuana, and drugs other than cocaine be one of the strongest of all craving triggers for cocaine use?"

Comments

A very similar segment is contained in the Addiction and Denial session, but the subject is important enough to repeat.

Should anyone object that alcohol or marijuana is not a problem, ask whether other members had once felt that way before learning differently, and allow them to share their experiences.

The discussion should cover at least the following points:

1. Alcohol and marijuana are among the most frequent causes of relapse to one's drug of choice. They are dangerous because they are associated with other drug use and with the addict lifestyle; because the act of changing one's mood by substances is itself a trigger for other drug use; and because alcohol and marijuana reduce self-control and warp judgment.
2. Using alcohol and marijuana puts clients in contact with the "wrong" people, even as it endangers and estranges clients from the "right" people (e.g., the members of their recovery groups).
3. Using any mood-altering substance interferes with learning new drug-free satisfactions.

Open Discussion

Ask for volunteers who have been to an inpatient cessation treatment facility and were able to complete the program. Ask them what made it possible to stop using while in the facility.

Comments

If there are no members with inpatient experience, the leaders may have to describe a typical day of residential treatment. Members will readily understand that confinement within a facility reduces access to drugs, which reduces craving. Other effective elements of inpatient treatment include a regimen of highly structured, recovery-oriented activities, much opportunity for support from staff members and other patients, minimal exposure to triggers such as stress, and insulation from triggers such as contact with active users.

Open Discussion

"How can you build similar 'walls' as an outpatient?"

Comments

The leader can prompt members' responses to this question by asking: "Who is successfully avoiding triggers? How are you doing it? How can you surround yourself with clean and supportive people? Can anyone share how this has helped? How can you plan your days and weekends to keep busy and avoid time spent idle and alone? Who is doing this? What are some ways that you make it harder for yourself to use drugs? Can you give examples from your experience? Does it help?"

Review the Handout

"The Foundation and the Walls II"

"This handout is similar to the one we gave you in Orientation and asked you to read at home. Today, we will review it as a group."

Comments

In the review of the handout, be alert to members' reservations about any of the safety measures.

Have each member identify "a foundation stone or a wall that needs strengthening." After considering a few examples that clarify the task for the group, ask members to complete the assessment at the end of the handout and to review their assessments with the group.

"Now that you have a list of steps to take, we will use this handout to help you plan your days."

Distribute and Review the Handout

"The Daily Chart"

Comments

If a member does not address here the trigger mentioned in the check-in, the leader should ask what wall and chart category might apply to it.

HANDOUT 2.1: The Foundation and the Walls II

Successful recovery requires much more than willpower. The real strength of early recovery lies in recognizing your limitations, in accepting help wholeheartedly, and in constructing solid structures of support — including a *foundation* and *walls*.

The *foundation* for long-term recovery consists of **a drug-free residence, a drug-free place to spend leisure time, a drug-free source of income, a drug-free immediate support group** (family, spouse, or closest friend), **and guidance in recovery.** You cannot live with active users, your job must be safe, and the person or persons you will depend upon most for support must be clean. If you cannot arrange for these conditions, then you may need residential treatment, a recovery or halfway house or day care.

The foundation supports the *walls*, which protect you during the vulnerable time of early recovery. The walls can be gradually lowered as recovery progresses. Like the walls of a residential "detox," outpatient walls reduce your exposure to drug use to a minimum. You build your outpatient *walls* by **avoiding "craving triggers," surrounding yourself with supportive people, making it harder for you to obtain and use drugs, keeping busy** with safe activities, and **attending recovery activities regularly.** Here are some "blueprints":

1. **Eliminate and avoid all unnecessary "craving triggers"** — that is, all avoidable dangerous situations such as exposure to dealers and users, excess cash, places where you used to use, emotional extremes (arguments, major decisions, intense occasions), casual sexual encounters, parties, rock concerts, celebrations, and anything that reminds you of getting high or makes you want to use. Throw away records you got high to, posters, books, and videos. By putting them in the trash, not just putting them away, you show that you are serious about never needing them again.
2. **Surround yourself with clean, supportive people.** Get in the habit of asking yourself, "Should I be accompanied? Whom can I call? Whom will I be with tomorrow?" Planning cements your walls.
3. **Make it harder for you to get drugs.** Have someone hold your money and have your paycheck deposited; destroy your 24-hour cash card; get rid of paraphernalia; destroy your address book; change your telephone number; move, if necessary; tell people clearly about your recovery in order to shut the door on future drug offers and to have more to lose from those you care about.
4. **Keep busy every waking hour.** Minimize time idle and alone. Plan for where you are going after work, especially on paydays, weeknights, holidays, and weekends.
5. **Attend recovery activities regularly.** These include our group sessions and NA and CA meetings — any place where you are accompanied by other people in recovery and where you can learn more about recovery. You must show up even when you don't feel like it. Recovery is hard but rewarding work.

Building Plans: Make a list of what you need to do to complete your foundation and walls.

A. Cornerstones of my recovery's foundation that are in place or need to be put in place:
   1. Residence   ___ in place ___ needs to be put in place
   2. Income   ___ in place ___ needs to be put in place
   3. Immediate
      support group   ___ in place ___ needs to be put in place
   4. Recovery guidance   ___ in place ___ needs to be put in place

B. Walls that need strengthening:
   1. Remove triggers   ___ solid ___ needs strengthening
   2. Surround with supportive people   ___ solid ___ needs strengthening
   3. Make obtaining drugs harder   ___ solid ___ needs strengthening
   4. Keep busy   ___ solid ___ needs strengthening
   5. Attend recovery activities   ___ solid ___ needs strengthening

HANDOUT 2.2: The Daily Chart for a Clean Routine

This chart will help you to answer the most common questions in early recovery: "What should I be doing?" and "How am I doing?" The *more* that you do, the better you are doing. The chart is a daily planning and record keeping guide for constructing your "walls"—for keeping busy, for staying away from avoidable craving triggers, for surrounding yourself with supportive people, for learning more about recovery, and for making it harder for you to use drugs.

Begin by setting out the times for your schedule of activities for tomorrow. Include work or school, treatment (professional or self-help), networking (face to face or by phone support), self-improvement (e.g., hobbies, reading), recreation and relaxation, and physical activities. Then use the Commitment Step and Common Triggers Keys below to identify any commitment steps you plan to take and common triggers you will take positive steps to avoid. At the end of each day give yourself one point for each item accomplished and two points for each commitment step. (You probably know whether you did well enough on a given item to merit a point, but if you have doubts, ask the group leaders.) After scoring your day, pencil in the next day's plans. You are responsible for copying this chart each week.

Use the chart to measure your progress. At week's end, total your points for the week, and complete the sentences on your progress and problems.

Commitment Step Key
A. Get rid of drugs and paraphernalia.
B. Stop dealing/drinking/smoking pot.
C. Deposit paycheck.
D. Destroy 24-hour card/dealer's #.
E. Tell recovery to loved ones, friends, boss.
F. Change phone #, move.
G. Plan new weekend activities.
H. Make new friends/ask for sponsor.
I. Others.

Common Triggers Key
1. Using drugs, alcohol.
2. Seeing drugs.
3. Old "hot" spots, such as bars, clubs, street corners.
4. Extra cash.
5. Weekends, holidays, vacation time.
6. Loneliness, boredom, anger.
7. Rock music, concerts.
8. Some sexual encounters.

The Daily Chart

ACTIVITY (Points)	SUN.	MON.	TUES.	WED.	THURS.	FRI.	SAT.	Weekly Total
Work/school (1)								
Treatment; Meetings/CA/NA/ AA (1)								
Phone/support (1)								
Self-improvement (1)								
Fun/quiet time (1)								
Workout/sports (1)								
Commitment steps (2)								
Avoided triggers (1)								
Others (1)								
DAILY POINT TOTAL								

I'm doing well at _____ I need to work on _____

152

Closing the Doors to Addiction

Background

How does an addict start wanting to get better? The desire to avoid the negative consequences of addiction produces some motivation for change and brings clients to treatment. But fear and misery do not by themselves sustain solid recovery. In a vacuum of alternative rewards, pain and fear are forgotten, and the high life retains its intrinsic attraction. Thus, if old rewards are to be avoided, they must be replaced. *Commitment steps* serve both functions. The commitment step is our term for an action that increases the rewards of a recovering lifestyle while making a return to the addict lifestyle more difficult.

The willingness to recover, like the desire to get high, may be increased bit by bit. Take the example of the client who enters treatment after her boss warns her that she will be fired for further absences. She may not tell her boss why she had been absent or that she has entered treatment, because she is not sure that she really wants recovery. If her boss knew the facts, he might *hold* her to a full course of treatment as a condition of continued employment. Now, suppose that with the group's gentle pressure and support this client is able to make the disclosure, and suppose that the boss reacts supportively. Maybe he is glad to have a rational explanation of her previous poor performance, and maybe he is even more pleased with her honesty as evidence of her new commitment. Indeed, this reaction is common enough. He offers to be flexible about giving her time off to attend her groups. His response encourages the client, as does the group's approval when she reports the disclosure. Perhaps a member who has been struggling with the same step will thank her for giving him the impetus to try a little harder. Now she feels more like a part of the group. Having disclosed her recovery once to good effect, she is now able to disclose it to family members. Maybe she will accept her mother's offer to screen her telephone calls and to hold her cash. This step in turn will win her more trust and reduce her craving for drugs on paydays.

During the course of this interlinked series of commitment steps, our hypothetical client, who is based on many real ones, will become increasingly committed to recovery. She will "want" it more wholeheartedly than before because she has experienced its benefits. The same actions that make discovery more likely should she backslide also produce specific gains, so that she will have more to lose by backsliding. The more she experiences the alternative rewards of supportive people, the more she will be deterred from exposing herself to addicted people. The same step that makes backsliding more difficult makes moving forward more likely.

The underlying principle is that a change of social membership is critical to recovery, and that new social membership and identity offer natural rewards that are incompatible with the old rewards. Especially at the outset, the recovering person's new membership is strengthened through concrete actions. The same act that cuts off one's retreat, or makes retreat more costly, also brings friendly overtures, a sense of belonging, and many other benefits which ultimately validate one's decision.

Like immigrants, most people new to recovery spend a period of time in a social no-man's-land. The challenge of cessation and early recovery training is to help them make this no-man's-land a "land of opportunity." Clinicians must be aware that the very discomfort of the displaced individual is an opportunity, for it makes him or her receptive to alternative solutions. The commitment step is a concrete piece of an alternative solution.

Materials

Handout: "Your Key Commitment Step"

Key Points

1. Because of ambivalence about recovery, many new clients leave themselves "escape routes." They make relapsing easier rather than more difficult.

2. "Commitment steps" are actions that make prorecovery changes more binding by increasing the cost of backsliding and by rewarding progress. Thus, they help to resolve ambivalence. Commitment steps close doors to addiction and to the addict lifestyle, and they open doors to further recovery.

3. The new client in social limbo is unusually receptive to taking the risks that provide alternative rewards and build momentum in recovery.

Session at a Glance

1. **Check-In:** A door currently left open.
2. **Open Discussion:** Examples of closing doors: dieter and prisoner.
3. **Open Sharing:** Past experiences of closed and open doors.
4. **Brainstorming:** Commitment steps—range of examples.
5. **Handout:** "Your Key Commitment Step"—common important steps.
6. **Next Step:** Explaining your next commitment step—why and how you plan to take it.

Format

Check-In

"Mention briefly a door you need to shut completely on the old way of life—a change that you could make (or complete) to make relapse less likely."

Topic and Goals

"It is natural to be 'on the fence' in the beginning of recovery. How many of you have fears of life without drugs? How many of you still wish now and then that you could control your use of drugs or alcohol, or that you could see your old drug-using friends or lovers, or that you didn't have to make all of the changes that we have suggested? [Ask for a show of hands after each question.] Principles of addiction and of human behavior explain that you will remain deeply attached to the old rewards until you actually start to experience the rewards of recovery. Perhaps you take our word for it that recovery is worthwhile, but that isn't the same as experiencing it. Only by taking small risks will you experience it.

"Tonight we will offer you a technique for experiencing some early rewards of recovery that will help you to get off the fence. This technique is a special sort of action that we call 'commitment steps.' Diving off a springboard into a swimming pool is a commitment to going in the water. No more thinking about it, no turning back. Just go for it. Once you are in, it feels great. Commitment steps help to increase your investment in recovery by making it harder for you to relapse and by offering you a 'payoff' for demonstrating your commitment. Commitment steps aren't easy, but you will find that they close doors to addiction in a way that opens doors to recovery. As the session proceeds, each of you should be trying to think of the commitment step that would be most useful now to your recovery."

Open Discussion

"Consider the following situations and what they have in common:

A. A woman who has been trying to lose weight has been making 'midnight raids' on the refrigerator. Her husband says he doubts she's serious about dieting. So she buys a lock for the refrigerator and gives the key to her husband.
B. An addict who keeps returning to prison because of crimes committed for drugs decides, while 'doing time,' to enter recovery. Realizing that in the past his good intentions have been overwhelmed on his first day out, he takes some new steps. First he tells his brother, who is in AA, about his stash and asks him to destroy it before his release. Then he arranges for a temporary sponsor to pick him up at prison and take him to his halfway house. Finally, he contacts the probation department and arranges to give regular urine samples.

"What will be the likely effects of these steps? Do you think that they show commitment to a new course of action (for example, compared to the commitment of another prisoner who felt just as enthusiastic about staying clean but took no similar steps)? Do you think that these steps could *increase* commitment to a new course of action? How might that come about?"

Comments

The woman in situation *A* might win more active and trusting support from her husband through the same act that cuts off her midnight raids.

The addict in situation *B* demonstrates commitment by his willingness to take concrete actions that restrict his access to drugs. He has taken self-restricting steps that show he knows where his real freedom lies. At the same time, he has probably won the trust and praise of his brother, his sponsor, and his probation officer. This addict is right not to overestimate his willpower.

Reminder

"Comments" contain points that the leaders should first try to elicit from group members in their own words. The points are learned most effectively when they come from the group, from its active participation. The leader can very briefly summarize or underscore the main points in his or her own words.

Open Sharing

"Let's apply this principle to your own recoveries. In each of the examples above, the person closed a door against retreat, and made it harder for himself or herself to backslide. Have any of you ever relapsed more easily or failed to stop using because you left open a door you might have shut? Give examples. Why did you leave the doors open? Has anyone closed any doors? Examples? What was the effect on your recovery?"

Comments

The leader may prompt the group by asking about the events leading to the decision to enter treatment and the effects of that decision on both individual clients and those in their lives who know about it. Direct clients to the key foundation for recovery areas: "What about closing doors against drugs at home? What about closing doors against drugs at work? What about closing doors against friends who use? How does joining recovering people in their activities close doors against users?"
    Members who have closed some doors can help others to see the perils of not closing them. Members are also sensitive to one another's hidden motives for leaving doors open. Ensure that members share the rewards of steps such as disclosing recovery to family members. These include making abstinence more secure, winning new allies, increasing

self-esteem and the esteem of others, and gaining confidence and support for taking further steps.

Brainstorming

"Let's make a list of all the useful commitment steps we can come up with—a menu of ways for the person new to recovery to make it harder for himself or herself to use drugs or slip back to old ways."

Comments

In this exercise, as in the previous ones, members will give the leaders opportunities to clarify the concept of commitment steps by proposing prorecovery changes that do not really close doors.

In order to sharpen the definition of commitment steps (which close doors) versus other prorecovery actions (which we also support), the leader may use these examples: "What about saying 'no' when a dealer calls? Is that a commitment step? How could you make it a commitment step? (You could disclose your recovery firmly, and you could change your telephone number.) What about putting away your free-base pipe where you can't see it? (Destroying it would be a commitment step.) What about refusing a drug offer by saying you don't feel well today? (Saying that you don't do drugs anymore because you are in recovery is a commitment step because it has a better chance of shutting the door on future offers.)"

Also point out that there are degrees of strength among commitment steps. Entering treatment is a commitment step that is strengthened by telling valued others about it. Having your paycheck directly deposited is a commitment step, but having it deposited to a supportive person's account is a stronger one. Attending an NA meeting is a commitment step, especially if the recovering addict attends during a time of the day and week when he or she is accustomed to using drugs. Identifying yourself at the meeting as a newcomer looking for help is a stronger step; and making a particular meeting one's home group and volunteering to do some of the group's business is still stronger. One can proceed from ordinary changes to commitment steps, which make the changes more binding, and then to stronger commitment steps that further solidify changes while enabling additional rewards.

It is not necessary for the leader to use all of the foregoing examples. These examples are given only to supplement the group's effort to give its own examples. As soon as the group seems to understand the difference between commitment steps and other changes, the leader may move on.

Distribute and Review the Handout

"Your Key Commitment Step"

Next Step

Allow members to discuss the handout and make personal additions to it. Now ask, "Who has left open a door? The rest of this session will be about preparing to take the step from the handout—or one of the personal steps that you have added to the handout—that is most important for you now. Perhaps your commitment step will be one that solidifies a change that you have already made. Perhaps it will be one that helps get you off the fence that you spoke about in the check-in. This could be your most important step since entering treatment. But it requires courage and self-honesty."

Poll members one by one on their intended steps. Caution members against committing themselves to actions that they aren't truly ready to take. "Just identifying your open door to the group can be an important step for now." Have members share any fears they have about their step or problems they have had taking the step in the past.

Ownwork

"For Saturday's Problems and Progress session, you will need a written 'progress report.' Using your Daily Chart for the week, jot down your step. If you haven't taken your step, jot down something you could do to make it easier. For example, you could talk to someone in the group who has taken a step like yours."

HANDOUT 3.1: Your Key Commitment Step

Key changes are required to build a foundation for recovery. Firmly closing doors to your old way of life makes it easier to open doors to your new way of life. Every new step makes others easier.

The list below is designed to help you identify a key step—a binding change that is a first priority for you now. You may identify more than one step, but don't let too many items distract you from what should come first. In each space below, insert a "1," a "2," or a "3": 1—Already taken; 2—To be taken now; 3—To be taken in the future.

___ Throw out drugs and/or paraphernalia. Tell someone supportive about it both before and after you do it.

___ Tell someone supportive about difficult situations for you. Use his or her advice and/or company.

___ Break off with users and dealers, and tell someone supportive about it.

___ Get a sponsor.

___ Move your residence to a more drug-free area, and don't tell users or dealers your new address.

___ Change telephone numbers and/or destroy telephone numbers of dealers. (Underline one or more.)

___ Tell a loved one, boss, or co-worker about recovery. (Underline one or more.)

___ Get a job that is more supportive of recovery.

___ Have paycheck automatically deposited/Destroy 24-hour cash card/Have someone hold your money. (Underline one or more.)

___ Try a new drug-free weekend activity with drug-free people.

___ Confide something not yet told to counselor/group leader.

___ Attend a new NA/CA meeting.

___ Identify yourself at a meeting/Volunteer to do a group job. (Underline one or more.)

___ Your own commitment step not listed here: _____

_____

Problems and Progress

Background

Sessions such as Erecting the Walls and Closing the Doors to Addiction carefully examine the scope and specifics of "what to do and how to do it." Problems and Progress acknowledges that doing is not easy, offers the group's extended attention to individual cases, and presents group belonging as a powerful alternative to doing it alone. The very acts of confronting problems and celebrating progress together create team spirit—a sense of everyone's being "in the same boat" and pulling together.

This session is somewhat less structured than the others. A more flexible format allows for extended individual participation even as it encourages the group to take active responsibility for its recovery. However, "less structured" does not mean undirected. Because many new clients have had no positive group experiences and may not know how to behave in groups, the leaders must carefully model good listening, openness, praise-giving, and respectful probing. The recovering peer leader should take a more active leadership role in this session than in the previous three by sharing relevant personal experience when appropriate.

Both leaders must also work to draw out infrequent participators. A point that bears repeating is that speaking openly is itself a powerful first step. Each member should be encouraged to ask for the group's help in defining a next step. The weekend planning segment of this session offers many opportunities for projecting next steps, for exchanging information, and for mutual help. The essential message of Problems and Progress is that the group's problem-solving and caring can replace isolation and emotional chaos even as it rewards progress.

Materials

12-step fellowship meeting lists and other listings of recovering community activities (e.g., notices of "sober dances")

Key Points

1. Emotional extremes and discomfort are normal in early recovery.
2. Talking about accomplishments and frustrations puts them in perspective and makes the client part of the group.
3. There is always a next step that the recovery addict can take to help feel better in the long run. The group is a valuable resource for defining and supporting that step.
4. Weekends are dangerous times for newly recovering people. One of the most immediate and concrete ways an early recovery group can express mutual support is by planning weekend activities together.

Session at a Glance

1. **Topic and Goals:** Members are to integrate the program principles and put them into practice. The goal is to formulate and support actions, including weekend plans, that will lead to feeling better.
2. **Review of Charts:** Members review their week's problems and progress using "The Daily Chart."
3. **Check-In:** Members update their progress on a key step and talk about their feelings.
4. **Open Discussion:** Members analyze two or three problem cases generated in the check-in. They formulate plans for coping with the problems during the coming week.
5. **Chart Planning:** Members return to their charts to plan for the coming week, including the current weekend.
6. **Weekend Plan Review:** The group helps individual members make and refine weekend plans.

Format

Topic and Goals

"During the weeknight sessions, you have learned much about addiction and recovery. The Problems and Progress session is an opportunity to apply what you have learned in more depth. If you have made progress on a critical step defined in an earlier session, sharing your success will help the whole group. If you are still stuck or hurting, maybe the group can provide suggestions and support. Especially for those of you who have not participated actively in the weeknight groups, now is the time to make this *your* group.

"Our other goal in this session is to help you firm up your weekend planning. Weekends are often critical for people in early recovery. These former 'party times' too often remain free times. Unplanned-for weekend time can reactivate an addiction. But the flip side is that good planning and follow-through on weekends can make recovery more real and rewarding. It depends on your response. This afternoon you can begin to help one another make positive responses."

Review of Charts

In preparation for check-in, each member reviews his or her progress over the past week using "The Daily Chart." (Members must always be reminded on the last weekday session to bring their completed charts to Problems and Progress.)

Check-In

Have each member mention one step that he or she is proud of and one area that is the biggest problem or stumbling block. Also give members the option of saying how they are feeling about recovery. The leader should repeat the three-part instructions of the check-in for each client, if necessary. For example, "Is there one bit of progress you are proud of? What do you most need to work on? How are you feeling about recovery?"

Emphasize that each member will be held to 2 minutes but that two or three personal situations will be targeted for further group discussion later in the session. These "live cases" should be partly self-selected and partly selected by the leaders according to their illustrative value for the group. Group leaders should try to focus on at least one case that illustrates the issues covered in the past week. Another principle of selection is urgency. Priority may be given to a member who feels especially shaky and at risk for relapse. However, not all shaky members offer sufficiently focused or universal examples. The leaders may decide that some needy members would be better seen individually after the session.

If more than three members request further discussion of their situations, the leaders may have to reserve time for one-to-one discussions or individual counseling sessions.

Open Discussion

[Reserve at least 30 minutes for this segment.] Announce that the discussion will return to the problem cases that were identified during the check-in.

"This segment is a chance to put the program's principles into actual practice. We will learn how to think about problems together and start to solve them." Solutions should emphasize concrete actions. Ask members to keep in mind that "changing what you do often changes how you feel."

If the discussion is slow, the recovering peer leader can model an appropriate response. For example:

"In the beginning of my recovery, I felt guilty and confused and I was always fighting with myself about whether or not to use. But after I took the suggestions of telling my family about my recovery and letting them hold my money, I was greatly relieved. I felt better about myself for having taken a step and for knowing that they were behind me; and I felt safer knowing that I couldn't get away with using drugs as easily as before."

Another example of a "bad feeling" mentioned during the check-in might be "feeling lonely and bored." An appropriate plan for the coming week would be to attend NA meetings with other group members.

Chart Planning

Have members go back to their charts to plan for the coming week, including the present weekend.

Weekend Plan Review

[Reserve at least 20 minutes for this segment.] "We know from years of experience that many people in early recovery do not make plans for their first weekends clean. Maybe they are too busy to give it any thought. Maybe they think that recovery is not supposed to be fun; maybe they are so used to getting high that they are afraid to go out clean; or maybe they are at a loss about what else to do. But we know that an unplanned weekend, even the first one, is a threat to recovery. Sometimes unrealistic plans can be a threat, too. So if you have not made plans yet, now is the time. If you have made them, let's hear what they are. You can use the group to check their wisdom and practicality."

After each respondent speaks, ask the group members whether they agree that the plans are solid and how they might be improved. For example, is all free time accounted for? Are the plans clear and specific? Are they truly safe? Are there backup plans? Have they considered likely difficulties?

The peer leader should distribute current NA and CA meeting lists so that members can refer to them while arranging to attend meetings together. The leaders should encourage members with experience in the fellowships to invite others to meetings. It is also desirable for the peer leader to attend a centrally located meeting to which he or she can routinely invite the group at large.

Ensure that every member volunteers a plan or identifies the need for a plan and that each member's situation is addressed, if only very briefly, by the group.

Some members may try to slip through the cracks during this segment. Be alert to plans that sound too pat—especially on the part of individuals who have resisted joining group outings. Ordinarily, however, this is a high-spirited exercise in which members reach out to one another as they begin to make recovery a reality.

Note

During the weeknight sessions, the leaders should poll members, when appropriate to the discussion, about their follow-through on proposed plans. Again, during the Problems and Progress session, members who followed through on the previous weekend should be commended, and members who failed to follow through should be offered extra support.

Family Invitation Reminder

On the weekend prior to the family session, the leaders should take a moment at the end of the Problems and Progress session to remind members of the importance of full attendance by families. Review who is coming and try to allay unrealistic fears about what will occur.

Addiction and Denial

Background

The drug high is a powerfully reinforcing experience that the addicted mind will deceive itself to retain. Self-deception can take the form of forgetting, rationalizing, ignoring, and minimizing the scope of the problem and the difficult steps required to change. It is not surprising that people still conditioned to regard drugs as the solution, the source of all pleasure and protection, are reluctant to see drugs as the problem. Until clients actually begin to experience the rewards of change, the pull of addiction can warp their perception of the need for change.

The diagnosis of addiction not only implies an initially painful prescription—giving up drugs; it is stigmatizing as well. Too often the image of a hopeless, down-and-out criminal comes to mind. This image is based on a stereotype of the heroin addict in the 1950s and 1960s, a time when addiction was poorly understood and when competent treatment and self-help resources were not widely available. Because many of today's addicts, especially earlier-stage cocaine addicts, do not fit the popular street addict image, they are tempted to dwell on the differences. Typically, addicts insist that because they are not physically dependent or don't have to use cocaine every day, and because they have jobs, spouses, cars, and so forth, then they cannot be "real" addicts. They can always point to cocaine users who are much worse off than they are. In this way, the very intact systems of social and economic support that usually favor recovery can, in combination with an outdated notion of addiction, contribute to denial.

The first job in dealing with denial is to present an up-to-date, science-based model of addiction. The conditioning model that underlies our program explains that addiction is a matter of degree. The rational response to a lesser degree is to take systematic actions to prevent its progression and to deactivate it. The model stresses that the ability of cocaine addicts to stop using cocaine for regular, limited periods represents a typical pattern of addiction to stimulants rather than a capacity for control. The conditioning model also explains why physiological withdrawal is not an essential feature of addiction and why trying to use cocaine in a controlled manner is likely to lead to a progressively higher level of addiction. The self-assessment instrument presented in this session pointedly asks not whether the individual is or is not an addict, but "how addicted" he or she is.

Although one must overcome a degree of denial in order to enter a cessation program, denial is as subject to recurrence as the addictive process it protects. The painful early days of treatment can occasion some of the most slippery efforts to back out. A client may accept that he or she has a problem with cocaine but continue to defend his or her ability to drink safely. Or the client may admit the extent of the problem, but insist that he or she can now deal with it on his or her own. The handout "Common Examples of Denial" is intended to familiarize clients with the shifty forms and functions of denial. It should also illustrate that denying the extent of the problem often takes the more subtle form of denying the need for comprehensive and binding solutions.

Because the most effective examples of denial are live ones, the session is structured to elicit examples of members' own denial, past and present. Respect is essential when confronting these examples, since acceptance by a caring recovery group is itself one of the most powerful antidotes to denial. It is a foretaste of an alternative way of life. Conversely, clients who feel judged may be placed on the defensive. The essential experience of this session should not be one of a group pitted against its recalcitrant members but rather of a group united against addiction and the self-deception it promotes.

This session has a large number of short segments. It is not necessary to cover them all. Rather, focus on covering the main points. Sometimes spending a few extra minutes on a segment will allow the group to cover some of the material of the following segment which may then be reduced by a few minutes, and so on. As with all of the sessions, the discussion's logical flow from segment to segment should take precedence over exhaustively covering each segment.

Materials

Handouts: "Addiction: Myths and Facts"
"How Severe Is My Addiction?"
"Common Examples of Denial"

Key Points

1. Denial is a major obstacle to recovery. Accepting the reality of a strong addiction is painful because it is stigmatizing and signals the necessity of giving up drug use and undergoing a demanding process of recovery. It is natural to avoid the "addict" label if possible.

2. The denial of many early-stage cocaine addicts is fed by their lack of physical dependence, their ability to stop using for regular periods, and the relative intactness of their work and family lives. An up-to-date conditioning model of addiction shows that addiction is a matter of degree. There is no specific point at which a person is or is not an addict, and in the early stages of addiction almost no one feels like an addict.

3. The denial of the newly abstinent outpatient is often displaced from cocaine use to alcohol or marijuana use. Because alcohol and marijuana are more socially acceptable than cocaine, it is easier to deny that their use is a problem. The conditioning model explains the experience of thousands of addicts who have relapsed because of this error.

4. Properly understood and accepted, the diagnosis of a severe addiction is a source of hope and relief. It allows a client to accept the principles of recovery along with the help provided by counselors and recovering addicts; and it helps him or her to convert the negative "addict" identity into a positive "recovering addict" identity. It also puts the client in a strong position to resist self-deception about controlled drug use and to refuse offers of drugs and alcohol. Recovery begins with the person facing his or her proven inability to control drug use or its harmful consequences.

Session at a Glance

1. **Check-In:** "Recovering addict." Introductions and reactions to the label.
2. **Topic and Goals:** Denial as a major obstacle to recovery; denial as not accepting the real nature of one's addiction or the full solution that is needed.
3. **Discussion Question:** The reasons for denial.
4. **Brainstorming:** Characteristics of addiction (the conditioning model corrects misconceptions that feed denial).
5. **Handouts:** Summaries of the characteristics of addiction, a self-test, the forms of denial.
6. **Partners' Communication:** Partners interviewing each other on handouts—seeing one's degree of addiction and forms of denial from the other's point of view.

7. **Open Discussion:** Groupwide corrections of and learning from partners' denial.
8. **Open Sharing:** Personal experiences and advantages of overcoming denial.
9. **Closing Sharing:** Admitting lingering deep reservations—using the group's modeling and support to examine and overcome denial.
10. **Ownwork:** (a) Practice disclosing recovery or reservations; (b) begin a diary of recovery including feelings about the recovering addict identity.

Format

Check-In

Open by saying, "Tonight we begin with an exercise. I'd like everyone to introduce himself or herself to the others in the tradition of 12-step fellowships: 'Hi, I'm _____ , and I am a recovering addict.'"

After all members have complied, ask, "How do you feel about identifying yourselves this way? Are you sure, deep down, that it fits?"

Comments

Allow the discussion to continue until it is clear that members are engaged in the issues that will be addressed. Ask those who do not volunteer to speak whether they would like to share their thoughts with the rest of the group. The members should begin to recognize any reservations about accepting the label or its full implications.

Another purpose of this exercise is to introduce the leaders to the range of responses in the group. If leaders can identify the group's levels and types of denial, they will be in a better position to address them.

Thank members for their honesty, and indicate that there will be "further opportunities for increasing self-honesty tonight."

Topic and Goals

"This session is designed to help you understand and overcome denial, one of the greatest obstacles to recovery. Given the negative image a lot of people still have of addicts, it is easy to understand why some of you resist the label. We'll see that the negative image is based on mistaken ideas about addiction. Being a 'recovering addict' is completely different from being an addict, and 'recovering addict' is an identity with great advantages.

"The fact that you are *here* indicates that you have made some headway against denial. You deserve credit for that. But some of you may still be thinking, 'I don't have this problem.' Like addiction itself, denial is not a black-or-white condition that you either have or you don't. There are various degrees and subtle forms of denial. You can admit that you are an addict and still deny the need for treatment or for taking some crucial suggestions of treatment.

"Denial resurfaces and takes different forms even after you have entered treatment. Many of you will accept that you cannot control cocaine while insisting, against the evidence, that alcohol is not a problem for you. Perhaps some of you will only discover the truth of what we are saying by wasting more life, if not all of it. Yet since every solution begins with facing the problem, tonight may be the beginning of a solution for some of you."

Discussion Question

"Why is it so hard for someone early in recovery to accept that he or she is strongly addicted?"

Comments

The discussion should bring out several points. First, denial can be thought of as the self-deception that allows addiction to continue. "Love is blind." "You ignore, forget, minimize, or rationalize facts that indicate the need to make painful changes." Second, "No one likes to be thought of as weak. That is a blow to your pride, but the idea of weakness is based on a mistaken idea of addiction." Third, "The down-and-out image of the addict, also a mistake, might allow you to think that you are not 'bad' enough to have to give up a whole way of life." Fourth, "You may be defending yourself against the guilt and fear associated with your addiction. You may not realize that accepting the problem is the best way to relieve these feelings."

Brainstorming

"Since you may have a mistaken idea about what addiction is, let's see if we can reach some agreement about what defines an addict. What behaviors have you noticed in yourself or others that add up to addiction?"

Comments

This discussion should anticipate the major points of the handouts:

1. Addiction happens gradually and is a matter of degree.
2. Since addiction is a conditioning of a part of the nervous system that is independent of reason and consciousness, almost no one feels like an addict in the early stages of addiction.
3. Addiction is progressive—so long as "you continue to use, you are headed toward the same self-destructive end-points as the most severely addicted individuals."
4. Individuals from all social and professional levels become addicted.
5. Addicts continue using drugs despite negative consequences to themselves and others and despite past resolutions.
6. Addicts cannot consistently limit the amount or the occasion of their use.
7. Bit by bit, addicts let go of normal social, familial, occupational, and recreational activities, values, and responsibilities.
8. Addicts tend to rationalize, minimize, or ignore both the consequences of their drug use and the necessity of making difficult changes.

Members should be encouraged to substantiate these points with examples from personal experience. If the discussion is slow or tentative, the leader might try asking, "Has any of you ever underestimated your degree of addiction?"

Distribute and Review the Handouts

"Addiction: Myths and Facts"
"How Severe Is My Addiction?"
"Common Examples of Denial"

Comments

Emphasize those points on the "Addiction: Myths and Facts" handout that have not been discussed in the previous segment. Also indicate which points *have* been anticipated.

Partners' Communication

Have members in adjacent seats pair off. The extra member in an odd-numbered group should be paired with the recovering peer leader. Now have each partner complete the "How Severe Is My Addiction?" checklist by interviewing the other. That is, partner *A* completes a checklist of partner *B*'s responses and vice versa. Instruct each partner to probe the other's responses in a friendly manner when skepticism seems warranted. Once each partner has completed a checklist of the other's responses, have the partners exchange lists so that each may see the results for themselves.

Now have each partner interview the other on "Common Examples of Denial." For example, instruct the partners to ask, "Have you told yourself or others [proceed down the items on the list]? Are any of these forms of denial still a struggle for you? What about others that do not appear on the list?"

Open Discussion

Allow 5 or 10 minutes for the partners to share their experiences and reactions with the whole group.

Comments

Occasionally, members become agitated or depressed by the "How Severe Is My Addiction?" checklist. Leaders should be alert for this reaction, which is usually relieved by group support. Throughout the session, the leaders must emphasize that although facing the problem may be painful, it is also a hopeful step toward a solution.

Open Sharing

"Have anyone's feelings about accepting addiction changed as the result of personal experience?"

Comments

In most groups, there quickly emerges a direct relationship between level of acceptance on the one hand and amount of experience or knowledge of recovery on the other.

The discussion should bring out the advantages of overcoming denial described in Key Point 4. They include acceptance of the principles of recovery and the help of the group, conversion of one's self-image to a more positive "recovering addict" identity, and increased ability to resist self-deception and offers of drugs.

Closing Sharing

The leader remarks, "From now on, we shall always begin our meetings using the same introduction that we used this session: 'Hi, my name is _____ , and I am a recovering addict.' "

Encourage members to share any deep, private reservations that they might have about being addicts or needing to abstain completely from drugs and alcohol.

Comments

Introduce this concluding segment as "an opportunity for self-honesty." If members cannot report current reservations, they may be asked to consider possible future reservations. In addition, they may share any feelings that came up during the check-in.

In responding to reported reservations, the leader should set a tone of respectful concern for whatever holds one back from full self-acceptance and full membership in the group. The recovering peer leader should model the technique of nonjudgmentally offering relevant personal experience.

Ownwork

1. For those who have been unable to identify themselves as addicts or to disclose a reservation to the group, a next step might be writing it down, saying it to a mirror, or disclosing it privately to a leader or a loved one. You might also merely disclose that you still have something to disclose.
2. Begin keeping a diary of your recovery. Make the first entry a full disclosure of your feelings about being an addict.

HANDOUT 5.1: Addiction: Myths and Facts

MYTH: Addicts have to use drugs every day.
FACT: Most cocaine addicts stop using for regular periods.

MYTH: Addicts are all "low-life" criminals.
FACT: People from all social levels become addicted.

MYTH: When addicts stop using they go into severe withdrawal.
FACT: Cocaine addiction has no severe physical withdrawal. Even heroin addicts usually become addicted *before* they become physically dependent.

MYTH: Addicts are weak. They just need more willpower.
FACT: Because of the very powerful conditioning of repeated drug use, willpower alone will not usually sustain recovery. Severely addicted individuals should have good information about addiction and solid external structures and supports. These structures and supports must remain in place until the recovering person deactivates addiction by learning new responses to craving.

MYTH: When addicts stop using they are no longer addicted.
FACT: Addiction continues long after addicts stop using. That is why stopping use from time to time is easier than "staying stopped." Every bit of the old drugging lifestyle reminds the addict's nervous system of the high and can reactivate severe addiction.

MYTH: There must be some way to control drug use. Others seem to do it.
FACT: The overwhelming majority of addicts who try to control drug use fail. Especially for one who has had a problem, all drug use is addictive. Sooner or later, it progresses to increasing levels of severity. Why play with fire?

MYTH: Alcohol and marijuana are not at all like cocaine and heroin. They are acceptable parts of normal social life. If someone has never had a problem with them, there is no reason not to use them.
FACT: A hard look at the addict's drinking/pot-smoking history usually reveals that he or she abused alcohol and marijuana long before and during cocaine use. But even if alcohol or pot had not been a problem (at least, compared with one's drug of choice), it is very likely to become one in recovery. Drinking and smoking pot put an individual in contact with users and they warp judgment and commitment. Most important, because they are central to the whole drugging lifestyle, they very commonly lead back to the drug of choice.

MYTH: Stopping drug use means no more good times.
FACT: Stopping drug use can mean the beginning of better sorts of good times. If you don't learn to have fun drug free, you will probably relapse.

HANDOUT 5.2: How Severe Is My Addiction?

Read each question. If the answer to a question is yes, put a checkmark on the line next to the number. Each checkmark indicates an increased degree of addiction.

____ 1. Do you or those close to you ever worry about your drugging?

____ 2. Are you ever unable to stop drugging when you want to?

____ 3. Do you work hard to get your drug? Does it take a lot of time, effort, and planning?

____ 4. Has your drugging ever created problems between you and someone close to you?

____ 5. Have you ever missed work or been late to work because of your drugging?

____ 6. When a time for getting high is approaching, do you think about it often and eagerly look forward to it? Are you extremely disappointed when the expected drug is not available or when it is of poor quality? When it is used up?

____ 7. Have you ever neglected your family, your work, or other important obligations because you were drugging?

____ 8. Have you ever been in the hospital or jail because of your drugging?

____ 9. Have you been unable to stop using until all the drug is gone or all the money is gone?

____ 10. Have you given up or reduced important social or recreational activities because of drugging?

____ 11. Have you been unable to enjoy yourself (e.g., at parties) without drugs?

____ 12. Have you continued to drug despite problems such as depression, financial difficulties, or inability to get up in the morning?

____ 13. Have you used in inappropriate places such as work? Are you very protective of and secretive about your supply?

____ 14. Has your use become more frequent or regular?

HANDOUT 5.3: Common Examples of Denial

Refusing to accept the label of "addict" is only one form of denial. Addicts minimize, rationalize, or ignore the harmful consequences of addiction and the need for making painful changes. They dwell on the differences between themselves and other addicts. Can you add to the list below from your own experience or observation?

1. "I'm not an addict. I can control it. I stop for days at a time."

2. "I use much less than a lot of the people I know. I don't use as much as a real addict."

3. "Drugs are not causing my problems with my wife (or my parents, or at work, etc.). They don't understand what I am going through. *They* are making my using worse."

4. "I take drugs only to enjoy myself. I work hard and I deserve some fun."

5. "I can't control drugs now, but maybe I can learn to in treatment."

6. "I know I can't control cocaine, but alcohol (or pot or pills) has never been a problem for me. I've already proven to myself that I can use it just on weekends (or on special occasions or in limited quantities)."

7. "I have a problem, but I can handle it my way. These programs are fine for other people, but I'm different." Or: "I don't really have to take *all* the program's suggestions. Some of them just don't apply."

8. "I still have a good job, a car, a spouse (etc.), so I can't be that bad."

Making the Most of Treatment

Background

Does treatment for addiction work? How does it work? How long does it take? How much effort does it require? What are the specific requirements of outpatient treatment? What other resources may be needed? Many clients who first enter treatment, and even many who have been in treatment before, need answers to such questions. If they are to use treatment well, they need to know what is involved and what is expected of them.

It is not surprising that most clients *don't* know what to expect. Treatment has undergone a revolution over the past 20 years. Not long ago, many people saw addicts as hopeless. Today examples of solid recovery have become commonplace—at least to addiction specialists and to the growing recovering community. There is also a growing body of formal studies (Gerstein & Harwood, 1990; McAuliffe et al., 1988; McAuliffe, 1990) documenting the effectiveness of treatment. In consequence, a well-informed client is now likely to be a realistically hopeful one.

Hope and realism are the twin themes of this session. In the previous session, we suggested that gaining access to systematic help was a benefit of overcoming denial. In this session, we discuss that help in detail, with special emphasis on the client's role. Treatment works, but not instantly and not without great effort. Clients who entertain the wishful notion that treatment is something "done to you" (like surgery) or administered like an antibiotic must learn there is no way around—

and no shortcut through—making difficult, long-term personal and lifestyle changes. Stopping drug use is only a first condition of these changes. Counselors, therapists, and other recovering people can offer guidance and support in both implementing cessation strategies and making long-term changes; but the ultimate responsibility for making treatment work well is the client's.

An essential challenge to the designers of this session was to keep members engaged rather than bored or burdened by the necessary bulk of information. This is accomplished in part by creating opportunities for those who have been in treatment before to share their experiences with those less experienced. Where possible, the essential information is elicited from the clients themselves. The "What's Wrong Here?" game is another strategy to engage clients actively. Each fictional case highlights a common misuse or under-use of the resources of treatment. Fictional cases free clients to grapple with relevant issues without fear of personal exposure and without stimulating personal denial. At the same time, they allow members to solve problems as a team, actively fitting the main points of the session into realistic contexts. The game format helps the leaders to maintain the sense of lively relevance and active learning that transforms a collection of facts and precepts about good treatment into an *example* of good treatment.

Materials

Handouts: "Questions about Treatment"
           "What's Wrong Here?"
           "The Keys to Treatment Success"
Literature on 12-step fellowships and other local treatment resources

Key Points

1. Addicts do recover in treatment. Recovery is a likely outcome when clients make the prescribed changes in their lives.

2. Addiction treatment is an intensive, long-term undertaking. Clients must follow the full regimen and complete the full course of treatment. Many clients need to use multiple resources.

3. Early treatment focuses on safely separating from drugs and the drug lifestyle. Gradually, the client learns to cope with a wide range of situations and to focus on personal development.

4. Treatment can offer guidance, training, and support, but it is up to the individual to make the changes that enable recovery.

5. Consistent attendance, respectfulness, open-minded listening, honesty, cooperative participation, learning from mistakes, taking credit for small successes, asking for help, willingness to try new ways of coping despite misgivings and discomfort, and planning ahead are among the behaviors and attitudes that help a client make the most of treatment.

Session at a Glance

1. **Check-In:** "How will you make treatment work?"
2. **Topic and Goals/Open Forum:** The new client's need to know what treatment is and how to use it.
3. **Distribute and Review the Handout:** "Questions about Treatment." Elicit additional questions from clients about the nature, effectiveness, extent, and length of treatment—answered by experienced clients where possible.
4. **Distribute and Review the Handout:** "What's Wrong Here?" Three cases that illustrate common failures to make the most of treatment.
5. **Brainstorming:** The components of success. How clients make the most of treatment.
6. **Distribute and Review the Handout:** "The Keys to Treatment Success." Summary and review of the components of success.
7. **Next Step:** Applying the components of success to each client. "How will you make this group work better for yourself?"

Format

Check-In

"Take 1 minute to tell the group how you plan to make sure treatment works for you. Mention whether you have been in treatment before."

Comments

The leaders need an early sense of members' levels of experience with different types of treatment. They will then be able to elicit relevant information later in the session. They will also be able to address specific misconceptions about treatment.

Topic and Goals/Open Forum

"Today we are going to work on making the most of your treatment. The first step is to know the basics. We understand that you have not learned these things in school or when you were getting high. People entering treatment have many questions about it. Some of you may not have the foggiest idea of what you can do to make progress in your recoveries. You may wonder about how exactly our program works, about how other programs work, about how much treatment you need, or about how long you need to be in treatment. If you have any of these questions – or any other questions about how treatment works or about what you can do to make it work better – now is the time to ask them."

Distribute and Review the Handout

"Questions about Treatment"

Comments

Leaders should involve members actively in the topic and help them identify specific concerns not addressed in the handout. When possible, members with more treatment experience should be encouraged to respond to the questions of those with less.

In reticent groups, the recovering peer leader may prompt questions by recalling his or her own questions in early treatment. For example, "I wondered why I had to go to so many meetings for so long; I wondered what I was supposed to learn aside from 'Don't use drugs'; I wondered how I would ever stop wanting to get high. How could just talking about my problem make it better?"

The leaders should answer questions when members do not; and they should correct, clarify, and expand upon members' answers when necessary.

Distribute and Review Fictional Case Studies Handout

"What's Wrong Here?"

Case Analyses

"Marvin."   Marvin is making two common errors. First, he is picking and choosing among the parts of the treatment regimen – deciding which principles apply to him and which do not. Second, and most crucially, he is doing this secretly. By not openly airing his reservation, he is depriving himself (and the group) of a possible learning experience. Using group treatment well means speaking *especially* about reservations and conflicts. This is the only way to bring the group's collective experience and the leaders' expertise into one's decision-making.

"**Luis.**" Too often, clients like Luis end treatment prematurely. They become overconfident once they start feeling better and once they understand some basic principles of addiction. One problem is that understanding, although important for change, is not the same thing as change. In addition to helping clients learn about addiction and recovery, treatment must help them make the systematic changes that lay a foundation for long-term recovery. Perhaps Luis needs to educate his wife and make her a "partner" in recovery. In any case, impatience with the responsibilities of treatment is a poor reason to cut treatment short.

"**Carol.**" Carol need not discuss all of the personal details of her past in order to talk about the common addiction and recovery problems that she shares with other group members. Some of the personal issues that cause her shame might best be discussed first in individual counseling or privately with the group leaders. With their encouragement she might gradually disclose a little more to group members, especially to members of a more close-knit long-term recovery group, once she has grown to trust and feel comfortable with them. Opening up in groups can be a great relief. Quite often a client's shame is lifted with the discovery that other members share or can easily relate to his or her problems. In addition, members are almost always very respectful of one another's confidentiality. However, any member who has concerns about it should air them openly so that the group's norms can be made as clear as possible.

Brainstorming

Explain that the cases bring out some of the client attitudes and behaviors needed to make treatment successful. For example, Marvin needs to be more open and honest, and he needs to become a wholehearted learner; Luis needs commitment and persistence; and Carol needs to risk being vulnerable. Ask members to list other elements of the client's role in "making the most of treatment." The leader may have to prompt the group by offering a few additional examples such as "good listening" or "follow-through." Write the brainstorming list clearly on a chalkboard or newsprint.

Distribute and Review the Handout

"The Keys to Treatment Success"

Comments

Point out that the handout addresses the client's role in making treatment work. "The handout will help you understand what is expected of you and how you can speed your progress." Also, point out which of the items from the handout had been anticipated in the previous brainstorming and which had not.

Next Step

"What can you do to make treatment work better for you, starting here and now with this group?"

Comments

During this exercise, the leader should refer to "The Keys to Treatment Success" handout and the brainstorming list. Each member should identify an area for improvement.

HANDOUT 6.1: Questions about Treatment

Does treatment work?

We know now that individuals who complete the full course of treatment have an excellent chance of an enduring, full recovery. The success rate can be as high as 90% in the year following completion of outpatient drug-free treatment.* Because of advances in research and because of the growth of recovering communities, the prospects for addicts who are serious about making changes are much better than they were 10 or 15 years ago.

How does treatment work, and why is it necessary?

Treatment allows each recovering person to benefit from scientific knowledge about addiction and recovery and from the experience of many others who have faced similar problems. The essence of treatment is to learn to do something other than taking drugs when you experience craving. The key is to change your lifestyle and ways of coping. The program helps you to avoid many common pitfalls. Proven strategies are quicker and less dangerous than going by trial and error. Counselors and other group members can help by showing you how to change, by giving you feedback, and by supporting your efforts to make difficult changes.

Some people have quit drugs on their own, but many people come to treatment because they have discovered that they cannot do it on their own. This lesson is an easy one to forget. Too often, the desire to "do it alone" is a disguise for not really wanting to do it. If you do it "your way," you can hold on to bits of the old way of life that keep you addicted. And there's nothing to hold you to a forward course. If mere willpower, so-called inner strength, has already failed you, you need *outer* strength—that is, solid structure and support from those who have your best interests at heart.

What is the difference between inpatient and outpatient treatment, and are there any options in between?

In general, treatment should be most intense at first, and decline in intensity as recovery progresses. At what level of care you begin depends on several things. Inpatient care is for people who have medical complications, a physical dependency that is potentially life threatening, or do not have a home or job situation in which they can separate from drugs. People who are physically dependent on drugs such as alcohol, tranquilizers, and sedatives may need close medical supervision in case of seizures.

Detoxification can also occur in a hospital if the person has severe medical or psychiatric conditions. The usual stay varies from 1 to 3 weeks. Clients who have no need for medical or psychiatric care, but who lack a safe and stable living situation, who have repeatedly failed to stay clean as outpatients, or who are so severely addicted that they need time away from everyday life are good candidates for a period in a halfway house or day treatment. If these facilities do not provide enough support, then a period of residential treatment may be the answer.

Intensive outpatient programs like ours—attending three group sessions and

183

one individual counseling session weekly—can be used either as a follow-up to residential and halfway house treatment or as an alternative to them. Once you are capable of establishing a foundation for recovery on the outside—that is, a clean living and working situation, a well-structured daily schedule, and clean leisure time and social support—intensive outpatient treatment is appropriate. If you find that outpatient care does not provide enough support initially, then you should obtain more intensive treatment.

How long does treatment last?

Although the length of treatment depends more on your degree of progress than on time, there are some rules of thumb that generally apply. The cessation phase of stopping drug use and separating from the drug lifestyle requires intensive support for at least a month. This treatment should be followed by 6 to 12 months in weekly individual counseling and a recovery group which meets one or more times weekly. During this period, most people need at least one daily therapeutic contact, so most must supplement their indivudual counseling and recovery group attendance with 12-step fellowship attendance and sometimes with family counseling or psychotherapy. During the second year of recovery, most clients are able to reduce the number of their weekly treatment contacts, but still need some continuing support. Addiction is deactivated as safe practices become second nature and you branch out to new social and recreational activities. The pace of recovery varies from individual to individual, but a rule of thumb for reducing structure is "better too slow than too fast."

*McAuliffe, W.E., Albert, J., Cordill-London, G., & McGarraghy, T.K. (1990–1991). Contributions to a social conditioning model of cocaine recovery. *International Journal of the Addictions*, 25 (9A & 10A), 1145–1181.

HANDOUT 6.2: What's Wrong Here?

Marvin

Marvin is proud of himself for entering treatment. It wasn't easy. What he has heard so far makes sense to him, except for all of the stuff about avoiding drug users. That's probably right for most people but in his neighborhood you *can't* avoid them. Users are everywhere. He realizes that he could move, but it would take him a while to find a place. Besides, he figures that he will run into temptation sooner or later, so he might as well learn to deal with it now.

Marvin hasn't mentioned this in his groups or to his counselors, because he already knows what they will say.

What's wrong here?

Luis

Luis has been coming to the program for three nights a week for almost a month, and he feels much better. His wife is beginning to complain about all of the time he spends at group meetings, especially since he spent so much time away when he was getting high. Luis himself is wondering if he really needs more of this. He is grateful to the counselors and group members for helping him to see how he kept relapsing. For example, he used to cash his paycheck and head down to "The Border" for drinks and conversation before heading home. Now he brings his paycheck right home and doesn't go out at all unless he has a treatment group scheduled. If his wife starts a fight, he just bites his tongue. Now that he knows the dos and don'ts of staying clean, he feels that he can make it on his own.

What's wrong here?

Carol

Carol has a hard time speaking in large groups. She is also very ashamed about some of the things that she did while on drugs, and she figures that it is no one's business. She doesn't mind speaking about other members' problems, but she feels unable to speak about her own. How does she know someone wouldn't use any personal confessions against her? She is beginning to feel that group treatment is not for her.

What's wrong here?

HANDOUT 6.3: The Keys to Treatment Success

"Counselors can talk, but clients have to walk" is one way of saying that you are responsible for making the most of your treatment. Recovery requires active, wholehearted participation. To make progress, you need:

Full, Punctual Attendance. The drug habit destroys responsibility and consistency. You can rebuild them by attending your groups and counseling sessions faithfully and on time, and by following through on new commitments and routines. Poor attendance and lateness are disrespectful and reveal a lack of commitment.

Patience and Persistence. Worthwhile gains take time. Someone who has been addicted for years cannot expect to change everything in weeks or even months.

Honesty. Dishonesty is a deep habit of addiction. Active addicts always have a lot to hide. Honesty is both a great relief and a key to new support.

Openmindedness. As honesty is to talking, so openmindedness is to listening. If you recognize that your own best efforts to make changes have not worked, then you will carefully consider what others are saying.

Willingness to Try. Some of the steps recommended in treatment will not feel easy. In order to get past the fear and discomfort, you must be willing to make the effort.

Asking for Help. Don't let false pride hold you back from using the help of your counselors and the other group members.

Learning from Mistakes. Early in recovery you are a beginner. You need to learn from your own mistakes and from the experience of others.

Taking Credit for Success. You should find ways to reward yourself for even small gains. Let your group and your counselors know about your progress.

Respect/Cooperation. Groups work by pulling together. You will learn that being helpful to others and respectful of their recoveries is an important part of being helped. Respecting others' confidentiality will also help you to feel free to talk in the group.

Planning Ahead. You can no longer afford to "take life as it comes." In some ways, your "natural" first responses are still addicted ones, so you must take responsibility for changing them. For example, you can no longer "play it by ear" on weekends. Using your group to help you plan is a good use of treatment.

Coping with Dangerous Situations

Background

Successfully dealing with craving and its causes is a key to achieving stable abstinence. In order to prevent being overwhelmed by powerful cravings, the client in early recovery must avoid many craving triggers. However, some triggers cannot or should not be avoided: for example, an upcoming day in court, the stress of resuming work, the unforeseeable drug offer at a bus stop, the distress accompanying drug withdrawal, social anxiety and depression, and the craving produced by a birthday, by the death of a loved one, or by the arrival of the weekend. One must learn instead to cope with craving stemming from these sources. This session examines techniques for coping with such craving triggers.

The client's first step in addressing this issue is to acknowledge the problem. Unavoidable cravings do not signify personal weakness and failure; rather, they are predictable events of early recovery. Once clients accept this fact, they can plan coping strategies—especially since many unavoidable triggers such as holidays or court dates are foreseeable. At the same time, clients must learn to distinguish between truly unavoidable triggers and triggers that they call unavoidable only because they do not want to avoid them. The group can do much to correct this sort of thinking. Once "avoidability" is clearly defined, the group can examine what has worked and what has not in past attempts to escape from or cope with unavoidable dangers. Coping strategies are usefully divided according to external or internal dangers because somewhat different responses may be involved. For example, the client's proper initial response to the presence of drugs at the work place may be to leave the scene, while the proper response to depression may be to call his or her counselor or therapist. Many situations, such as the arrival of weekends, combine external and internal triggers. These situations call for a variety of responses including making plans to be accompanied for as much time as necessary and designating "escape routes" and back-up plans. For unavoidable dangers that occur without warning, this session offers an "emergency kit" of easy-to-remember guidelines.

A repeated theme of the session is that, although *wanting* to use drugs may be inevitable for the newly recovering person, *using* drugs is not. Craving can be reduced by changing one's environment and one's consciousness. This session offers training in both sorts of change and explains how to combine the two.

Materials

Handouts: "HEDS"
            "Three Ways to Stop Craving"

Key Points

1. Many sources of craving in early recovery are unavoidable and must be coped with immediately. A first step is acknowledging the problem.

2. Since many unavoidable dangers are foreseeable, one may productively plan for them and rehearse coping strategies.

3. Clients often classify avoidable triggers as unavoidable, in part because they do not want to avoid them. Many triggers are inherently appealing or have become appealing because of their long association with drug use. Some triggers that cannot be *completely* avoided (e.g., free time or anger) can nonetheless be limited or minimized.

4. Some unavoidable triggers are internal, such as boredom, anger, or depression; others are external, such as white powders. The best response to both internal and external triggers is often to seek out social support. The best *first* response to external triggers may be to leave the scene immediately.

5. Most crises may be coped with by having a plan, by asking immediately for support, by learning to slow down and think the craving through, and by developing a routine of alternative, distracting activities.

Session at a Glance

1. **Check-In:** Identifying an unavoidable trigger and defining "unavoidable."
2. **Brainstorming:** Identifying other common unavoidable triggers.
3. **Open Discussion and Brainstorming:** Dividing the list into external and internal triggers and generating strategies for each.
4. **Handouts:** Reviewing basic strategies in "HEDS" and "Three Ways to Stop Craving."
5. **Individual Plans:** Applying the strategies to members' individual situations.

Format

Check-In

"Tell the group about an unavoidable situation or feeling that stimulates your drug urges."

Comments

The leaders should take this opportunity to help the group distinguish between *truly* unavoidable triggers and those that just seem unavoidable. Point out, if the members do not, that some triggers such as free time, boredom, loneliness, or anger may be reduced and avoided when possible but may not be entirely eliminated. Also point out that denial and attachment to triggers can lead recovering people to call avoidable triggers unavoidable.

Brainstorming

Make a list of the unavoidable dangers mentioned so far. Now ask the group to add to the list. "What are some other common unavoidable dangers that you have experienced or that you might experience?"

Comments

Once again, the leaders must determine whether the dangers are truly unavoidable.

Open Discussion and Brainstorming

Have the group divide the list into internal and external triggers, indicating that the distinction is not absolute. (Many situations present combinations of internal and external triggers.) First ask for an example of each sort of trigger: for example, boredom versus an unexpected tax refund. Then ask for coping strategies in each category. "What has worked for you, or what might work?"

Comments

Point out the similarities and differences in coping strategies for internal and external triggers. Using support is recommended in all cases, as is distraction and reflecting on the consequences of drug use. However, one can frequently escape from external triggers physically. Some unavoidable internal triggers—for example, anger and stress—may be reduced by avoiding *their* external triggers—such as raising old sore points with a spouse or making major decisions. Planning to have support available can reduce the internal consequences of unavoidable external situations such as court dates or dental surgery.

Distribute and Review the Handouts

"HEDS"
"Three Ways to Stop Craving"

Comments

The acronym HEDS is an easy-to-remember guide for crises.

If members are struggling with withdrawal-related tensions, the leaders can demonstrate the relaxation techniques in the "Three Ways" handout.

As usual, point out which of the strategies in the two handouts have been discussed by the group in the brainstorm. Also pay special attention to the strategies in the handouts that have *not* been discussed in earlier exercises.

Next Step/Individual Plans

Distribute two sheets of paper and a pencil to each member. Now announce, "We are going to apply our strategies and those in the handouts to making personal plans for dealing with unavoidable triggers." Have each member write his or her most pressing unavoidable trigger once on each sheet of paper. (This may be the same danger that was identified in the check-in.) If members cannot identify a pressing or "probable" trigger, have them identify a "possible" unavoidable trigger. Allow 5 minutes for members to write a plan on one of their sheets of paper. Ask members to label each part of their plans with the letter of the HEDS strategy employed.

Then ask members to place their second sheets (those with the unavoidable trigger identified but without a plan) at the center of the table. Shuffle the second sheets and have each member choose a sheet grab-bag style. If a client chooses his or her own sheet, he or she should replace it in the pile or exchange with someone else. Now allow 5 minutes for each member to devise a plan for the *other* member's identified trigger. In the ensuing discussion, have each member compare his or her own plan with the other member's plan for dealing with the trigger. Have the whole group evaluate the relative strengths and weaknesses of each plan and make alternative or additional suggestions.

Comments

For each member's trigger, ask whether anyone else can offer guidance from personal experience: "Who has coped successfully with a similar situation? How?" Ask which of the coping strategies from the brainstorming or the handouts applies.

HANDOUT 7.1: HEDS

When coping with craving, use your HEDS:

Help. Always ask for help as a first response. Have plenty of telephone numbers and meeting lists and use them. Tell counselors, friends, sponsors, and relatives right away when you feel shaky.

Escape. Don't hang around when that "little voice" tells you not to. Always have a planned escape route, including transportation and a destination. Move now and think about it later.

Do something. Get busy with some distracting activity. Chores, a hot bath, or good food may soothe you. Exercise is good for reducing stress. Exactly what you do is not as important as having your own little "drill" and practicing it faithfully.

Slow down. Breathe deeply, recite a prayer, and think the craving through. Focus on how you will feel after the drug is gone. Make a mental list of the advantages and disadvantages of using. Think about what your recovering friends, your counselor, and your sponsor would say if they were with you.

HANDOUT 7.2: Three Ways to Stop Craving – Debate, Distract, Deep-Breathe

When you let yourself dwell on the idea of getting high, your heart may start to beat faster in anticipation. The more excited you become, the more your craving is stimulated. If you do not stop this predrug upswing early, you may be too late. Probably the most reliable method of stopping craving is to ask someone supportive to be with you. But in crises, you can also use **debating, distracting, and deep-breathing.** Debating is a way of thinking through a craving. Distraction works by replacing drug-seeking with other activities and by replacing drug thoughts with thoughts about those activities. Replacing is always a more effective strategy than just removing because it refocuses your attention and offers new motivations. Deep-breathing is a form of meditation that works by slowing you down. You are not likely to be racing toward a high when you are feeling peaceful. **But remember that debating, distracting, and deep-breathing all require practice.** You will not be able to use the techniques in a crisis unless you practice them on a daily basis. They must already be second nature when thoughts about drugs begin.

Debate

Addicts often speak of the "little voice" that tells them to get high. This voice is a natural result of addiction. The recovering person must learn to oppose it with a recovering voice. The recovering voice debates the addict voice and exposes its false arguments. When the addict voice tells you to take drugs to feel better, the recovering voice asks immediately, "But for how long? And then what?" When the addict voice dwells on lost pleasures, the recovering voice speaks of the more solid rewards that drug use prevents. When the addict voice suggests that things might be different this time, the recovering voice should object that you have told yourself that before and deceived yourself. When the addict voice makes getting high sound glamorous, normal, or exciting, the recovering voice should remind you how ugly and sick getting high can be. For every "pro" that the addict voice puts forth, the recovering voice should have a strong list of "cons." But remember that the recovering voice is new and needs strengthening by other positive voices. If you carry on your debate only in solitude, you will start to lose it.

Distract

At the first thought of drug use, *do something else.* Useful distractions are ones that (a) you enjoy; (b) you can do at any time of the day and in many places; (c) are immediately rewarding (eating a favorite snack); (d) increase self-esteem (working out, doing chores); (e) require some concentration (building a shelf, writing a letter, reading a thriller); (f) are soothing and repetitive (doing the dishes, mopping the floor, folding the laundry); and (g) require energy and reduce tension (running).

Deep-Breathe

(1) Find a comfortable position in a quiet room. (2) Let go of muscle tension by contracting and then relaxing deeply each group of muscles (from your feet to your face). (3) Take a deep breath and hold it for as long as you can. Let it all out, and imagine that your tensions and drug urges are expelled with it. Feel yourself letting go of harmful attachments and coming to a peaceful place in yourself. Repeat this ten times. (4) As you let your breath flow in and out, you may begin focusing on a peaceful image, such as moonlight on a lake, or a peaceful word, such as "calm" or "serene." You will notice that all sorts of thoughts keep jumping in. Just let them flow past and keep returning to your image or word until it is your only focus. Notice the slowing of the breath. (After a few weeks of practice, you will be able to slow your breathing and heart rate rather quickly.) **You should practice this at least 20 minutes a day.**

Family and Partners in Early Recovery

Background

For better or for worse, recovery is likely to be a family affair. Some family members can provide the most powerful and meaningful support to the recovering person; they become part of the solution. Other loved ones who are uninformed about recovery or who are invested in the status quo of addiction can become part of the problem. Many clients enter treatment specifically to maintain the support of loved ones. Yet others must learn to make peace with the absence of supportive family members. When feelings about family are not part of the motivation to recover, they may be among the unavoidable triggers addressed in the previous session. The goals of this session are to explore ways of bringing the family into recovery and, where this is not possible, to help clients prevent family members from contributing to continued addiction.

Loved ones are best positioned to provide support if they understand the principles of addiction and the necessity for lifestyle change. Family members also need to know where they can turn for help (e.g., counselors, self-help groups) during the course of recovery. They need to understand why most clients need daily therapeutic contacts, why the foundation and the walls must be put in place, and why stopping all drug and alcohol use is a necessary first step—but *only* a first step—in recovery. Common family problems of early recovery include intense distrust, overprotectiveness, confusion about the difference between helping and "enabling" addiction, uncertainty about new family roles, drug use by family members, clients' unwillingness to reach out to potentially supportive family members, and family members' objections to the demands that treatment makes on clients' time and energy. This session is intended to address all of these issues in terms of the client's and the loved one's roles. Key family members are invited to this session so that these roles can be clarified. For example, family members can learn why and how they should help to keep a residence drug free; but everyone must understand that remaining abstinent is ultimately the client's responsibility. Similarly, clients and family members can help one another to understand the difference between supporting and controlling one another: Individuals can encourage one another to make use of various treatment and self-help resources by providing relevant information, praise, and a positive example, but each individual's attendance at recovery activities is up to that individual. One cannot force recovery on another.

Family members cannot support a client's recovery if they do not know about it. One of the client's first responsibilities is to be open with potentially supportive family members and to educate them. Yet some clients are reluctant to invite their loved ones to treatment sessions precisely because recovery-wise family members would pose additional barriers to future drug use. Their knowing what to look for would close doors to the old lifestyle. Leaders must address this reluctance well in advance of the session. As early as the Orientation session, inviting key family members to the family session should be presented as a vital step in each client's commitment to successful treatment and recovery. Having family members meet the leaders and participate in a session with the client and other members helps greatly to develop family support for the client's participation during the program. A reminder on the weekend prior to this session can greatly increase attendance by family members.

Family and Partners in *Early* Recovery (emphasis added) does not attempt to address the whole range of family recovery issues. Many family issues, such as conflicts caused by family members recovering at different rates and the delayed surfacing of buried resentments, should be addressed later in recovery, as they are in the Recovery Training and Self-Help family session (Zackon et al., 1991). Even those issues which are relevant to both the cessation phase and the longer-term group, such as the family's response to relapse, have different emphases at each stage. For example, any relapse in the first days of recovery might reasonably make a loved one question whether outpatient treatment is enough, but 4 months later a brief relapse might indicate a need for the client to become more involved in the recovering community and for loved ones to support this involvement.

When the occasional "blaming match" between clients and family members erupts, it is essential that leaders not appear to take sides. Leaders must demonstrate by example as well as precept that the time for blaming is past. Instead, leaders can join *all* parties by acknowledging the pain of past injuries, while pointing out the present common interest in recovery. During the course of this session, as members learn more about the common enemy of addiction, and as clients and their loved ones begin to understand one another's experiences, there is often a widespread sense of relief and forgiveness, of rebuildable bridges. At its best, Family and Partners in Early Recovery fosters an atmosphere of new hope and solidarity.

Materials

Handouts: "Robert and His Family"
            "Suggestions for the Family in Early Recovery"
Information about Al-Anon and Co-Anon

Key Points

1. All family members are affected by any member's addiction. Many clients enter treatment in order to retain family support, and loved ones can become key partners in recovery.

2. Family members will be in a better position to support recovery if they learn more about addiction and treatment and if they understand why a major commitment of time and energy is required by treatment. They must understand that the client is not "cured" because drug use has stopped. Stopping drug use is a necessary and commendable first step.

3. Each client is primarily responsible for his or her own recovery. The client must take the initiative to bring potentially supportive family members into treatment and to involve them in some of his or her new activities.

4. Many family members who are unwilling or unable to become "part of the solution" tend to become "part of the problem." Clients may have to avoid or detach from family members who continue to use drugs or otherwise tempt clients to use drugs.

5. Family members often need support independent of the client's. This can be provided by organizations such as Co-Anon. Family counseling can be another useful resource.

6. Relapses are dangerous but not unusual events in early recovery. They are setbacks that usually signify the need to redouble one's active commitment and to accept increased restrictions. Relapses at the cessa-

tion phase can indicate the need for a period of halfway house, day-care, or residential treatment. Family members as well as clients should have plans for responding to relapses. Productive plans spell out clear, enforceable limits. In crises, family members should focus on preserving their own well-being rather than on trying to protect or to control the addicted one.

Session at a Glance

1. **Welcome.**
2. **Introductions.**
3. **Topic and Goals:** The client's and family members' or companions' new roles in recovery.
4. **Check-In:** Members' family situations/questions. Assessing concerns.
5. **Brainstorming and Discussion of Problems:** Other family problems. Eliciting more participation and perspectives.
6. **Brainstorming and Discussion of Suggestions:** Suggestions for clients and for family members—sharing what has worked and what has not.
7. **Optional Fictional Case Study:** "Robert." Applying the suggestions.
8. **Review the Handout:** "Suggestions for the Family in Early Recovery." Summarizing the suggestions.
9. **Open Discussion:** Applying the handout suggestions to members' problems and/or to the problems of Robert's family.
10. **Closing Communication:** ("I love you"; "I need your help"; "Forgive me"; "Thank you"; etc.) Creating a sense of solidarity among family members and partners and with the group.

Format

Welcome to Family Members

Commend family members for coming and clients for inviting them. "This can be a new beginning, the start of pulling together instead of apart."

Introductions of Leaders and Members

Introductions at this point should be limited to giving first names and, for family members, relation to the client.

Topic and Goals

"Addiction affects whole families, not just addicts, and recovery is most effective when family members and clients are on the same team. Teams share priorities and assign roles. Yet addiction badly disrupts normal family roles, and in recovery these roles must be redefined. Family members often ask, 'How can I help?' And just as important, 'How can I avoid doing harm?' And clients are often uncertain what *they* can do with and for their family members. Tonight we will examine these questions: What is helpful? What is harmful? What is the loved one's responsibility? And what is the client's? We hope to arrive at some practical suggestions for some common family problems in early recovery, and we hope to bring everyone a bit closer in the larger 'family of recovery.' "

Check-In

Have each member introduce himself or herself again (first name and relation), and "describe very briefly a current family problem or present a question or issue for later discussion. This is not the time to explain your whole family history or to go deeply into complicated family issues. Our task now is just to get an early idea of where everyone is and to *label* or *headline* key concerns for later discussion."

Comments

This segment should take no more than 10 minutes, so leaders may have to paraphrase core concerns and defer further discussion to later in the session. Where the family's living situation is not clear, the leader should ask clarifying questions. As common issues emerge, the leader should underline that they are shared.

Brainstorming and Discussion of Problems

The leader should summarize the issues that have emerged so far and ask, "What are some other common family problems in recovery?"
    Exhibit the list on a large sheet of paper or a chalkboard.
    "For the rest of the session, we shall look more carefully at the effects of these issues on recovering families, and we shall try to come up with responses: ways that family members can help and avoid doing harm."

Brainstorming and Discussion of Suggestions

Reread aloud the list of family issues generated by the members and ask, "What has worked for you with these problems, and what hasn't worked? Let's generate a list of helpful suggestions for both clients and family members. These may include attitudes, actions, and general guidelines. When you offer a suggestion, label it as a suggestion for family members, for clients, or for both."

Distribute and Review Fictional Case Study (Optional)

"Robert and His Family"

Have members go around the room reading the case study aloud. Then have members analyze what is wrong with this family situation and why. Ask, "What is Robert's responsibility? What steps can he take?"

Case Study Analysis

This family is not communicating. Part of the problem is the family's ignorance about the needs of recovery. If Robert invited Annette to the family session of his treatment group, she would receive support for opposing Robert's hanging out with Willie, and she might learn how to confront him constructively. She would also learn "what goes on in those meetings" and that she can't "make" Robert relapse (or recover). Annette seems to be hanging on to a lot of understandable resentment about the past; at a family session, she could be directed to support groups and agencies that help with such feelings. The group would probably validate her need to communicate with Robert and to spend more time with him. She might be encouraged to express her needs directly. And she would learn that recovery must include some fun for the entire family.

The father would also benefit from attending a family session. He would get support for his position that Robert needs to prove himself by consistent actions before a loan would be appropriate. He would also be encouraged to express his reasons directly to Robert, and he might be helped to see that his being hurt by Willie's addiction has shaped his attitude toward Robert's recovery.

If Willie were willing and able to stay clean for a day in order to attend the family session, he would learn why the other family members are wary of Robert's hanging out with him. Finding out more about treatment could persuade Willie to try it, and he would certainly learn that having beers isn't supportive or harmless.

It is Robert's responsibility to educate the other family members, and he is avoiding it. He resents not being trusted, but he is not doing what is necessary to begin to regain trust. His keeping the other family members in the dark about the needs and priorities of recovery suggests shaky commitment on his own part. Perhaps he resists inviting Annette to the session because he is not ready to shut the door on drinking with Willie. And perhaps it is easier to blame his father for not understanding him than it would be to work to earn his father's trust and understanding.

Because Annette is the person closest to Robert, and because she wants to be supportive, inviting her to a family session is the most logical first step. Additional steps might include asking his group and counselors for help with his family situation, inviting his father and brother to the family session and/or to meet with his individual counselor, distributing program handouts to all of his family members, and entering couples and family counseling.

Distribute and Review the Handout

"Suggestions for the Family in Early Recovery"

Comments

Indicate the points on the handout that have been anticipated in the previous discussion and emphasize the points that have not been anticipated.

Open Discussion

Have members apply the suggestions from the handout to their own identified family issues. If the discussion is slow, have members apply the suggestions to "Robert" and his family.

Closing Communication

Ask members to make an essential communication to a loved one, whether or not that loved one is present. Offer a menu of core communications (making clear that members need not limit themselves to the list):

"I love you."
"I'm sorry."
"Thank you."
"I need your help."
"I'm angry at you."
"I forgive you."

Point out that recovery is a new beginning based upon honest communication and cooperation. The unity of recovery groups helps to promote new family unity—and vice versa.

Thank everyone again for coming. State that this session should be only the beginning of family participation in recovery. Review any other family services available in the agency or community.

Al-Anon and Co-Anon meeting lists should be available on a table for family members. All of the cessation program handouts should also be available. The leaders should plan to remain about 20 minutes after the session ends to answer family members' questions.

HANDOUT 8.1: Robert and His Family

Robert: "Between giving up all my friends, getting back to work, attending recovery meetings every night, and putting up with all the crap at home, recovery seems almost too much. I swallowed my pride and asked my father for a loan to get a truck, but he refused and acted as if he thought I was still out there using.

"My wife, Annette, is worse. She heard that I went to the ballgame with Willie the other night, and she almost flipped out. Sure, Willie is a user, but he also happens to be my brother. Why should Annette begrudge me a ballgame? She's sure no fun to be around.

"My treatment group is having a session with family members, but I really have no one to invite. My father wouldn't come, Willie is too busy, and it would make Annette too nervous. She worries enough about my relapsing as it is, and once she learned how many dangers there are to worry about . . . forget it."

Annette: "I want to support Robert in recovery, but I am not sure what to do. He seems to have such a short fuse lately, and I am afraid that I will say something that will make him relapse. I know that I shouldn't have gotten angry when I heard he was hanging around with his brother again, but Willie gets crazy, and he makes Robert crazy.

"Besides, I'd like to know why he doesn't hang around more with *me*. After his staying out all night getting high and doing God knows what else for so long, and after his using up all of our savings, you'd think that he'd want to make it up to me. That is, when he isn't at one of his ten thousand meetings. I wonder what really goes on at those meetings."

Father: "I knew it. As soon as I wouldn't give him money, Robert started acting like that no-good Willie again. He even *defended* Willie. Is that what they teach them in treatment? I might consider making him a loan, but only after he's proven that he won't throw the money away and that he will repay me."

Willie: "I'm really proud of Robert. Maybe if he can do it, I can do it. At any rate, I'd like to find out more about treatment. I know that dad and Annette think I'll pull Robert down, but I think that just having a couple of beers together and not doing any coke is a supportive thing for both of us."

What mistakes is this family making? What is a next step for Robert? What would be some other productive steps?

HANDOUT 8.2: Suggestions for the Family in Early Recovery*

For the Recovering Addict

1. You've earned distrust, and you must re-earn trust.
2. Help your family learn about recovery, what your groups and meetings are like, and what you are trying to accomplish in treatment.
3. Invite your family to family sessions, and make opportunities for them to meet your new friends.
4. Be open to "meeting" your loved ones anew. You may see sides of them now that you have never noticed.
5. Try to make at least one family member a "partner in recovery," someone you can be fully open with and on whom you can rely.
6. Do as much for yourself as you can without relying on family. Take on some extra responsibilities to express thanks to those who support your attendance at recovery meetings. But don't be too proud to ask for help when necessary.

Remember: Your recovery depends on you, *not* on your family.

For the Other Family Members

1. Keep your home free of drugs, psychoactive medicines, and alcohol.
2. The client is not "cured" by stopping drug use. Full recovery requires daily therapy for many months and continuing support for years.
3. Learn more about recovery and the family. Attend appropriate treatment sessions with your recovering person.
4. Have a written contract spelling out the self-protective measures that you are prepared to carry through in the event of relapse. Make your needs and rules clear, but without lecturing.
5. Get outside support through groups of recovering families or family counselors.
6. Be open to meeting the client's new friends and joining in some social-recreational activities.

Remember: You cannot make someone recover, and you should not try to protect someone from normal responsibilities. The most that you can do is to offer support and love, and to keep yourself well.

For Both

Honest discussions do not have to turn into arguments about who is right or wrong. Communicate, compromise, and do things together. Be patient. Lasting changes take time, but they are worthwhile.

*This handout was adapted from Zackon, F., McAuliffe, W.E., & Ch'ien, J.M.N. (1985). *Addict aftercare: Recovery Training and Self-Help* (DHHS Pub. No. (ADM)85-1314). Rockville, MD: National Institute on Drug Abuse, p. 98.

Making Changes

Background

In some ways, demonstrating the need for behavioral change is the easy part of cessation training. Knowing that one must change does not ensure that one can or will change, and knowing what changes are needed may be useless if one does not know how to make the changes. It is normal to avoid frustration, anxiety, and unpleasantness and to hold on to familiar rewards. Even cocaine-addicted clients who understand quite well that they need to stop drinking or to end a relationship with a drug user may be stuck, unwilling or unable to act on their knowledge. Typically, resistant clients hope that half-measures will suffice. They tell themselves that a dangerous relationship need not be broken off completely or that drinking can be limited to weekends or special occasions. Even clients who recognize that more thorough changes are needed often put them off. "Every afternoon I tell myself I should go to a meeting, and every night I end up alone with the TV" is a too-common confession. In the face of predictable resistance to change, the message of this session is clear: "Now is the time to find a way to reduce that resistance."

In our conception, treatment must not merely tell one what to do, but must also help one to do it. Both clinicians and clients must acknowledge honestly that major behavioral changes are difficult. If the cessation group is not made safe for expressing resistances, they may be driven "underground." Intimidated by others' reports of success, clients may clam up or falsify progress. The more helpless one feels, the less likely one will be able to ask for help. Rather than allowing members to feel like hopeless failures, we must show that normal resistances may be

204

overcome by practical strategies. The strategies that we use include breaking larger objectives down into manageable steps, making the most of natural and artificial incentives and rewards, and using the accompaniment, encouragement, applause, experiences, and examples of other group members. Even if this session does not result immediately in a productive action for every member, everyone should be left with a sense that group support can empower individual change.

Materials

Handouts: "A Key Change Checklist"
"Making Hard Changes Easier: Tips for Taking Steps"
"Steps of Change"
"Case Study: Roger"
Pencils
Chalkboard or large sheet of paper

Key Points

1. It is normal to resist change. In order to stop chronic drug use, one must replace familiar rewards and solutions with untried and frightening alternatives.

2. Small pockets of resistance to change commonly undermine recovery. Such pockets often indicate deeper resistance, for the lifestyle of addiction is an integrated structure, each part of which leads to the others.

3. By acknowledging their resistances, recovering people can get help in overcoming them. Openly discussing difficulties makes them seem less shameful and helps to place them in rational perspective. Conversely, clients often increase resistances by not discussing them.

4. Among the techniques for overcoming resistance to change in a group are encouragement, group approval, group pressure, successful models, and using the group's experience and wisdom to scale down overambitious goals to small steps.

5. Some people can plunge into a new lifestyle while others must "test the waters." Because it is important to experience success in early recovery, one should not overreach oneself. However, one must take *some* action in the initial phase of treatment when one has the support, the guidance, and the momentum to do so.

Session at a Glance

1. **Topic and Goals:** Resistance to change as a normal obstacle and steps to overcome it.

2. **Open Sharing:** General experiences of resisting change.
3. **Open Discussion:** The general reasons for resistance.
4. **Handout:** "A Key Change Checklist." Some necessary changes for recovery.
5. **Open Discussion:** Identifying specific individual resistances already overcome and still to be overcome.
6. **Open Sharing:** Beginning to define individual steps, necessary changes.
7. **Handouts:** Strategies for making change easier.
8. **Next Step:** Announcing individual steps and strategies for making them easier to the group.
9. **Optional Case Study:** "Roger." Illustrating unwillingness to make changes.

Format

Topic and Goals

"Our topic for tonight is finding ways to help you make changes for recovery. We talk a lot about these changes, yet you already know, or you soon will find out, that despite your best intentions, making these changes is not easy or certain. People tend to cling to their old ways until they are forced to let go or until they start to experience the rewards of new ways. I am certain that you can point to some area where you are hanging back or hoping that you can get away with a little less than the program has prescribed."

At this point, ask for a show of hands of members who have "at least a bit" of resistance to change. Poll individual members about "where you are hanging back." Unguarded responses may be facilitated by first asking the peer leader to recall his or her areas of resistance in early recovery.

"Before too long this resistance to change will limit your recovery, and frustration and disappointment about lack of progress will replace your hope that you can make it without changing. Tonight each of you will speak about a personal obstacle or sticking point. Then the group will arrive at general strategies for making difficult changes a bit easier. Finally, each person will apply our strategies to his or her area of difficulty and define a small doable step."

Open Sharing

"Who has had difficulty making desired life changes in areas other than drug addiction? For example, losing weight, saving money, changing jobs, or ending a relationship? Why was the change difficult?"

Allow all members with relevant experiences to contribute. Ask frequently, "What were you giving up? What were you afraid of? How did you avoid changing?"

At the blackboard or on a large sheet of paper, begin to generate two lists: one list of the factors that hold people back from making desired changes (e.g., fear of rejection or incompetence, loss of familiar comforts, not knowing where to begin); and another list of strategies people use to avoid and resist change (e.g., procrastination, rationalization, half-measures, wishful thinking). Accept lack of "willpower" as an answer, but go beyond it to find out what is at the root of willpower or its lack. Ask, "What finally helped you change? How did it feel? Did you have unfounded fears?"

Open Discussion

"How are these experiences similar to making the changes that we have recommended in this program? Give examples."

The leader can prompt, "What about stopping drinking or going to nightclubs? What about breaking off with people who use drugs? What about coming clean with loved ones? What about participating fully in the recovering community?"

Keep the discussion general here. The principal purpose of this segment is to identify difficulty and resistance as common and predictable.

As soon as the main points of this segment are made and summarized (see points 1, 2, and 5 of the Key Points, above), the leader should move on. Together, this and the previous segment should take no more than 15 minutes.

Distribute and Review the Handout

"A Key Change Checklist"

Read the directions aloud, and ask whether everyone understands how the checklist is scored. Leave time for members to reflect on the items and complete the checklist. Emphasize the need for self-honesty, for "one cannot begin to work on a problem until one admits that it is a problem."

Open Discussion

Allow a brief discussion of responses to the checklist. When a member reveals a self-rating, ask the group if it feels the rating is justified based on the facts given. Is more information required?

In the discussion, make sure that members who identify as "number 3" (Not started yet, but don't expect problems) are being realistic. Probe their reasons for not having begun yet. Also, where appropriate, probe those who choose number 2 (Making concrete progress, don't need extra help) and number 6 (Doesn't apply).

Now announce that for the remainder of the session "we are going to break further into the number 4 (See the need, but is hard) and number 5 (Seems unnecessary) items."

Open Sharing

Have each member discuss his or her major "See the need, but is hard" item. If people cannot identify a primary difficulty, the leaders may inquire about probable difficulties. Members may identify more than one area, but for the purposes of defining a step in this session they should be encouraged to examine a single area closely.

Brainstorming

Ask the members who have dealt successfully with any of the "See the need, but is hard" items mentioned in the Open Sharing to contribute to a group-generated list of coping strategies. Ask, "What helped? Let's create a list of tips and strategies for making changes a little easier."

Distribute and Review the Handouts

After the group has made its own list, distribute "Making Hard Changes Easier: Tips for Taking Steps" and "Steps of Change."

Indicate the points on the "Making Hard Changes Easier" handout that were anticipated in the foregoing discussion, but pay special attention to the points that were not mentioned. Then, in reviewing the specific steps on the "Steps for Change" handout, ask for each step a member selects from or adds to the list, "What 'tips' from the other handout would be especially useful in taking this step? Who has had firsthand experience?"

The handouts, taken together, summarize the main points of the session.

Next Step

The Next Step exercise grows out of the handouts. Having chosen one of the steps on the "Steps of Change" handout or added their own primary step to the list, members should each announce a proposed step to the group. Even a very small step should be presented as a *goal* if there is reason to doubt the member's ability to perform it during the current week. Leaders must continually counsel realism, specificity, and practicality in the definition of steps. The leader should remind everyone that the group will follow up on the step at the Problems and Progress session.

Optional Case Study

"Roger"

Time permitting, introduce this segment by announcing, "Now we will work on the number 5's."

Comments

The case study is intended to illustrate Key Point 2.

Roger is comfortable in his old job and his old social role, which have become intertwined. Beyond comfort, he is probably still excited by the proximity to the old lifestyle. He is flirting with danger, but denial protects his resistance. Because he doesn't want to change, he tells himself that he doesn't have to change.

He enjoys his "image" at work, and the desire to hang on to familiar people and familiar pleasures has blinded him to the fact that the 5 years of his employment coincide with the worst period of his addiction.

The danger is all around him. Even if one of his old acquaintances doesn't offer him drugs, Roger will remain aware of how easily available the drugs are. If Roger knows that cherished friends are getting high, that may make getting high seem more desirable and more harmless to him, especially if he has had a beer or two. Furthermore, when a client is surrounded by the sights and sounds of the old lifestyle every night, his or her craving will often be stimulated without the client's being aware of the specific cause.

Roger is right about the program's advice to have good times and to socialize, but the program says that the social recreation must be drug and alcohol free. Part of Roger's problem may be his fear of the discomfort and inconvenience of making new friends in the recovering community and committing himself to an untried way of life.

Finally, Roger hasn't mentioned his resistance to the group, because he suspects what its response would be. This sort of omission is itself cause for concern, and it defeats the purpose of treatment. Roger needs to remember that commitment to recovery is best expressed by actions, not how solid one feels.

Suggested Strategies

1. Talk about it. Seek out his counselor, group leaders and, especially, other recovering people who have learned through experience that a similar job change was necessary after all.
2. Examine the source of his resistance. Does he secretly enjoy and long for more parts of the old lifestyle? Has he been reluctant to try new drug-free social recreation and involvement in the recovering community?
3. Examine the possibilities for relapse in great detail. Have any of the circumstances of bartending contributed to past relapses, past lapses in control, or binges?
4. Define a red flag. What behavior that he now thinks is unlikely would convince him that he was wrong? Define a plan should the behavior occur. Whom should he tell immediately? How might he increase his commitment with a commitment step?
5. Have him imagine himself in a different job. What might be some of the benefits? And he could begin to look into the job listings in the paper and ask around about different jobs, without committing himself to changing jobs yet.

Ownwork

Taking one's next step is the main ownwork assignment. But an additional or alternative step for everyone can be to target an area on "The Daily Chart" where one needs improvement and to report on one's findings in the Problems and Progress group.

HANDOUT 9.1: A Key Change Checklist

This is an exercise in recovery awareness and self-honesty. Circle the number that best describes the status for you for each of the key changes listed below. If you can think of other important changes that apply to you, add them to the end of the list.

1 = Already done; 2 = Making concrete progress, don't need extra help; 3 = Not started yet, but don't expect problems; 4 = See the need, but is (or will be) hard — need help; 5 = Seems unnecessary, or unwilling (unable) to do this; 6 = Doesn't apply.

1 2 3 4 5 6   Stop using drugs and drinking.

1 2 3 4 5 6   Stop dealing.

1 2 3 4 5 6   Stop seeing active users.

1 2 3 4 5 6   Establish a drug-free place to live.

1 2 3 4 5 6   Establish a drug-free or safe workplace (change jobs or get help at work).

1 2 3 4 5 6   Stop attending bars or nightclubs.

1 2 3 4 5 6   Let someone hold your cash and/or have your paycheck automatically deposited to a safe account.

1 2 3 4 5 6   Tell a key person, friends, spouse, boss, or family member about your recovery — someone whose knowledge would make it harder for you to use and who might give you support.

1 2 3 4 5 6   Bring a key loved one to the family session and individual counseling.

1 2 3 4 5 6   Stop going unnecessarily to a place or engaging in an activity linked to past drug use.

1 2 3 4 5 6   Commit yourself to a safe weekend activity with other recovering people.

1 2 3 4 5 6   Attend a 12-step fellowship meeting and identify yourself.

1 2 3 4 5 6   Break off with or set clear, enforceable rules with an intimate who uses.

1 2 3 4 5 6   Tell a counselor or group leader about a problem that you haven't yet mentioned.

HANDOUT 9.2: Making Hard Changes Easier: Tips for Taking Steps

Change is never easy, and the thoroughgoing changes necessary for secure and satisfying recovery from addiction can be especially difficult. However, they are worth it. The following list of suggestions to ease difficult changes is based both on behavioral science and on the concrete experience of many recovering people.

- Talk about it. Examining a resistance openly often makes it smaller and sometimes brings surprising solutions. Others have dealt with the same problems.

- Tell the group what you are going to do. Then reward yourself by telling the group when you have followed through.

- If you are afraid to take action, ask yourself what is the worst that could happen if you make the change. Would you be better or worse off than you are now? Separate real from imaginary results.

- Consider the advantages of taking action. Would it help recovery? How would it make you feel about yourself, and how would it make others feel about you?

- Discuss a desired action with someone who has taken a similar action. What helped the other? What were the pluses?

- Plan a special treat or good time for yourself when the action is completed.

- Ask for company. Having others along can help you to perform certain key steps such as attending your first NA meeting or throwing out your stash. (*Two* people should accompany you in the latter step.)

- Don't seek the ideal action or the perfect person or moment. Better to take *some* step now and then build on it or find a better step later.

- Examine your proposed action with your counselors and group members and break it down to a practically doable step or series of steps. Sometimes people confuse steps and goals. Resolving to do what you think you *should* be able to do can be setting yourself up for failure. "Small" successes are important. You should take credit for them. Making an early success will improve your confidence and get you moving.

HANDOUT 9.3: Steps of Change

Here are some examples of doable steps for specific goals. Target one important but doable step and focus on it. Remember that these are only *sample* steps. If your own key step and goal are not included, add them to the bottom of the list and tell the group about them.

Step: Throw out all mood-altering substances and paraphernalia.
Goal: Reduce craving, secure abstinence, and increase commitment to recovery.

Step: Tell a family member who is in AA about your recovery.
Goal: Get closer to solid people / Expand support network.

Step: Ask someone trusted to hold your cash.
Goal: Reduce danger and craving until you can handle cash.

Step: Have your paycheck automatically deposited.
Goal: Make paydays safer.

Step: Announce at a recovery meeting that you are trying to get away from a drug-using partner and that you will need a recovering roommate.
Goal: Separate from users (partner, friend, spouse); make new friends; find a new residence.

Step: Tell a boss about recovery.
Goal: Make work safer and more supportive.

Step: Stay 10 minutes after group to talk with leaders and members.
Goal: Become more involved in the group.

Step: Change your telephone number. Buy a new address book; throw out the old one.
Goal: End contact with users. Increase commitment.

Step: Announce at an NA meeting that you are looking for a safe job.
Goal: Change to a safe job.

A Key Step for You:
Your Goal:

HANDOUT 9.4: Case Study: Roger

Roger is working as a bartender. The group leader has suggested that bartending might not support recovery. However, Roger doesn't buy it. He figures that even though he has been surrounded by drinkers for years in this job, it has never interested him in drinking. And he claims never to have taken a drink on the job.

Actually, he has decided that the job puts him in a good position to see the effect of drinking and drugging on others. Sometimes an old acquaintance will show up acting like a fool, and Roger can see a reflection of his own old behavior.

Roger also wonders if the group leader realizes that good jobs don't grow on trees. Roger has been in the same place for almost 5 years. They appreciate him there; everyone knows him and vice versa. In fact, as long as he works there he would never forget where drugs took him, because his partying has become legendary, and now everyone is amazed by and supportive of his recovery.

Roger resists making another suggested change as well. Occasionally, he still watches Sunday football and plays Friday night cards with guys he used to party with, and he sees no reason to stop. But he hasn't even mentioned this to his group or counselor, because he knows what their reaction would be. The group just doesn't realize what a nice bunch of guys his old friends are. They would never try to get him high. And doesn't the program say that it's healthy to socialize and enjoy yourself?

Most of Roger's old friends have stopped doing coke since they saw what happened to Roger. So Roger feels that he is a good influence and that it probably wouldn't hurt to have an occasional beer with them — just to show that he hasn't become some sort of fanatic. An occasional beer would be only normal, he thinks.

Can you think of any tips or strategies that would help Roger?

A Road Map to Recovery: Where You Are and Where You're Headed

Background

A person doesn't need a map to drive to a long-familiar home. Steering there becomes almost automatic. Similarly, the long-addicted person returns automatically to the familiar "home" of getting high. However, in order to arrive at a new destination, the addict must pay attention and think ahead. A thoughtful look ahead can show how far one has come, how far one has to go, and whether one is on course.

The "road map" presented in this session is not intended to be rigid or definitive. In practice, the timing of the phases varies widely among individuals, and at a given moment, the phases are likely to overlap. The map is intended rather to suggest the probable groupings and sequences of the key events of recovery. Members can use it to integrate their own experiences with their new knowledge of recovery. The very process of actively deciding what belongs where will give members a better sense of the big picture and of the benefits of persisting.

Materials

Handouts: "Defining the Phases of Recovery"
           "The Phases of Recovery"

Large pad or blackboard
Drawing paper
Colored pencils

Key Points

1. Just as there is a typical progression of addiction, there is a typical course of recovery. Although there are many individual variations, as people move forward at different rates and with different styles, experiences are similar enough to provide guidance to beginners.

2. Having a larger picture of recovery can help addicts identify where they are currently, what is "normal," and what they need to work on in order to move ahead.

3. Learning to recognize the common pitfalls and signposts of recovery can help addicts to stay on course.

4. An overview of the "new neighborhood" of recovery can show how different it is from the old neighborhood of addiction—and how much more attractive.

Session at a Glance

1. **Topic and Goals:** Members examine the stages of recovery. The goal is to figure out at what stage of recovery they are and where they want to be.

2. **Check-In:** Members relate an important turning point in their recoveries.

3. **Self-Drawing and Discussion:** Members' views of themselves before, during, and after treatment.

4. **Handouts:** Summaries of phases of recovery and common emotions and events associated with them.

5. **Written Exercise:** Members assess the stages of their own recoveries.

6. **Next Step:** Members evaluate their assessments and plan a next step.

7. **Ownwork:** Integration of future elements of recovery into the present.

Format

Topic and Goals

"Recovery is similar in important ways for most people. There are common stages and turning points, and some well-known pitfalls and help stations. Tonight we'll look at some of these. The purpose of the session is to help you apply what you have learned so far and to determine where you really are in recovery. Once you understand how far you've come, you will be better able to decide what should come next for you.

"We know that it can be uncomfortable to look too far ahead when you are struggling with staying clean *today*. But an occasional look ahead can bring today into clearer focus. It can help you see *how* and *why* to stay clean today."

Check-In

"Can you think of a turning point or landmark in your recovery that you have recently dealt with or are dealing with now— something that has made or will make a great difference? If you cannot think of *any* turning points or landmarks, either past, present, or future, then just mention some event from your week that gives the group an idea of where you are in recovery."

Comments

This check-in is intended to stimulate thinking about current issues in the context of a coherent recovery process. It should also generate a fund of events that can be tapped later in the "map-making" segment of the session.

The leader may have to stimulate participation by first asking the group at large for examples of turning points in recovery. The leaders may supply examples if they are not forthcoming from the members. For example: "How about the day Luis admitted he was an addict and told his family about his recovery?" Or: "What about when Hannah broke up with her addicted boyfriend?"

Leaders can also stimulate members' thinking by directing them to the key areas of recovery: "What about family issues? What about old friends? What about new friends? What about a safe residence? What about work and money? What about intimate relationships?"

This check-in may be longer than the average check-in. If it is engaging members appropriately, allow it to run for up to 20 minutes.

Self-Drawing and Discussion

"Using the colored pencils and pads, draw three pictures of yourself. Call them, 'Past,' 'Present,' and 'Future.' The past should show you just before entering treatment. The present should show you now, and it should include some symbols of your current progress and problems in recovery. The future should show you a year or two into recovery. Include meaningful settings, symbols, and other people in each picture. Don't worry if you can't draw well. Make a stick cartoon if you like, or just use words for things you cannot draw. Have fun with it."

When the drawings are complete, have members volunteer to show and explain their drawings. If the group is small enough (eight members or fewer), have everyone "show and tell." Pay special attention to the elements that must be added to or removed from each member's picture of the present in order to realize a realistic picture of the future.

Comments

Laughter during this exercise can help to lighten a sometimes difficult and self-searching session. At the same time, clear reminders of the purpose of the exercise should keep members focused on the task.

Distribute and Review the Handouts

"Defining the Phases of Recovery" and "The Phases of Recovery"

Make a column for each phase on the blackboard or on a large sheet of paper. Review the main kinds of events that were mentioned in check-in and point out those that correspond to items on the handout. Events, landmarks, or turning points that are not on the handout should be added to the appropriate column.

Written Exercise

At this point, ask members to work individually, marking those items that they have already gone through with a "P" (for "Past") or an "N" (for "Now"). Items that were not or are not yet relevant to an individual should be left unmarked. Allow time for most members to complete their sheets and to reflect on them.

Comments

Make sure that everyone understands the five phases of the handout. Point out that in practice the phases overlap and that individuals may be "mainly" in a particular phase while "partly" in another.

The leaders must remind the group throughout this exercise that the person who deserves the most credit is the one who is honest about his or her status and who keeps pushing ahead steadily.

Next Step

"How do you feel about where you are, and what is your next step?"

Ownwork

Choose one important item from your *next* phase. Add it to your drawing of yourself at present. Also decide whether anything in your drawing of yourself now must be eliminated before you can move on to your future picture.

HANDOUT 1O.1: Defining the Phases of Recovery

Recovery is a process of growth and development that involves changes in every area of life. In each phase, your entire style of learning and coping can change.

Entering Treatment. You have just made the break with drugs and are entering treatment. You are confused and scared. You are experiencing the symptoms of cocaine withdrawal: depression, craving, and an inability to experience pleasure. You want help desperately.

Ambivalence. You are on the fence, pulled at once backward into addiction and forward to change. During this phase, you are feeling out the possibility of a drug-free life, but you are still full of self-doubt and afraid to burn your bridges.

Commitment could also be called "Forward." During this phase, you begin to act instead of just wishing and talking. You work hard at treatment, making safety second nature, and building new relationships. As you cut off your exits, you find yourself more securely part of a recovering community. You are also starting to feel more at home with normal day-to-day routines.

New Frontiers is a phase of new learning and expansion. Now you begin to cope with situations that you had been putting off. The walls are gradually lowered and you branch out into more areas of a full, normal life.

Citizenship used to be called "Integration." During this phase you consolidate your gains, and you become absorbed in achieving normal goals and satisfactions. Self-knowledge and self-acceptance increase. You begin to feel like part of the larger community.

Not everyone deals with all of the items on the accompanying list, and not everyone deals with them in the same phase or in exactly the same order. Some people will have issues that are not on the list at all. Yet the overall process is uniform enough so that individuals starting out can learn much from "mapping" it.

HANDOUT 10.2: The Phases of Recovery*

I. Entering Treatment
Think a lot about using; craving
Confused, depressed, scared, desperate
Life seems bleak, gray
Trouble enjoying anything; can't have a good time
Emotional roller coaster; moody
Want someone to trust
Feel alone, isolated
Jittery; trouble sleeping

II. Ambivalence
Resist making all the needed changes
Recovery desirable, but don't want to cut off retreat
Back and forth, neither here nor there
Enthusiasm grows but so does doubt
Want to change, but not sure if you can
Awkward around recovering people
Learning about addiction and recovery
Starting to avoid some main dangers, but maybe not all
A lot of craving when drugs available
Who am I?

III. Commitment
Focus primarily on recovery
Cut off user friends for good
Commitment steps: close doors to drug use
Implement treatment suggestions faithfully
Start regular daily schedule with meetings
Start to make new friends
Renew positive family relationships
Get a sponsor
Join "home" NA group
Open up, proud of recovery

IV. New Frontiers
Begin coping with sex and money
Explore new social and fun activities
Get out of debt
New career possibilities
Making big decisions that had been on hold
Marrying, children, saving for house
Leadership role in NA
Craving gone in once tough situations

V. Citizenship
Active in larger nonrecovering community
Help others in fellowships
Achieve family and financial goals
Can reveal addict past without shame
Feel like a citizen

*This handout was adapted from Zackon, F., McAuliffe, W.E., & Ch'ien, J.M.N. (1985). *Addict aftercare: Recovery Training and Self-Help* (DHHS Pub. No. (ADM)85-1314). Rockville, MD: National Institute on Drug Abuse, p. 65.

References

Akers, R.L., Burgess, R.L., & Johnson, W.T. (1968). Opiate use, addiction and relapse. *Social Problems, 15*(4), 459–469.

American Psychiatric Association. (1987). *Diagnostic and statistical manual of mental disorders* (3rd ed., rev). Washington, DC: American Psychiatric Association.

Amini, F., Zinberg, N.J., Burke, E.L., & Salasnek, S. (1989). A controlled study of inpatient vs. outpatient treatment of delinquent drug abusing adolescents: One year results. *Comprehensive Psychiatry, 23*(5), 436–444.

Anker, A.L., & Crowley, T.J. (1982). Use of contingency contracts in specialty clinics for cocaine abuse. In L.S. Harris (Ed.), *Problems of drug dependence, 1981* (NIDA Research Monograph 41). Rockville, MD: National Institute on Drug Abuse.

Annis, H.M. (1986). A relapse prevention model for treatment of alcoholics. In W.R. Miller & N. Heather (Eds.), *Treating addictive behaviors: Processes of change.* New York: Plenum.

Annis, H.M, & Davis, C.S. (1988). Self-efficacy and the prevention of alcoholic relapse: Initial findings from a treatment trial. In B. Baker & D. Canon (Eds.), *Assessment and treatment of addictive disorders.* New York: Praeger.

Ashery, R.S., & McAuliffe, W.E. (1992). Implementation issues and techniques in randomized trials of outpatient psychosocial treatments for drug abusers: Recruitment of subjects. *American Journal of Drug and Alcohol Abuse, 18*(3), 305–329.

Bandura, A., & Walters, R. (1963). *Social learning and personality development.* New York: Holt, Rinehart & Winston.

Biernacki, P. (1986). *Pathways from heroin addiction: Recovery without treatment.* Philadelphia: Temple University Press.

Bigelow, G.E., Stitzer, M.L., & Liebson, I.A. (1984). The role of behavioral contingency management in drug abuse treatment. In J. Grabowski, M.L. Stitzer, & J.E. Henningfield (Eds.), *Behavioral intervention techniques in drug abuse treatment.* Rockville, MD: National Institute on Drug Abuse.

Corcoran, K.J., & Carney, M.D. (1988). Situational preference and alcohol consumption: Heavier drinkers prefer drinking opportunities. *Psychology of Addictive Behaviors, 2*(1), 14–19.

223

Daley, D.C. (1987). Relapse prevention with substance abusers: Clinical issues and myths. *Social Work, 32*(2), 138–142.

Deese, J., & Hulse, S.H. (1967). *The psychology of learning* (3rd ed.). New York: McGraw-Hill.

Drug Abuse Warning Network. (1989). *Annual data 1988: Data from the Drug Abuse Warning Network*. Rockville, MD: National Institute on Drug Abuse.

Edgehill Newport. (no date). Patient outcomes from a four-year study. Newport, RI: Edgehill Newport.

Edwards, G., Arif, A., & Hodgson, R. (1982). Nomenclature and classification of drug- and alcohol-related problems: A shortened version of a WHO memorandum. *British Journal of Addiction, 77*(1), 3–20.

Gawin, F. (1991). Cocaine addiction: Psychology and neurophysiology. *Science, 251* (5001), 1580–1586.

Gerstein, D.R., & Henrick, H.J. (Eds.). (1990). *Treating drug problems* (Vol. 1). Washington, DC: National Academy Press.

Grabowski, J., & O'Brien, C.P. (1981). Conditioning factors in opiate use. In N. Mello (Ed.), *Advances in substance abuse: Behavioral and biological research.* Greenwich, CT: JAI Press.

Halliday, K. (1992). *The efficacy of a modified dynamic group therapy for cocaine abuse: A test of Khantzian's self-medication hypothesis.* Unpublished manuscript, New School for Social Research.

Hasin, D.S., Grant, B.F., Endicott, J., & Harford, T.C. (1988). Cocaine and heroin dependence compared in poly-drug abusers. *American Journal of Public Health, 78*(5), 567–569.

Hayashida, M., Alterman, A.I., McLellan, A.T., O'Brien, C.P., Purtill, J.J., Volpicelli, J.R., Raphaelson, A.H., & Hall, C.P. (1989). Comparative effectiveness and costs of inpatient and outpatient detoxification of patients with mild-to-moderate alcohol withdrawal syndrome. *New England Journal of Medicine, 320*(6), 358–365.

Kang, S.Y., Kleinman, P.H., Woody, G.E., Millman, R.B., Todd, T.C., Kemp, J., & Lipton, D.S. (1991). Outcomes for cocaine abusers after once-a-week psychosocial therapy. *American Journal of Psychiatry, 148*(5), 630–635.

Khantzian, E.J., Halliday K.S., & McAuliffe, W.E. (1990). *Addiction and the vulnerable self: Modified dynamic group therapy for substance abusers.* New York: Guilford.

Lindesmith, A.R. (1947). *Opiate addiction.* Bloomington, IN: Principia Press.

Lindesmith, A.R. (1968). *Addiction and opiates.* Chicago: Aldine.

Malow, R.M. (1989). Treatment of drug abuse problems: A broad-spectrum approach. In P. Keller & S.R. Heyman (Eds.), *Innovations in clinical practice: A source book.* Sarasota, FL: Professional Resource Exchange.

Marlatt, G.A. (1979). A cognitive–behavioral model of the relapse process. In N.A. Krasnegor (Ed.), *Behavioral analysis in treatment of substance abuse.* Rockville, MD: National Institute on Drug Abuse.

Marlatt, G.A., & Gordon, J.R. (1980). Determinants of relapse: Implications for the maintenance of behavior change. In P.O. Davidson & S.M. Davidson (Eds.), *Behavioral medicine: Changing health styles.* New York: Brunner/Mazel.

Marlatt, G.A., & Gordon, J.R. (Eds.). (1985). *Relapse prevention: Maintenance strategies in the treatment of addictive behaviors*. New York: Guilford.

McAuliffe, W.E. (1989). From theory to practice: The planned treatment of drug users. *International Journal of the Addictions, 24*(6), 527–608.

McAuliffe, W.E. (1990). A randomized controlled trial of Recovery Training and Self-Help for opioid addicts. *Journal of Psychoactive Drugs, 22*(2), 197–209.

McAuliffe, W.E., Albert, J., Cordill-London, G., & McGarraghy, T.K. (1990–1991). Contributions to a social conditioning model of cocaine recovery. *International Journal of the Addictions, 25*(9A & 10A), 1145–1181.

McAuliffe, W.E., Breer, P., White, N., Spino, C., Goldsmith, L., Robel, S., & Byam, L. (1988). *A drug abuse treatment and intervention plan for Rhode Island*. Cranston: Division of Substance Abuse, Rhode Island Department of Mental Health, Retardation and Hospitals.

McAuliffe, W.E., & Ch'ien, J.M.N. (1986). Recovery Training and Self-Help: A relapse-prevention program for treated opiate addicts. *Journal of Substance Abuse Treatment, 3*(1): 9–20.

McAuliffe, W.E., & Gordon, R.A. (1974). A test of Lindesmith's theory of addiction: The frequency of euphoria among long-term addicts. *American Journal of Sociology, 79*(4), 795–840.

McAuliffe, W.E., & Gordon, R.A. (1980). Reinforcement and the combination of effects: Summary of a theory of opiate addiction. In D.J. Lettieri, M. Sayers, & H.W. Pearson (Eds.), *Theories on drug abuse: Selected contemporary perspectives* (NIDA Research Monograph 30). Rockville, MD: National Institute on Drug Abuse.

McLellan, A.T. (1983). Patient characteristics associated with outcome. In J.R. Cooper, F. Altman, B.S. Brown, & D. Czechowicz (Eds.), *Research on the treatment of narcotic addiction*. Rockville, MD: National Institute on Drug Abuse.

Meyer, R.E., & Mirin, S.M. (1978). *The heroin stimulus: Implications for a theory of addiction*. New York: Plenum.

Miller, N.S., Millman, R.B., & Keskinen, S. (1990). Outcome at six and twelve months post inpatient treatment for cocaine and alcohol dependence. *Advances in Alcohol and Substance Abuse, 9*(3/4), 101–120.

Miller, W.R., & Hester, R.K. (1986). Inpatient alcoholism treatment: Who benefits? *American Psychologist, 41*(7), 794–804.

National Institute on Drug Abuse. (1990). *National household survey on drug abuse: Main findings 1988*. Rockville, MD: National Institute on Drug Abuse.

Nichols, J.R. (1965). How opiates change behavior. *Scientific American, 212*(2), 80–88.

Nichols, J.R., & Davis, W.M. (1959). Drug addiction II: Variation of addiction. *Journal of the American Pharmaceutical Association, 48*(5), 259–262.

Nichols, J.R., Headlee, C.P., & Coppock, H.W. (1956). Drug addiction I. Addiction by escape training. *Journal of the American Pharmaceutical Association, Scientific Edition, 45*(12), 788–791.

Ogborn, A.C. (1978). Patient characteristics as predictors of treatment outcomes for alcohol and drug abusers. In Y. Israel, F.B. Glaser, H. Kalant, R.E. Popham, W. Schmidt, & R. Smart (Eds.), *Research advances in alcohol and drug problems* (Vol. 4). New York: Plenum.

Sells, S.B. (1979). Treatment effectiveness. In R.I. Dupont, A. Goldstein, & J. O'Donnell (Eds.), *Handbook on drug abuse*. Rockville, MD: National Institute on Drug Abuse.

Shaffer, H., & Jones, S. (1989). *Quitting cocaine*. Cambridge, MA: Lexington Books.

Skinner, B.F. (1953). *Science and human behavior*. New York: Macmillan.

Stanton, M.D., Todd, T.C., Steier, F., Van Deusen, J.M., & Cook, L. (1982). Treatment outcome. In M.D. Stanton, T.C. Todd, & Associates, *The family therapy of drug abuse and addiction*. New York: Guilford.

Vaillant, G.E. (1969). The natural history of urban narcotic drug addiction: Some determinants. In H. Steinberg (Ed.), *Scientific basis of drug dependence*. New York: Grune & Stratton.

Vaillant, G.E. (1988). What can long-term follow-up teach us about relapse and prevention of relapse in addiction? *British Journal of Addiction, 83*(10), 1147–1157.

Wikler, A. (1965). Conditioning factors in opiate addiction and relapse. In D.M. Wilner & G.G. Kassebaum (Eds.), *Narcotics*. New York: McGraw-Hill.

Zackon, F., McAuliffe, W.E., & Ch'ien, J.M.N. (1985). *Addict aftercare: Recovery Training and Self-Help* (DHHS Pub. No. (ADM) 85-1314). Rockville, MD: National Institute on Drug Abuse.

Zackon, F., McAuliffe, W.E., & Ch'ien, J.M.N. (1992). *Recovery Training and Self-Help: Relapse prevention and aftercare for drug addicts*. Rockville, MD: National Institute on Drug Abuse.

Index

227